Current Perspectives in Psychology

Social Support and Physical Health

Understanding the Health Consequences of Relationships

Bert N. Uchino

YALE UNIVERSITY PRESS   NEW HAVEN AND LONDON

Set in Adobe Garamond type by The Composing Room of Michigan, Inc.
Printed in the United States of America.

Library of Congress Cataloging-in-Publication Data

Uchino, Bert N.
    Social support and physical health : understanding the health consequences of rela-
tionships / Bert N. Uchino.
        p.   cm. — (Current perspectives in psychology)
Includes bibliographical references and index.
    ISBN 0-300-10218-6 (alk. paper)
    1. Patients—Social networks.   2. Social networks—Therapeutic use.   3. Health.
I. Title.   II. Series.
    R726.5.U26 2004
    615.5—dc22   2003016570

A catalogue record for this book is available from the British Library.

The paper in this book meets the guidelines for permanence and durability of the Committee on Production Guidelines for Book Longevity of the Council on Library Resources.

10 9 8 7 6 5 4 3 2 1

Contents

Series Foreword

Current Perspectives in Psychology presents the latest discoveries and developments across the spectrum of the psychological and behavioral sciences. The series explores such important topics as learning, intelligence, trauma, stress, brain development and behavior, anxiety, interpersonal relationships, education, child-rearing, divorce and marital discord, and child, adolescent, and adult development. Each book focuses on critical advances in research, theory, methods, and applications and is designed to be accessible and informative to nonspecialists and specialists alike.

In *Social Support and Physical Health,* Bert Uchino discusses the role of interpersonal relationships and health. Social support and our relations with others can have great impact on health and longevity, but the research findings are more nuanced than that general statement implies. The type of support we receive and who provides the support both influence the effects. Moreover, it is not always the support we receive that has impact but also the *perception* that support is available. Dr. Uchino discusses many different types of social support and the conditions under which support can provide beneficial effects. Critical topics include stress, loneliness, marital relations, aging, gender differences, and cultural influences. Specific diseases that are covered include cardiovascular disease, cancer, and human immuno-deficiency virus infection and acquired immunodeficiency syndrome.

The benefits of social support in relation to disease and death are detailed. Equal attention is accorded to describing the effects of social support and explaining the processes through which they occur. The processes refer to why and how support influences health: it may reduce the experience of stress, increase the perceptions of personal control, and foster health-related behaviors (such as exercise) that directly contribute to physical health.

Establishing the connections between social relations in everyday life and physical health is important from the standpoint of scientific research, health care, and social policy. The bifurcation of mental and physical health—between our psychological experience and disease—limits greatly what we can do to improve health care and the quality of life. One of many interventions that could improve health and health care, social support is firmly anchored as a pertinent domain in which to effect change. Dr. Uchino's comprehensive, authoritative, and readable book relates to each of us in everyday life.

ALAN E. KAZDIN
Series Editor

Acknowledgments

I would like to express my sincere appreciation to Manuel Barrera, John Cacioppo, Timothy Smith, Julianne Holt-Lunstad, two anonymous reviewers, and series editor Alan Kazdin for their invaluable comments on aspects of this book. Special thanks to Angela Newman and Erin Carter for their excellent editorial assistance, and my sister Debbie for her support through this writing project. I am also appreciative of past and current members of my laboratory who influenced my thinking on this topic including Lindsey Bloor, Rebecca Campo, Tim Garvey, Julianne Holt-Lunstad, John Ruiz, and Darcy Uno. I'd also like to thank John Cacioppo, Janice Kiecolt-Glaser, and Tim Smith for the many wonderful discussions that have informed my perspective on these issues. Of course, all final errors of fact or inference are mine. Part of this work was also generously supported by a grant from the National Institute of Mental Health (RO1 MH58690).

Finally, I'd like to dedicate this book to four people who have had a profound influence on me: my parents, Evelyn and Harold Uchino, for providing me with the support that will last a lifetime; my mentor John Cacioppo for patiently teaching me how to be a scholar; and my wife, Heather Llenos, who supplies me with my companionship.

1

Introduction and Historical Perspectives

In my hour of need, I truly am indeed alone again, naturally
—Gilbert O'Sullivan (1972)

The hit song by Gilbert O'Sullivan tells the story of a person who, like all of us, encounters life's tribulations. He recalls such events as being left by a lover and his father's death. His conclusion is always the same: alone again, naturally. This is indeed a tragedy, as the science of relationships suggests the importance of close ties for our happiness and to help in our deepest hour of need. In fact, when people are asked what is most important to them, the most common response is not their jobs or material possessions but their personal relationships (Berscheid, 1985). In a Gallup poll (13 October 2000), the presence of a spouse was reported as having one of the strongest influences on happiness. As a test, think about how you would want to spend your time if you had only six months to live. How about two weeks? Many of us would want to share that time with the individuals who have given us the most joy in our lives. If placed in that situation, I would not be sitting here alone writing this book! When it comes down to it, our close relationships matter the most.

Individuals with satisfying and supportive relationships find it difficult to imagine not having such people in their lives. Much research shows that socially supportive relationships protect individuals from a multitude of mental health problems, ranging from mild depression to suicidal tendencies (Cohen, Underwood, and Gottlieb, 2000). This book focuses on the less-obvious possibility that a lack of supportive relationships places an individual at risk for mortality from various diseases, ranging from cardiovascular disease and cancer to infectious diseases.

What overall evidence exists to show that a lack of supportive relationships can contribute to mortality from serious physical health conditions, such as coronary artery disease? Every few months the popular media report on a research study that finds that our social environment influences our health. For every one popular news report, probably five other well-conducted research studies are published that the public does not hear about. The next section examines the contributions of several researchers whose work provides the basis for this research and continues to influence how researchers think about the association between social relationships and physical health outcomes.

Historical Perspectives

The study of social factors and physical health has a long research tradition. Renowned French sociologist Emile Durkheim is credited for jump-starting an examination of social relationships and mortality. In his classic analysis, he argued persuasively for the scientific study of suicide (Durkheim, 1951). His analyses of suicide rates across social classes, cultures, religious affiliation, and gender led him to conclude that there were three basic forms of suicide. Although suicide would seem like an intensely personal event, Durkheim concluded that each form of suicide was so closely intertwined with the larger society that it could not be understood without reference to the larger social structures in which an individual was situated.

The most well-known form of suicide was what he termed egoistic suicide. Egoistic suicide results from a lack of integration of the individual to society or family life. As a result, individuals are left to face the challenges of life on their own. A second form of suicide he termed anomic. Anomic suicide can result from a sudden or more gradual change in societal regulation (for example, spousal death or economic changes). These changes may result in dramatic changes in standards (for example, role confusion) with subsequent suffering that can lead to suicide. Durkheim also argued that too much social integration might be harmful for the individual. He called the third form of suicide altruistic, and it occurs when the social situation is governed by rigid rules that result, for instance, in an individual taking his or her life at the command of a leader.

Durkheim's analysis was impressive in scope and careful in conclusion. Several points are particularly important for the social relationships and mortality studies that I later review. He clearly demonstrated that the social environment could influence significant outcomes, such as mortality rates. He also realized that the social environment could have both health-promoting and health-damaging effects on individuals, although this last point has been less emphasized in contemporary research. Durkheim's analysis had an influential role on subsequent researchers' interest on whether relationships influence mortality patterns.

Durkheim's analysis made it easy to see how the absence or presence of relationships might influence mortality from suicide. This link between relationships and mortality was much less obvious when applied to the medical domain, in which researchers have historically focused on the biology of disease. The more traditional medical model drew a separation between body and mind, a distinction that left little room for the incorporation of psychosocial factors in health and disease. However, medical researchers whose orientation questioned the mind-body separation provided a paradigm for examining the link between psychosocial factors and disease processes (Levenson, 1994). In 1939, the journal *Psychosomatic Medicine* was launched, and the American Psychosomatic Society was founded in 1942. The goals of the society were to formally study the links between the environment, mind, and disease. It thereby set the groundwork for asking questions about social support and disease processes.

One of the founders of the American Psychosomatic Society, George Engel, published an important article in 1977 on that general approach in the journal *Science*. His paper formally criticized the reductionist medical model on the grounds that it ignored the different levels of analysis that may influence health. He proposed the now-classic "biopsychosocial model" of health and disease that has since served as the cornerstone for the interdisciplinary fields of psychosomatic medicine, behavioral medicine, and health psychology. The biopsy-chosocial model made evident that human health could be influenced by diverse factors that ranged from the sociocultural milieu (for example, socioeconomic status) to the biological (for example, atherosclerosis). Further, these factors or levels of influence were not independent of each other but instead represented embedded and interacting processes.

The general approach endorsed by psychosomatic medicine and the biopsychosocial model was evident in two seminal papers on social support and health published in 1976 by Sidney Cobb and John Cassell. Cobb carefully defined social support as information from others that one is cared for, loved, esteemed, and part of a mutually supportive network. Social support was ultimately based, according to this perspective, in the meaning behind the supportive messages from others. He then reviewed evidence suggesting that these social support resources were important in dealing with a range of stressful life events such as pregnancy, hospitalization, and bereavement. The range of outcomes examined by Cobb made it difficult to argue that social support was not an important predictor of health outcomes.

While Cobb focused more on the nature and meaning of supportive interactions that might in turn influence disease, Cassell approached his review from a biological perspective. He argued that social support might best be seen as a protective factor provided by important network members that modifies an individual's biological resistance to disease. He reviewed studies suggesting that such relationship factors may modify bodily processes (for example, blood pressure, endocrine activity) that might then influence disease states depending on the disease agent, genetics, and prior experience.

Those two papers are important not only in the early nature of their conclusions that social relationships matter for health, but also in their complementary approaches. Cobb called attention to a more precise definition of social support and how it fostered adjustment to life events. Cassell pointed to a more precise biological and medical analysis of the protective effects of social support. These two approaches continue to dominate contemporary research on social support and health outcomes.

A few years after these groundbreaking reviews, one of the first well-controlled longitudinal research studies was published that linked social relationships to mortality. Lisa Berkman and Leonard Syme surveyed thousands of participants from Alameda County, California (Berkman and Syme, 1979). They linked questions about the extent of peoples' social connections to overall mortality and found that people who had fewer social ties had higher mortality rates. This classic paper was also able to rule out possible alternative explanations (for example, results due to poorer initial health status) and hence provided the most compelling empirical links at the time between social relationships and mortality.

In 1985, an important paper was published by Sheldon Cohen and Thomas Wills. In their review of the burgeoning literature on social support and health outcomes, they drew attention to the different ways of measuring social support and how these measures might be related to health. They noted that researchers measured support in at least two ways: structural measures and functional measures of support. Structural measures examined the existence or interconnection among various social ties, for example, the number of close friends or amount of contact with family members. Functional measures of support assessed the actual functions served by social network members, for example, examining expressions of caring or useful advice from close relationships. (A more careful distinction between the measures is discussed in depth in chapter 2).

Cohen and Wills found that structural measures of support were more likely to have general health-promoting effects because they provided an overall sense of stability and self-worth. However, we are sometimes exposed to events (for example, stressors) that challenge our sense of stability and esteem. Under such circumstances, actions provided by supportive networks that help us cope may lessen the impact of stressors on our health and well-being. Consistent with this reasoning, Cohen and Wills found that functional measures of support were more likely to "buffer" the potentially harmful effects of exposure to stress. Their work thus served to link several broad perspectives on social support (for example, social support as a stress buffer) with specific measurement approaches.

In 1988, a review entitled "Social Relationships and Health" was published in *Science* by James House and colleagues (House, Landis, and Umberson, 1988). The authors examined evidence from available prospective studies indicating that being socially integrated had an independent protective effect on mortality. They argued that these effects were of similar magnitude to standard medical variables such as blood pressure, smoking, and physical activity. They concluded that medical practice might be improved by the future examination and implementation of this impressive body of literature. Their careful analysis of well-designed prospective studies has served as the most recent basis for many researchers interested in the links between relationships and physical health outcomes.

Overview

Many other important papers have been published on this topic (for example, Broadhead et al., 1983; Cohen, 1988; Umberson, 1987). An underlying theme of those papers and this book is an emphasis on interdisciplinary research that integrates across different levels of analysis (Cacioppo and Berntson, 1992; Engel, 1977). These levels of analysis range from the macro or sociocultural level to the more micro or biological level of analysis. Interdisciplinary research is critical because of the complexity of the links between social support and physical health that undoubtedly influences just about every level of analysis. Each discipline can bring a unique set of perspectives, skills, and methodologies to each level of analysis and facilitate a more complete understanding of this important phenomenon.

Combining social and biomedical approaches has historically been difficult. Tension existed between the medical community and social scientists because both sides have had reason to be critical of the other's research. Social scientists may not have been sensitive to the rigorous biological approaches of biomedical research, and biomedical researchers may not have been sensitive to the appropriate measurement and theory of the psychosocial phenomenon. There is now much more acceptance of the mending of social science and biomedical research that is, in part, due to the progress and impressive findings made by various interdisciplinary research teams around the world.

In this book I discuss the current research and theory in the area of social support and physical health outcomes that have been informed by interdisciplinary perspectives. An important point of such research is that social support is an extremely complex process. The supportive statement "I know you will be fine in due time" to a person dealing with the loss of a loved one might be interpreted differently depending on who is saying it. If said by a loved one, it might comfort by underscoring the fact that you are not alone. However, if said by a person with whom you have a lukewarm relationship, it could be seen as minimizing your loss. Likewise, the disease outcomes to be considered in this literature are similarly complex. The natural progression of cardiovascular disease differs from the natural progression of cancer, and these issues need to be taken into account in order to understand how and when social support may influence these disease outcomes.

This book is divided into eight chapters. In chapter 2, I review the often difficult question of how one measures and conceptualizes social support. Although the term social support is used by many, its meaning and measurement differ dramatically depending on the background of the researcher. Recent thinking on this question is reviewed, especially in regard to potential links with health outcomes. A broad measurement model is proposed that can serve as a guide for researchers. In chapter 3 I review the main theoretical models linking social support to health outcomes. That chapter helps form a bridge between social and biomedical approaches. It also sets the stage for interpreting the actual evidence for an association between social support and mortality that is discussed in the next chapters.

The next two chapters take us to the main focus of the book and review the studies that provide direct evidence for a link between social support and all-cause mortality (chapter 4) and specific causes of mortality (chapter 5). In those chapters I review the results from more than eighty published studies in order to summarize major findings and address some important conceptual questions raised by the prior chapters. In chapter 6 I discuss the possible pathways by which social support may influence health as informed by the findings in chapters 4 and 5 as well as the larger social support literature. Such an analysis is critical because of its importance for building theory to guide effective applications. In chapter 6 I also reexamine the existing theoretical models covered in chapter 3 and propose a broader theoretical framework for how social support influences physical health. In chapter 7 I

examine the implications of this book for interventions seeking to utilize social relationships to promote positive health outcomes. In chapter 8 I summarize the major conclusions of this book and highlight
what I view as the most important future areas of study. All together,
this book examines the impressive literature linking social support to
physical health outcomes and provides an interdisciplinary perspective
on an important but complex phenomenon.

2

The Meaning and Measurement of Social Support

What exactly is a socially supportive person? A common answer would probably be "someone who is there for you." Although this definition captures part of what is labeled social support, researchers have reason to believe that it is much more. Definitions of social support range from the actual supportive acts that are exchanged between individuals to a personality-like factor based in early interpersonal experiences that then influences how an individual views the likelihood that someone is supportive.

Social support has been measured in numerous ways. One frequent criticism of social support research is the lack of consensus about a definition and how best to measure social support. In my opinion, the lack of consensus is primarily the result of the diverse research interest that social support has generated. The concept of social support has been investigated by researchers in anthropology, epidemiology, medicine, nursing, psychology, and sociology. Given the different backgrounds of researchers in these fields one can appreciate why reaching consensus for a definition of social support has been difficult.

Taking a broad perspective based on this literature, social support is usually defined to include both the *structures* of an individual's social life (for example, group memberships or existence of familial ties) and the more explicit *functions* they may serve (for example, provision of useful advice or emotional support). That approach will be taken in this book to try to interpret the existing research literature linking social support to mortality covered in the subsequent chapters. However, care is taken to define each component of social support commonly used in the research literature. This issue is crucial because the types of measures can tell us much about how social support may operate to influence physical health. I first start with an examination of structural measures of social support.

Social Integration or Structural Aspects of Social Support

Social integration measures often tap into the extent to which individuals are situated or integrated into a social network. These measures are often called integration or structural measures because they assess the existence and interconnections among differing social ties and roles. These measures rose to prominence in the social support literature of the late 1970s and early 1980s, when some of the early epidemiological evidence for a link between social ties and health often included measures of marital status, number of people living in the household, or participation in formal or informal organizations (for example, clubs). The importance of social integration, however, was also evident in the early work of Emile Durkheim (1951), who emphasized how different social structures can affect individual well-being.

Much of the conceptual work on social integration and health has its roots in the ideas of symbolic interactionism (Mead, 1934). Symbolic interactionism highlights the importance of society for normal personal and social development. According to this perspective, we form our sense of self or identity in the context of meaningful social ties and roles (Stryker and Burke, 2000). An example of this process would be athletes who, via this role, can develop their identity as fair competitors.

This body of work has been applied to the health domain by researchers such as Peggy Thoits, who argued that social integration provides the basis for a strong sense of self-identity, appropriate norms for behavior, and greater meaning or worth to life (Thoits, 1983; Umberson, 1987). According to this view, social integration is beneficial in part because of the social roles that accompany such integration. The view that social integration is health promoting stands in contrast to early work in role theory. Early role theorists argued for the possibility that too many social roles can have negative effects and lead to role conflict or overload. Social identity researchers acknowledge the possibility for role conflict but add that on average the benefits of social integration outweigh the negative effects (Thoits, 2001).

The benefits of social integration can most clearly be illustrated within the existence of one of our most intimate social structures—marriage. Although the stereotype of misery in marriage depicted in the 1990s television show *Married with Children* is common, the married are usually happier than their single counterparts (Gallup Organization, 13 October 2000). According to identity theorists, an important reason for this effect is that the marital role of being a wife or husband provides greater meaning and purpose to life (for example, someone to live for). In addition, marriage can influence more normative behavior (and hence less risky behavior) because the spouse can directly regulate the other's behavior by way of social reminders and sometimes sanctions. For example, your husband can remind you to drive carefully after you drop him off at work or not speak to you if you insist on not wearing a seatbelt.

There is a diversity of ways to represent the structural aspects of support. As shown in table 2.1, there are measures of the extent or composition of one's social network, as well as the interconnections among them (Brissette, Cohen, and Seeman, 2000; Walker, Wasserman, and Wellman, 1994). The existence of a spouse, parents, siblings, other kin relationships, and friends are among the most common social network members assessed in the health literature. In addition, the extent of contact with different network members can be examined. More complex analyses include an examination of the connection between different network ties such as density (how many of these network members have relationships with each other) and multiplexity (relationships with multiple roles). Most of these more complex measures have received little attention in the social support and health literature. Depending on the goals of the research, these social network measures are

Table 2.1. Definition of different social integration measures ranging from simple to more complex

Network Measure	Definition
Size	Number of people in social network
Contact	Amount of contact with network members (weekly/monthly)
Type	Existence of specific relationships, such as spouse, relatives, friends
Density	Interconnection among network members
Centrality	Importance of the network tie as evidenced by links with others
Multiplex	Relationships that share multiple roles
Reciprocity	Degree of exchange in the relationship or network
Strength of tie	Ties that are voluntary, are high in intimacy, and pervade across contexts

either looked at individually or averaged to provide a composite measure of social integration.

The social network index (SNI) is one example of a social integration measure that examines a variety of social ties (Berkman and Syme, 1979). For the SNI, participants complete questions about four sources of social integration, including (1) marriage, (2) contact with close friends and relatives, (3) church membership, and (4) informal and formal group memberships. A total social integration score is based on these four sources, with important social relationships weighted more heavily in this summary assessment (that is, marriage, close friends). In their seminal paper in which they used the SNI, Berkman and Syme found that people scoring lower on this measure were more than twice as likely to experience early mortality compared to those people scoring higher on the SNI.

I have used the SNI as an illustrative social integration measure, but there are many other well-developed measures available (for example, Cohen et al., 1997). The SNI is often a social integration measure of choice because it has been shown to predict morbidity and mortality. However, the ability of a measure to predict important outcomes is not the only reason to select a measure; issues related to reliability (is it replicable over time?) and validity (does it measure what we think it is measuring?) are also important for theory building and testing. Interested readers are referred to the recent review of social integration measures by Brissette and colleagues (2000).

Discussion and Evaluation of Social Integration Measures

Epidemiological evidence such as that presented for the SNI certainly makes clear the health importance of being integrated in a social network. However, significant issues need to be considered when using such social integration measures, including the possible negative effects of social integration and the different ways in which researchers should characterize social ties or roles.

Positive and Negative Influences of Social Integration
The most important question raised about social integration measures probably revolves around the assumption that integration measures primarily tap into the availability of positive social resources. Social integration researchers assume that on average multiple roles and ties are healthy (Thoits, 2001). Although this may be the case, research does suggest that social ties can have negative influences on health outcomes (Burg and Seeman, 1994; Rook and Pietromonaco, 1987).

One potential negative outcome of being socially integrated was highlighted by early research from Emile Durkheim (1951). In his discussion of altruistic suicide, Durkheim argued that social structures can leave individuals open to deviant social control. Subsequent research suggests more subtle ways in which social integration can have negative effects on the individual. For example, network ties can set a negative example and promote risky health behaviors (see review by Burg and Seeman, 1994). Having a parent who smokes is often a strong predictor of adolescent smoking. The peer group can also have a strong influence on experimentation with illicit drugs. Clearly then, the simple presence of close social ties does not automatically mean that they have positive influences on us.

There are also more direct ways in which social ties or roles can be negative. One possibility is that these ties can be a source of significant interpersonal stress in their own right (Shumaker and Hill, 1991). For instance, women are often socialized in Western societies to be the providers of support. As a result, women who are well integrated may benefit from the advantages of having access to social support but their additional role as support provider can be stressful (for example, stress caused by having to listen to other peoples' problems). Future research using social integration measures will need to examine more closely the conditions in which being integrated has positive or negative effects, and these insights would need to be incorporated into existing social integration models (Rook, 1998).

Different Ways of Examining Social Ties and Roles
The literature on social integration acknowledges that there are a number of different ways to examine structural measures of support. The implications of this research are only recently being considered in the social relationships and health literature. One issue relates to the possibility that not all social roles and ties are equally consequential. In some studies, researchers examined the importance or salience of the social tie or role. The rationale behind this approach is that if social ties provide meaning to the self, then this should especially be the case for more important roles (for example, parent). Although research to this point is mixed (Thoits, 1995a), one study did find that older individuals who felt control within their most important social role evidenced lower mortality rates (Krause and Shaw, 2000). However, control related to their other important roles did not predict mortality. More research will be needed to test the potential boundary conditions of this identity-importance hypothesis.

Researchers have also begun to examine the possibility that different combinations of social ties and roles may be necessary in order to have an influence on well-being (Menaghan, 1989; Thoits, 1992). For instance, it could be the case that being married is more important in combination with meaningful work roles so that one has a sense of being able to provide financial support for the family. This approach is noteworthy because it starts to address more complex modeling of different identities than has been the case in the past. In one study, it was found that positive effects of employment were primarily evident in married fathers (Menaghan, 1989). More research will be needed to further validate this interesting proposition.

One clearly important distinction among these structural measures of support is the extent to which the social tie is voluntary or obligatory (Thoits, 2001). Voluntary ties should be better for well-being because one can choose to engage in more rewarding voluntary ties or exit such ties if they become nonrewarding. On the other hand, obligatory roles have facets that make them difficult to exit during tough circumstances (for example, familial conflict). Research does suggest that roles that are voluntary—that is, one chooses to enter or engage with such ties (friends, church membership)—are related to greater self-esteem, feelings of control, and less psychological distress (Berbrier and Schulte, 2000; Thoits, 1992). In comparison, more obligatory roles have less consistently been related to positive mental health outcomes (Thoits, 2001).

It may also be important to distinguish between what are called "strong" and "weak" social ties (Granovetter, 1973). Strong ties are those that are voluntary, are high in intimacy, and pervade across a variety of contexts. We might guess that such ties tend to be health promoting because much of the social support literature has focused on these relationships (spouse, confidant). In a now-classic analysis, Mark Granovetter (1973) argued for the less-obvious "strength of weak ties" (for example, acquaintances, neighbors, past classmates). From an information transmission viewpoint, he reasoned that strong ties facilitate information dispersion within the group because of the close, overlapping nature of strong ties. However, this closeness comes at a cost because the close-knit nature of strong ties results in the same information being shared. Thus, new information may not penetrate into the group, which is one situation where weak ties may be important. Weaker ties can serve bridging functions that result in more shared informational support between social networks. In one study, researchers found that people were more likely to get important family planning information from such weak ties (for example, neighbors) (Liu and Duff, 1972). To date, this remains a relatively unexplored distinction in the broader social support literature.

Overall, the issues regarding structural measures of support make a simple point: structure does not map into function in a simple way. Therefore, the limitation of integration measures is that unless supplemented by additional data they do not tell us exactly what function is being served. At the end of this chapter, several existing measures that elucidate both the structure and function of relationships are discussed. One unfortunate reaction, however, to the initial limitations of structural measures was to argue that perhaps it is not the structural aspects of relationships that matter but their quality or function. This approach to examining the specific functions of social relationships is discussed next.

Functional Components of Support

More recent studies of social support conceptualize it as the functions that are provided by social relationships. These functions are usually organized along two dimensions: what support is perceived to be available and what support is actually received or provided by others. What is perceived as available may or may not correspond to what is actually provided, and such discrepancies are discussed in the later part of this chapter.

So what exactly is made available or provided by supportive individuals? Sidney Cobb defined these social resources as information that one is cared for, loved, esteemed, and part of a mutually supportive network. Other researchers have taken a broader approach to defining these supportive behaviors. For instance, researchers sometimes include tangible aid such as providing money as a form of social support (Barrera, Sandler, and Ramsey, 1981; Cohen et al., 1985). Although the question of what exactly is provided by supportive individuals varies between researchers, many agree that supportive individuals provide or make available what can be termed emotional support, informational support, tangible support, and belonging support (table 2.2) (Barrera, 2000; Cutrona and Russell, 1990). Although I define each component in isolation, these functional aspects of social support are often highly related to each other and not easily separated in everyday life. This issue is also discussed in detail later in this chapter.

Emotional support is probably what most of us imagine when we think about a supportive individual. It is often defined as expressions of caring and concern such as "I'll be there for you no matter how difficult things get." Emotional support is thought to be beneficial because it provides the recipient with a sense of acceptance and may bolster one's self-esteem during life challenges (Wills, 1985). Informational support is defined as the provision of advice or guidance. It can

Table 2.2. Definition and examples of different support functions

Type of Support	Definition	Example
Emotional	Expressions of comfort and caring	Someone who makes you feel better because they listen to your problems.
Informational	Provision of advice and guidance	A person who can give you trusted advice and guidance on an issue.
Tangible	Provision of material aid	A family member who could give you a personal financial loan.
Belonging	Shared social activities, sense of social belonging	A friend with whom you enjoy just "hanging out."

be a very powerful form of support to the extent that it provides useful direction. Of course, as noted by researchers such as Sidney Cobb, such advice and guidance may also carry an emotional message. It is often the case that useful guidance from close friends can be seen as emotionally supportive in that the person cares enough to speak with you about important decisions.

Tangible support refers to the direct provision of material aid. Parent-child relationships are often characterized by high levels of tangible support because important material resources such as clothing, shelter, and food are provided. This form of support is not limited to parent-child relationships; people may also provide friends and family with a loan or a temporary place to stay. Belonging support is defined as the presence of others with whom to engage in social activities. An example of belonging support would be a friend with whom to go shopping or to watch a basketball game. Belonging support may be beneficial because such positive social and leisure activities may enhance one's mood and sense of acceptance by others.

One widely used functional measure of social support is the interpersonal support evaluation list (ISEL) (Cohen et al., 1985). The ISEL measures the *perceived availability* of the four types of support defined above and, like many perceived support measures, assumes that socially supportive behaviors ultimately have their effects because of how they are interpreted. Example questions include "There is at least one person I know whose advice I really trust" (informational support) and "There are several different people with whom I enjoy spending time" (belonging support). Research with this measure has documented its reliability and validity across diverse populations (Cohen et al., 1985).

Studies using the ISEL suggest its usefulness as a predictor of mental and physical health indices. For instance, in one study our laboratory examined whether the ISEL predicted age-related differences in resting blood pressure for young and older women who differed in age by almost fifty years (Uchino et al., 1995). Aging is typically associated with increases in resting blood pressure, which confers increased vulnerability to cardiovascular diseases. However, we reasoned that an individual's level of social support should influence the strength of this association if it is indeed health protective. Results were consistent with our prediction; only individuals low in support showed the typical age-related elevations in resting blood pressure. Participants high in social support showed low and comparable blood pressure regardless of their age.

Discussion and Evaluation of Functional Support Measures

Given the myriad ways that individuals can possibly support one another, there are a number of questions or areas of discussion that have been of interest to researchers using these measures. One of the most important distinctions is between the perceived availability and receipt of social support, because these measures are not highly related and are often associated with different effects on well-being. Other questions relate to the origins of perceptions of available support and the types of support functions that are most effective. Important questions also remain about the level of specificity in which one measures functional support because one can examine it from the network as a whole or from specific individuals such as the spouse.

Association Between Perceived Available and Received Support
As noted earlier in this chapter, different types of support can be measured as their perceived availability (available support) or the actual

support received (received support) from individuals in one's social network. One widely used measure of received social support is the inventory of socially supportive behaviors (ISSB) (Barrera et al., 1981). The ISSB measures the obtained frequency, usually within the past month, of the four types of support. Example questions include "Told you were OK just the way you were" (emotional support), or "Gave you over $25.00" (tangible support). Research using the ISSB is consistent with the fact that social support is usually received during stressful episodes (Barrera, 1986).

Studies suggest that received support is not related to the perceived availability of support in a straightforward manner (Dunkel-Schetter and Bennett, 1990), although agreement between these two measures is usually better for closer relationships (Antonucci and Israel, 1986). One study had participants complete a daily diary of actual supportive behaviors and also a questionnaire used to determine the perceived availability of support (Cutrona, 1986). Illustrating the complexity of the association between these measures, results of this study showed that what participants viewed as available and what was actually received corresponded highest on days in which a stressful event occurred.

There are a number of reasons why measures of available and received support are not highly related. Measures of available support are related to one's cognitive representation of social support. In some cases, these representations may be accurate, but the social network could provide too little or too much support depending on the specifics of the situation. For instance, under times of severe stress individuals in your social network may be anxious because they may not know exactly how to provide you with effective support. Take the case of a person whose friend may have just been diagnosed with cancer. Many individuals report being anxious in interacting with cancer patients, and this anxiety may contribute to less provided support (Dunkel-Schetter and Bennett, 1990). In addition, received support may decrease over time because individuals in your social network expect you to begin "picking up the pieces" on your own. Bereaved individuals, for instance, usually receive much support soon after the loss of a spouse, but that support dissipates over time, often much faster than is preferred by the individual (Lehman, Ellard, and Wortman, 1986).

There are also times in which the person needing support may be hesitant to ask for it. Individuals in Western cultures are generally taught to be independent. This implies that we should attempt to handle many of our problems on our own. In fact, research in this area suggests that individuals may experience a drop in self-esteem when asking for aid (Nadler and Fisher, 1986). As a result, a person might perceive a high availability of support but decide not to utilize it because of concerns about network members' perception of their competence.

Issues Related to Received Support

Some studies have found that received support is not as highly related to successful coping compared to the perceived availability of support (Barrera, 2000). For instance, research has on occasion found that the amount of support received did not predict, or predicted increases in, distress (Helgeson, 1993). As a result, some researchers have argued that perceived available support may be the component most highly related to positive outcomes. This suggestion would seem consistent with several laboratory studies on the availability of support and its influence on coping with stressful tasks. One study found that simply letting participants know that support would be available if they needed it was associated with better performance on a task than when support was not made available (Sarason and Sarason, 1986). Importantly, participants did not actually ask for help, so it appears that the simple perception that support is available is calming and helpful. Our laboratory replicated and extended the findings from this study by also showing that simply making support available decreased cardiovascular reactivity to a speech task (Uchino and Garvey, 1997).

There are several explanations for why received support may not be as beneficial as the perceived availability of support. One possible explanation is based on the finding that stressful circumstances are usually associated with increased support seeking. As a result, those who report greater levels of received support are actually under more severe stress (Barrera, 1986). One implication of this argument is that researchers may need to follow the effects of received support in stressed populations over longer periods of time because initially it may represent an individual's attempt to mobilize support. However, only over time may received support eventually help one resolve the stressor.

A second reason why received support might not be as effective a social resource is due to the quality of the support that is received. We can all recall awkward moments when we know someone is trying to be supportive but it does not come across in a helpful manner. For instance, individuals providing support may sometimes rely on automated or stereotypic responses that can be viewed as minimizing a difficult situation. Let's again take the example of someone who is undergoing a very stressful event such as the loss of a spouse. What exactly does one say to that person in order to help?

In one study group of bereaved participants, researchers tested the possibility that some support attempts may be unhelpful (Lehman, Ellard, and Wortman, 1986). These researchers found that bereaved participants were readily able to recall support attempts that were both helpful and unhelpful. Actions such as expressing concern and contact with similar others were viewed as helpful, whereas giving advice and encouraging recovery were seen as unhelpful. They then asked a separate group of nonbereaved participants what they would do to support an individual in such a situation. Contrary to the possibility that individuals don't know what to do or say, participants' reports of what they would do to be supportive matched quite well with the reports of what was helpful in individuals who had experienced bereavement. If people know what to do, then why did so many individuals report unhelpful support attempts by individuals in their network? The authors hypothesized that people interacting with someone undergoing a stressful event feel anxious about the interactions. They do not want to do or say anything that will upset the individual at such a vulnerable time. Ironically, this anxiety makes it difficult to be an effective support provider because individuals may slip into more automatic or casual responses (for example, "I'm sure you will get through this with time") that may then be viewed as unhelpful.

A final possible explanation for why received support may not be beneficial is related to our prior point that asking or receiving support may be associated with a drop in self-esteem. This decrease in self-esteem may in turn offset any benefits of received support. For example, if you receive help to answer a question during a company presentation, you might feel disappointed that you did not know the answer to the question.

Acknowledging the potential negative effects of receiving support, Niall Bolger and colleagues (2000) argued that the best form of received support may be those acts that are not actually noticed by the recipient as supportive. For instance, a spouse might do extra (unnoticed) chores around the house so that the other person has more time to concentrate on studying for an important exam. According to these researchers, individuals in this situation can still benefit from the provided support but not take the self-esteem hit that may come had they known explicitly about the support. In one intriguing study of what Bolger and colleagues have termed "invisible support," they followed couples in which one member was preparing to take the New York State Bar Exam. Diaries on received support were completed over a one-month period. Results of the study revealed that there were many instances in which the partner reported providing support but the person preparing for the exam did not notice it. Further, the provision of "invisible support" from the partner was associated with the lowest levels of depression in the person preparing for the exam during the study period.

Not all studies have found received support to have negative effects, and some researchers have argued that we need to be more careful in accepting this proposition too generally (Barrera, 1986). One important consideration already discussed is that we may need research that follows participants over longer periods of time to adequately test the longer term effects of received support. In addition, received support can be of several types (for example, informational, belonging, emotional), and few studies have looked at how specific dimensions of received support predict adjustment.

There is good reason to take a closer look at specific dimensions because recent research suggests that the receipt of informational and tangible support tends to be viewed as less nurturing and more controlling than either emotional or belonging support (Trobst, 2000). In one study, researchers found that received tangible and informational support predicted increased depression, whereas received emotional support did not predict depressive symptoms (Finch et al., 1997). However, received positive interactions (belonging support) predicted lower levels of depression, a finding that was obscured if one only looked at total received support. Thus, it is possible that received belonging support may provide a necessary distraction from problems or affirm other aspects of the person's life. Other research in patients with chronic diseases also suggests a detrimental influence of received tangible support on depression but a beneficial influence of received emotional support (Penninx et al., 1998). More research is needed that examines the differential prediction of various components of received support, especially in clinical populations such as cancer or cardiac patients who may be forced to rely more heavily on received support.

Other researchers have tried to reconcile these discrepancies by arguing for a more complex view of how received support is related to perceived available support (Krause, Liang, and Keith, 1990; Wethington and Kessler, 1986). Those authors have pointed out that most studies have assumed that perceived available support represents a "reservoir" of support that may then be called upon during times of need. However, some researchers have argued that the reverse may be true in that received support may be the inlet feeding perceptions of available support.

One perspective consistent with this more recent view is the support deterioration-deterrence model (Norris and Kaniasty, 1996). According to this model, stressful events can deteriorate an individual's perceived availability of support from others. This may occur because stressful events can challenge one's basic beliefs. In addition, if the stressor is widespread enough, then immediate support providers may also be coping with the event as well, which would curtail their ability to provide support. Received support may then be beneficial because it prevents the deterioration of perceived support from others. Results from two large studies of victims of hurricanes Hugo and Andrew provided support for this model; received support was a predictor of greater perceived support over time, which in turn predicted lower levels of distress (Norris and Kaniasty, 1996). Received and perceived support may therefore be related in fundamental ways, and received support may be especially beneficial for stressful events that have a wide influence on one's social network (for example, familial crises).

Studies finding received support to have no effect or a detrimental influence on adjustment stand in stark contrast to laboratory studies that have found received support to be beneficial in helping individuals adjust to acute stress (Gerin et al., 1992; Lepore, Allen, and Evan, 1993).

In those laboratory studies, either a friend or the experimenter provided participants with support while they underwent a standardized stress task (for example, speech). The most common support provided was emotional support conveyed in a nonthreatening manner. Those laboratory studies suggest that there is nothing about received emotional support per se that precludes it having a beneficial effect.

The laboratory studies linking received support to better physiological adjustment during acute stress are also noteworthy because they are able to disentangle received support from current levels of stress. In those studies, the manipulation of received support is independent of stress levels because participants were randomly assigned to different support conditions. In more natural settings, the mobilization of support during stress can present difficulties in disentangling the harmful effects of stress versus the beneficial effects of support (Barrera, 2000). Intervention studies also provide a strong platform for testing the potential effects of received support on adjustment because participants can be randomly assigned to different support conditions.

Issues Related to Perceptions of Available Support

Important questions exist concerning perceptions of available support. As noted earlier, most prior research has assumed that perceived available support is related to the actual support received in the environment. However, because perceived support measures are not usually highly related to measures of received support, the question arises as to what else is being measured when we look at perceived available support.

Some researchers have argued that it may be fruitful to think about perceived available support as reflecting relatively stable expectations for relationships based on our early childhood experiences (Sarason, Sarason, and Shearin, 1986). In a series of studies, it was found that perceptions of social support were stable in a college population across at least a three-year period (Sarason et al.). College is usually a time when relationships are in a state of flux (for example, new relationships being formed), so why were these perceptions so stable? Consistent with their perspective, these researchers also found that perceived support was related to the quality of individuals early relationships with their parents (Sarason et al.). More specifically, individuals with high levels of perceived support reported more early parental affection and care. This perspective can explain in part why measures of perceived and received support are not more highly correlated because it raises the possibility that part of social support perceptions are established much earlier in life. This research is consistent with attachment theorists who propose that early caretaker-child interactions provide a "working model" for the developing child on the potential trustworthiness of others (Hazan and Shaver, 1987).

The Importance of Specific Types of Support

Another issue concerns the conditions under which different support functions are most beneficial (Berkman and Glass, 2000; Thoits, 1995b). Researchers have proposed what they term the *matching hypothesis* to address this question (Cohen and Wills, 1985; Cutrona and Russell, 1990). According to the matching hypothesis of social support, the effectiveness of any form of support will depend on the extent to which it meets the demands of the particular stressful event. For controllable stressful events such as having to find employment, action-facilitating social support such as informational or tangible support is predicted to be more important because it helps one deal directly with the stressor. That is, others can give advice on interviewing or help obtain an important interview. However, if the event is less controllable, such as in the case of spousal betrayal, then emotional or belonging support may serve to facilitate adjustment by reassuring one's sense of self or providing suitable social distractions that provide the person time to cope with the event.

The research evaluating the matching hypothesis is mixed (Barrera, 2000). For instance, in one study consistent with the matching hypothesis, researchers found that financial stress was associated with an increased risk for alcohol involvement (Peirce et al., 1996). They next examined whether different types of support would help individuals cope better with their current financial situation. Of the different types of support measured, only tangible support consistently decreased the association between financial stress and alcohol involvement. However, other studies looking specifically at individuals with low financial resources have not found tangible support to be the most effective form of support (for example, Krause, 1987a).

There are several reasons for these discrepancies in prior research that represent real difficulties in conducting a clean test of the matching hypothesis. One issue is that many stressful events are not easily classified as either controllable or uncontrollable, and these classifications may change over time. For instance, coping with a serious medical diagnosis may be uncontrollable early on (nothing can be done about the diagnosis); however, successful adaptation will often require informational support from one's physician (treatment regimen) or tangible support from a spouse (help with daily activities). A second problem is that many of the components of support are often highly related to each other, which presents statistical difficulties in showing specific effects. This overlap makes sense: a person who gives valuable informational support would probably also be viewed as emotionally supportive.

Despite these difficulties in testing the matching hypothesis, research continues to favor this approach for several reasons. First, studies that statistically model the structure of functional measures of support suggest that these components of support are distinct lower-order processes that together make up the higher-order concept of social support (Cutrona and Russell, 1987). Second, the use of specific functional measures of support demonstrates why social support is beneficial. For instance, an association between emotional support and mental health gives researchers more specific guidelines in attempting to develop an effective support intervention.

Although there are conceptual advantages to the future examination of the matching hypothesis, there is evidence that some types of social support are helpful across many different life events. In particular, both emotional and informational support seems to foster adjustment across a wide variety of situations. In a review of the literature it was found that these two support components had the most consistent effects on varied outcomes such as depression, physical symptoms, and smoking cessation (Cohen et al., 1985).

As suggested by Cohen and colleagues, emotional and informational support may be particularly beneficial because people can usually benefit from useful information or reassurances of their worth. Take the example of a person going through the stress of a divorce. Adjustment to this major life event requires adequate informational (legal advice) and emotional (reassurances of brighter future) support. In fact, many stressful life events are complex and elicit multiple challenges (for example, threats to self-esteem, need for advice), and the combination of these support types appears to provide a powerful means to help the individual cope.

General and Specific Sources of Support
Cutting across the present discussion of the meaning and measurement of social support is the issue of at what level is social support measured. We can measure social support as general views of support (presumably reflecting their overall sense of support) or as support from specific individuals in the social network. For instance, research examining general perceptions might ask the question, "Are there people you can go to if you need advice on dealing with a difficult problem?" Much of the social support research has been conducted using this approach. On the other hand, this question can also be asked for specific individuals in one's network (for example, "Can you go to Glenn if you need advice dealing with a difficult problem?"). If this latter approach is performed across a wide range of the social network, then one starts to merge both structural and functional approaches to measuring social support.

There are several arguments for why one might examine such specific sources of support. Much research has demonstrated the importance of perceptions of support from the network as a whole (Cohen et al., 1985). However, research suggests that these different ways of measuring support are not highly related, and measures of support from specific network members may uniquely predict adjustment even after considering general perceptions of support (Davis, Morris, and Kraus, 1998; Pierce, Sarason, and Sarason, 1991). In addition, research suggests that certain network sources tend to be characterized by the provision of many different support types (for example, strong ties, parents), whereas other ties tend to be limited to the provision of one kind of support (Wellman and Wortley, 1990). These data suggest the potential importance of separating specific sources of support.

At a broad level, it has also been argued that a focus on general perceptions of support provides less information on the specific close relationships that serve as the basis for support transactions (Gottlieb,

1985; Sarason, Sarason, and Gurung, 2001). Researchers have generally assumed that these are the relationships assessed by their measures. However, given the other processes that may influence general perceptions of available support (for example, quality of early parental-child relationships), it may be preferable to assess support from these close relationships if the goal is to make more specific inferences about these ties (Pierce et al., 1991).

Besides the importance of examining close relationships, is there evidence on the centrality of other social ties? The answer to this question appears to depend in part on the person's life circumstance and the sociocultural context. For instance, studies examining individuals dealing with medical problems (such as cancer or cardiac disease) have fruitfully examined support from the spouse, other family members, and sometimes the physician. These are the support sources that seem to be directly counted on during these specific circumstances. Studies examining adolescents also suggest the importance of separating peer and familial relationships. Both of these support sources appear to have differing influences on adolescent outcomes such as substance abuse and mental health (Barrera, 2000; Wills et al., 2000). Also important to consider are cross-cultural differences in preferences for support. William Dressler (1994) has shown the potential importance of carefully considering the social context of relationships by demonstrating predictable associations between culturally important relationships (for example, compadres in Mexican communities) and lower blood pressure levels.

The ultimate decision to assess support from specific sources or more globally will most likely be influenced by the research question (that is, what sources are likely to be of most importance) but also time considerations. A simultaneous assessment of structural measures of support, followed by more detailed questions of the support functions they provide, can be lengthy. The advantage is in the unique sources of information that might be gained as well as the specificity of the findings. This specificity may be particularly important if potential interventions based on the natural support system are to be undertaken (for example, family and peer interventions for substance abuse). When possible, it would seem important to assess both global and specific sources of support; such an assessment would provide a powerful means by which to integrate the functional and structural components of support.

Summary and Discussion

In this chapter, I reviewed the major ways in which social support has been conceptualized and measured. Each of these approaches captures a piece of the social support puzzle. Figure 2.1 illustrates how these different measures are related to each other. The innermost box represents the functional types of support that can potentially be exchanged between individuals. These support types can be measured as either received or available support, with research indicating that these are at least somewhat related to each other. The next box highlights that received and available support can be measured at different levels of specificity from the network as a whole to specific network members. I should note that one can also measure support between these levels if one asks about received support from categories of relationships such as family or friends in general. Finally, the outermost box specifies the structural aspects of support. It provides the sociocultural context for the other measures and is the broadest measurement approach that social support researchers presently pursue.

An examination of figure 2.1 makes salient several points. It emphasizes that these measures are embedded strategies and that each captures part of the phenomenon of social support. It also highlights the limitations of taking only one measurement strategy because each approach makes certain insights easy and others more difficult. For instance, measures of social integration can tell researchers about the types of social structures that may be beneficial. However, this broad approach has less specificity, so information on mechanisms may be more difficult. Examining functional components of support (for example, emotional) tells us much about what is being received or available, but it does not highlight the larger social structures that provide the opportunities or constraints for such social exchanges.

Some researchers will disagree with the broad approach I have taken in this chapter because it goes against the claims of some that social support needs better definitional specificity. I do not advocate a dismissal of a broad approach in favor of a much more narrow defini-

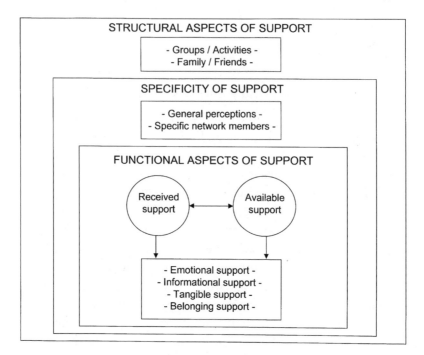

Figure 2.1. Potential links between structural and functional measures of social support and associated measurement strategies.

tion and measurement strategy. In my opinion we can do both: a broad approach that makes salient the conceptual links among these measures and specific definitions for each domain. It is the case, however, that researchers should more explicitly acknowledge the strengths and limitations of their measurement choice than is presently the case.

The model depicted in figure 2.1 also makes clear the need for a more integrated measurement approach. There are measures that illuminate aspects of both structural and functional support, but there are pros and cons to such comprehensive assessments. On the positive side is that one combines the strengths of both approaches to ask questions related to social support; one can also model the association between these structural and functional measures. One recent study illustrates the potential importance of this point. Researchers found that when the role of being a parent was combined with high levels of functional support it predicted the greatest evening reduction in ambulatory systolic blood pressure compared to any of these measures in isolation (Steptoe, Lundwall, Cropley, 2000). However, a serious drawback to a more comprehensive approach is the time-intensive nature of such an assessment. In many large-scale epidemiological studies social support may represent one of many different risk assessments; hence, researchers need to consider the measure of social support that is relatively brief but most relevant.

To date, there are only a few measures that might allow for a more comprehensive assessment of social support, including scales such as the Arizona social support interview schedule (ASSIS) (Barrera, 1980), social support questionnaire (Sarason et al., 1983), and the social relationships index (Uchino et al., 2001). The ASSIS asks individuals to list the people in their lives who provide various support functions (for example, emotional or informational support) and to rate their need and satisfaction with that support. A relatively unique aspect of the ASSIS is that individuals are asked to also list the individuals who are sources of negative interactions. This broad assessment allows the ASSIS to extract measures of both structural and functional support as well as the negative qualities of social relationships (Barrera, 1980; Sandler and Barrera, 1984).

Although the ASSIS allows a simultaneous assessment of the negative qualities of social relationships, very few measures of support have this capacity. An important issue that cuts across the assessment of both structural *and* functional measures of support is the tendency for most assessments to ignore the negative aspects of social ties (Uchino et al., 2001). The fact that social integration measures simply assess the existence of certain types of social relationships or roles makes them vulnerable to tapping into both positive and negative features. At face value this issue appears less relevant for researchers using functional measures of support because these measures directly assess the positive qualities of relationships such as emotional support. However, many close relationships are characterized by both helpful and upsetting qualities (Fincham and Linfield, 1997; Uchino et al.). Ambivalent relationships can involve an overbearing parent, a volatile romance, a competitive friend, or any positive relationships characterized by a past or recent history of conflict on important dimensions (for example, lifestyle decisions).

The existence of ambivalent relationships suggests more hetero-geneity in social networks than has been examined in past research. There appears to be a subset of social network members that are char-acterized primarily by helpful qualities, whereas another subset is more mixed or ambivalent in nature, with both helpful and upsetting quali-ties (Uchino et al., 2001). If researchers simply assess the helpful quali-ties of a network member, it is unclear whether they will be assessing a network member who is primarily supportive or a network member who has both helpful and upsetting qualities (ambivalent). This is im-portant because prior research suggests that ambivalent ties may have negative effects on well-being (Sandler and Barrera, 1984; Uchino et al., 2001). We have argued that some inconsistencies in prior social support research may be a result of this practice of lumping primarily supportive and ambivalent ties together. Future research will deter-mine the full implications of this argument for the measurement of so-cial support and its association to various outcomes.

3

Theoretical Perspectives Linking Social Support to Health Outcomes

Social support has been defined and measured in a variety of ways. At a broad level there exists the distinction between structural and functional measures of support. Structural measures of support assess the existence or interconnection among social ties, whereas functional measures of support assess the specific functions that such relationships may serve. Within each of these broad measurement approaches are even more specific ways of assessing social support. Research on structural measures of support highlights the important distinction between voluntary and obligatory social ties as well as strong and weak ties. Studies examining functional measures of support suggest the utility of distinguishing between the perceived availability and actual receipt of support as well as the potential importance of examining specific support functions. Research that incorporates both structural and functional aspects of support is not common. However, several instruments exist (for example, the Arizona social support interview schedule) that allow for a more comprehensive approach and can help highlight the links between these different ways of defining social support.

Because of the different approaches to measuring social support, it has sometimes been difficult to evaluate theories linking social support to health outcomes as conflicting findings may reflect ambiguities in how one defines and measures support. In this chapter, I provide an overview of various conceptual frameworks linking social support to health outcomes and tie them more specifically to the measures defined in chapter 2. Each model emphasizes different processes by which social support may influence health outcomes. In fact, as emphasized by others, these models are likely complementary approaches to studying the health effects of social support (for example, Berkman et al., 2000).

Most of the models linking social support to health outcomes are variants of what are termed stress-related and direct effect models. The most prominent stress-related perspective is the buffering model. It predicts that social support is primarily healthy because it diminishes or "buffers" the deleterious effects of stress in a person's life. In comparison, the direct effect models operate across a wide range of circumstances and suggest that social support is beneficial irrespective of life stress. The popularity of this distinction resulted from an influential review done by Cohen and Wills (1985) on the conditions and specific measurement strategies linking these perspectives to various outcomes. Cohen and Wills reasoned that functional measures of support (for example, emotional support or informational support) are more likely to be associated with stress-buffering effects because they can more directly meet the needs elicited by stressful events (for example, loss of control or uncertainty). On the other hand, structural measures of support are more likely to be associated with direct effects because they tap into more general social resources. Their review of the many studies published at the time was consistent with this reasoning.

One issue to keep in mind is that these models were developed largely from the social support and mental health perspective. It would be fair to say that in many cases, researchers examining the association between social support and mortality have not been as attentive to these models and the basic research on measuring social support. Many researchers have simply tried to examine whether indicators of social support predict mortality rates. These theoretical models, how-

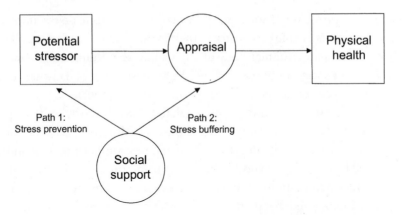

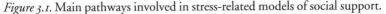

Figure 3.1. Main pathways involved in stress-related models of social support.

ever, provide an excellent opportunity to better understand the nature of any association between social support and mortality.

Stress-Related Models of Social Support

The models that have received the most attention in prior research emphasize the role of social support in stress-related processes. Of these, the buffering model of support has been the most widely researched (Cobb, 1976; Cohen and Wills, 1985). A model that has received much less attention is the stress-prevention model (Gore, 1981; LaRocco, House, and French, 1980). This model suggests that social support is beneficial because network members may provide us with the resources to avoid or reduce our exposure to some types of negative life events. The stress-prevention model is illustrated in path 1 of figure 3.1.

A good example of the way the stress-prevention model works can be illustrated with the "Y2K" problem a few years ago. The months prior to 1 January 2000 saw rising concern over the potential impact of glitches in computer operating systems around the world. The Y2K problem was associated with uncertainty over the future, and many individuals stocked up on water and food and took money out of their accounts in case of emergency. However, if one had had a trusted friend who provided informational support on why Y2K would not be a problem, then it might not have been viewed as a stressor. In this sense, the provision of social support may actually decrease the number of stressors people experience in their lives. This point was nicely illustrated in a longitudinal study of older adults that found individuals with higher social support experienced a lower number of daily hassles over an eleven-month period (Russell and Cutrona, 1991).

The most well-known stress-related model is the buffering model of support. According to this model, social support is beneficial because it decreases the negative effects of stress on both mental and physical health (Cohen and Herbert, 1996), and this buffering is more apparent when examining functional measures of support. This process is highlighted by path 2 in figure 3.1. How does this stress-buffering process occur? It is first useful to consider how the stress process operates. Models of stress and coping suggest that life events and daily hassles ultimately have their influence on well-being by what is called an appraisal process (Lazarus and Folkman, 1984). The appraisal process is a psychological one in which information from the environment is processed in reference to our perceived coping abilities.

One example of this process was illustrated at a gathering I attended a few years ago in which two individuals were asked to perform public speeches. The person giving the first speech was an accomplished speaker (a clergy member). The other person was an experienced musician. Before his turn to speak, he remarked to the pastor that he was nervous. He said he didn't understand it because he could play his musical instrument in front of hundreds of people with no problem. These two individuals were faced with the same objective event, but because of their different experiences they appraised the situation differently, which influenced their reactions to the task at hand. In this case, the absolute level of experienced stress depended on the combination of the potential threat specific to the event (public speaking) and the individual's perceived ability to cope with that specific event. This point was further punctuated by the pastor's response in which he jokingly replied, "Oh, you place me in front of a hundred people with a musical instrument in my hands and I'd be terrified!"

There is strong evidence for the buffering model of support on adjustment to stress (Cohen and Wills, 1985). Even when faced with extremely stressful events (for example, death of a spouse), having individuals who can provide a person with support can help reduce the intensity of the stress response and facilitate coping over the long term. In fact, social support has been shown to decrease the negative effects associated with a wide range of stressful events, such as unemployment, bereavement, and medical problems (Cutrona and Russell, 1990).

A major variant of the stress-buffering model is the matching hypothesis (Cohen and McKay, 1984; Cutrona and Russell, 1990). The matching hypothesis predicts that stress buffering is most effective when the type of support matches the needs or challenges of the stressful event. As reviewed in chapter 2, the matching hypothesis predicts that informational and tangible support should be most effective for controllable events (for example, preparing for a job interview), whereas emotional and belonging support should be most effective for uncontrollable events (for example, job layoff). Research on the feasibility of the matching hypothesis is presently inconclusive (Barrera, 2000). However, there are several difficulties in testing the matching hypotheses, including the problems of specifying an event as controllable or uncontrollable and how this classification may change over time. There are conceptual advantages (specificity of findings) to examining whether more specific types of support predict adjustment that highlight the need for a more thorough examination of this perspective.

Critiques of Stress-Related Models

The stress-buffering model is probably the most widely researched model linking social support to mental health outcomes. However, a number of important critiques and questions surround this perspective and the stress-prevention model. First, some research appears inconsistent with these models. Second, there are significant gaps in our knowledge. Third, some important processes are not explicitly addressed by the framework of these stress-related models. Because of the lack of research on the stress-prevention model, many of these critiques are predictably centered on the stress-buffering model of support.

Research Inconsistent with These Models

Although measures of available support often find stress-buffering effects, measures of received support have not always found such effects (Helgeson, 1993). This may be related to (1) a confounding between the level of stress and the mobilization of support, (2) negative effects of asking for support, (3) the receipt of unhelpful support, or (4) an oversimplification of how researchers have conceptualized received support and adjustment (see chapter 2). Nevertheless, the fact that measures of received support sometimes do not show stress-buffering effects is problematic for this model. Just how problematic depends on whether one views measures of the perceived availability or receipt of support as equally relevant to the stress-buffering model (Lakey and Cohen, 2000). Although there is no resolution to this issue at this point, it is clear that future research on the stress-buffering model must more closely examine the conditions under which measures of received support reduce or exacerbate stress.

Gaps in Understanding

One issue is that most research has examined the possibility that social support decreases the magnitude of stress responses. Much less research has been focused on the intriguing possibility that individuals with strong social support experience less stressful events during their lives (path 1 in figure 3.1). This has been termed the stress-prevention model, but evidence on this pathway is surprisingly scarce (Barrera, 2000). In one early study, researchers found that the combination of community level and individual support was associated with fewer negative life events during the one-year study period (Lin, 1986). This study and others (for example, Russell and Cutrona, 1991) suggest the importance of considering how social support can help individuals avoid stress in the first place.

Although much research is consistent with the stress-buffering perspective, it has mostly focused on measures of mental health. Whether this model has implications for physical health outcomes has yet to be fully demonstrated. More recent data, however, are beginning to link this perspective to health-relevant physiological processes. Most of us have experienced our heartbeat racing when we are momentarily stressed. Although we cannot feel it, our blood pressure during stressful situations is also increasing to a level that one normally observes during exercise. Is this healthy? The reactivity hypothesis of stress suggests that this exaggerated cardiovascular reactivity (heart rate, blood pressure) may play a role in both the development and exacerbation of coronary artery disease (Manuck, 1994). Repeated reactivity during stress may be linked to injury to the insides of the coronary arteries that may contribute to the plaque-forming process. In addition, increased blood pressure reactivity in cardiovascular patients during stress can lead to silent myocardial ischemia, a potentially dangerous imbalance in the supply and demand of oxygen to the heart (Krantz et al., 1991).

If social support is an effective stress buffer for physical health outcomes, then according to the reactivity hypothesis it should be associated with decreased cardiovascular reactivity to stressful circumstances. This hypothesis has been tested in a number of well-controlled laboratory studies, and results suggest that the receipt of social support is associated with lower reactivity to stressors (Lepore, 1998). In one noteworthy study, researchers had participants engage in a discussion task in the presence or absence of social support (Gerin et al., 1992). In the no social support condition, two confederates (people who pretend to be naive participants) attacked the participant's views while a third confederate sat silently. The discussion task was identical for the social support condition; however, the third confederate now defended the participant's views. Results of the study revealed that social support during the conflict discussion was uniformly associated with lower increases in heart rate, systolic blood pressure, and diastolic blood pressure. In another study conducted by our laboratory, we found that simply telling participants that support was available if needed was enough to lower blood pressure reactivity, despite the fact that no support was actually given (Uchino and Garvey, 1997). Thus it appears that both the availability and receipt of support may be effective stress buffers on physiological outcomes. Given the results of these laboratory studies, more research is needed to examine the stress-buffering effect of social support on physiological processes and how it may ultimately influence physical health outcomes.

As we try to link the stress-buffering model with long-term health outcomes, another important gap in our knowledge is how to best make this link. An examination of coping with discrete life events (for example, cancer diagnosis) can tell us about stress-buffering effects for individuals who already have significant health conditions. However, there are data that do suggest that social support may influence the *development* of health problems with a long-term etiology, such as cardiovascular disease. (This issue is covered in the following chapters.) The laboratory research on social support and cardiovascular reactivity is one attempt to link social support with such long-term disease end points. In order to have a strong test of social support as a risk factor in the development of health problems, we need to consider how to adequately test and measure these processes over significant time periods. It is here that the incorporation of more "intermediate" health indicators may be useful. For instance, intermediate outcomes as simple as resting blood pressure or as complex as imaging scans of the coronary arteries are known to predict future coronary risk (Rumberger et al., 1999; Vasan et al., 2001). Long-term studies that include repeated assessments of stress-buffering processes, intermediate outcomes, and health status will be necessary.

Processes Not Explicit
The stress-related models are elegant in their simplicity and parsimony. However, this simplicity may also be a weakness because it results in unexplained processes with implications for these models. One of these is that the stress-related models do not really specify how support events unfold and change over time, especially in response to stressors. This issue is evident when examining potential limitations of support when faced with certain life events. For instance, there are some stressors that not only impact the person under stress but also their social network. This process can erode critical support during times of need. In one study, researchers tested this possibility by examining how support was influenced when couples attempted to cope with the diagnosis and treatment of breast cancer (Bolger et al., 1996). These researchers found that although support was initially mobilized in response to the diagnosis, the patients' distress was related to an erosion of received support from the spouse over time. Of course, this erosion in support has important implications for the future effectiveness of social support in helping the patient deal with the stress and challenges of living with cancer.

In other contexts, however, stressful life events may not erode support but instead provide an important opportunity to foster the growth of personal relationships (Holahan and Moos, 1990). For instance, the experience of stress may lead to a greater need for self-disclosure. When appropriate, self-disclosure can facilitate the development of a person's social ties (Altman and Taylor, 1973). Such a process may in turn foster better adjustment during the course of a long-term stressor or subsequent stressful circumstances because it increases a person's comfort level in receiving support from these individuals (Burleson and Goldsmith, 1998). By strengthening a person's social network this process may also be associated with stress-prevention effects over time.

The stress-related models predict what happens once support is provided or perceived by the recipient. This focus on the support receipt process ignores another important issue: why and when will individuals seek support in the first place? It is often assumed that stress will lead to support seeking but research suggests a more complicated picture. Barbee and colleagues (1990) argued that persons under stress consider a number of factors that may determine whether they actually seek social support. Persons under stress decide to seek support based on their emotions (do they feel embarrassed about the problem?), thoughts (can they handle the problem on their own?), and the quality of their existing relationships (is there someone that they can turn to about this problem?). Clearly, stress is not related to seeking support in a simple fashion.

Individuals may also have differing preferences and motivations for seeking social support. Some researchers have suggested that individuals can seek support for self-evaluation or self-enhancement reasons (Stroebe and Stroebe, 1996). Self-evaluation refers to processes aimed at gaining accurate information about the self. Such information is thought to be critical so that we can make well-informed decisions and place ourselves in proper (not overwhelming) situations (for example, taking too many hard courses in a semester). Self-enhancement is aimed at helping the self feel better (Wood, 1989). This comes into play primarily when we feel threatened, and it can motivate us to gather social information that boosts our self-esteem (for example, patients can compare themselves with those who are not doing as well as they are, or they can seek emotional support).

Stroebe and Stroebe (1996) further argue that support seeking during stress for evaluation or enhancement depends on the perceived controllability of the stressful event. Controllable stressors are events that can be coped with most effectively using direct action. The authors hypothesize that individuals are more likely to seek support for evaluation when faced with controllable stressors so that their plan of action can be evaluated or other options considered. However, uncontrollable stressors are those in which little can be done to influence the outcome (for example, being the person in a marriage who does not want a divorce). In such cases, individuals can do little to directly alter the situation, so they instead try to get a handle on their emotions. Under these conditions, it is predicted that support seeking for enhancement is more likely so that individuals can make themselves feel better by validating their feelings via emotional support. Although some similarities can be seen here with the matching hypothesis of support, this perspective addresses the often neglected question of why people seek certain types of support in the first place.

People may also be motivated to seek out support consistent with their preference for one type of support over others. Such motivations may influence when social support is effective because, all else being equal, getting the preferred types of support should be associated with a more beneficial outcome. For example, some researchers have argued that socialization processes result in women both preferring and benefiting more from emotional support than other support types (Flaherty and Richman, 1989). To test this proposition, the authors examined psychological adjustment in women and men during the first year of medical school. Results suggested stronger associations between emotional support and well-being in women compared to men. Future research will be needed to more directly incorporate these motivational processes with the stress-related models of support.

Another important factor relevant to stress-related models is personality processes that can influence whether individuals seek support in the first place as well as the benefits that they receive from support transactions. Hostile individuals, for instance, are less likely to seek support because of their mistrustful nature (Smith, 1992). One study also directly tested whether hostile individuals under stress benefited from social support provided by a stranger (Lepore, 1995). Researchers found that hostile individuals did not appear to benefit from support as evidenced by their high levels of blood pressure changes during the task. Of course, the number of potential personality processes or individual difference factors that can influence support processes is daunting. A sustained analysis at the interface of conceptually relevant personality factors and stress-related support processes will be important for future research (see Pierce et al., 1997 for a discussion of such issues).

Finally, stress-related models do not explicitly take into account how the type or quality of relationship may influence the effectiveness of social support. In one interesting study, participants performed a stressful task while either a friend or stranger provided them with social support (Christenfeld et al., 1997). Despite the fact that the same objective supportive behaviors were performed, blood pressure reactions to the stressful task were lower for participants who were given support from a friend versus a stranger. Even among friends there are differences in relationship quality that may impact on the effectiveness of support. In one of our studies we found that women provided with support from an ambivalent female friend (that is, a friend for whom they had both positive and negative feelings) actually showed heightened cardiovascular reactivity during stress (Uno, Uchino, and Smith, 2002). Findings such as these make it clear that not all relationships will result in stress-buffering or -prevention effects. Relationships contain expectations for appropriate interactions and a personal history that can facilitate or hinder the support process (Berscheid and Reis, 1998). These issues need strong consideration in stress-related models.

Direct Effect Models of Support

The second set of models linking social support to health emphasizes the overall benefits of being embedded in a social network (Berkman, 1995; Cohen and Wills, 1985). The types of measures that tend to find such evidence are structural measures of support because they tap into the existence of a variety of social roles and ties. The main question here relates to what exactly is healthy about being socially integrated. One answer to this question is suggested by identity theorists who argue that being imbedded in a social network is health protective because it gives

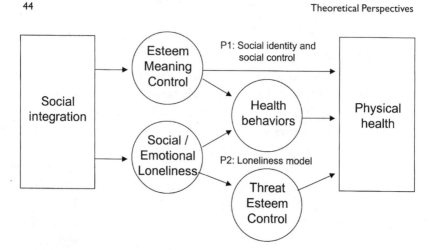

Figure 3.2. Main pathways involved in direct effect models of social support. P1=Pathway 1, P2=Pathway 2.

individuals meaningful roles that provide esteem and purpose to life (Thoits, 1983). Other researchers have argued that being imbedded in social networks also provides a sense of both physical and emotional security (Stroebe and Stroebe, 1996). These pathways may in turn have a direct effect on health. Figure 3.2 illustrates this effect (path 1).

Also shown in figure 3.2 is the pathway (path 1) made explicit by the social control hypothesis, which is a major variant of the direct effect model (Umberson, 1987; Lewis and Rook, 1999). According to this view, social networks are health promoting because they facilitate healthier behaviors such as exercise, eating right, and not smoking. This can happen in at least two ways. One way postulates an indirect route in which integration may be healthy. As noted by identity theorists, having multiple social roles can provide greater personal incentive to remain healthy because our roles provide a sense of meaning and obligation to life. Simply put, relationships can provide us with important reasons to live. The second route is more direct in nature because it suggests that our social networks can place pressures on us to act in healthy ways. For instance, your spouse may serve as a source of control by gently (or perhaps not so gently) reminding you to eat healthier or see the doctor when you are not feeling well. The research that does exist is consistent with the social control hypothesis. These studies provide evidence that measures of social integration (for example, marital or parental status) tend to be associated with healthier behaviors such as lower risk taking, alcohol intake, and substance abuse (Umberson, 1987; Lewis and Rook, 1999).

One unique prediction of the social control perspective is that although social network members can influence us to behave in healthier ways, they may also be a source of psychological distress (Hughes and Gove, 1981). This distress can occur because people resent being directly controlled by others. Research on this tenant of the social control hypothesis is mixed. However, one recent study examined network distress at a general level (overall network) and from specific network members and its relation to health behaviors (Lewis and Rook, 1999). They found that only when social control was measured from specific network members did it predict greater distress and healthier behaviors. One interesting implication of the social control hypothesis is that attempts at social control that are not as obvious to the individual may be the best because they might be associated with better behavioral *and* psychological outcomes.

A second perspective under the direct effect model is what I will term the loneliness hypothesis (Stroebe and Stroebe, 1996). As depicted in figure 3.2 (path 2), loneliness may be an important pathway linking social integration to health outcomes. Although the specific pathways depicted in figure 3.2 are not explicit in Stroebe and Stroebe's model, they are implicated in recent research. For instance, loneliness appears to be related to negative health-related outcomes because of more chronic appraisals of threat during daily life and health behaviors such as poorer sleep (Cacioppo et al., 2002; Hawkley et al., 2003).

In their analysis of the loneliness hypothesis, Stroebe and Stroebe distinguish between social and emotional loneliness (Weiss, 1973). Social loneliness is thought to have its origins in the absence of engaging social interactions (for example, friends), whereas emotional loneliness is thought to be caused by the absence of close attachment relationships (for example, spouse). A recent study on the social networks of young and older adults provided support for the predicted associations between specific social integration measures and different types of loneliness (Green et al., 2001). However, more research is needed linking these specific network ties and types of loneliness to various outcomes. One study found that the depression caused by the death of a spouse (attachment figure) was associated with variations in emotional and not social loneliness (Stroebe et al., 1996).

An interesting and emerging perspective on social integration measures involves its contribution to what has been termed social capital (Kawachi and Berkman, 2000; Putnam, 1995). Social capital is defined as the aspects of the social environment, such as the degree of integration, that set the foundation for collective action (Kawachi and Berkman). It is measured as the degree of membership or involvement in relatively formal group activities, and it is viewed as a form of capital because it appears to be a resource for social good. Most of this research has examined the influence of social capital on community outcomes such as crime and social cohesion. This research has shown that social capital is consistently related to higher levels of community trust and lower rates of violent crimes such as robbery and homicide (Kawachi and Berkman).

The concept of social capital has been applied to the examination of community health. In one of the first studies to examine this issue on physical health outcomes, researchers used data from the General Social Survey, which is based on a representative sample of U.S. English-speaking individuals who are eighteen years or older (Kawachi et al., 1997). These researchers found that states with lower overall social capital, as measured by the amount of group memberships or degree of community trust, had the highest mortality rates.

Social capital may contribute to mortality patterns via distinct pathways (Kawachi and Berkman, 2000) (figure 3.3). One possibility is that social capital may influence healthier behaviors because communities high in social capital appear to have greater access to innovative health-relevant information and endorse healthier norms. Notice that this is different from the social control hypothesis in its level of analysis. Social capital theorists focus on community-level control, whereas social control theorists focus more on control from the network or specific network ties. A second pathway is that social capital may influence access to health services. Communities high in social capital tend to be more effective in ensuring that budget cuts do not influence important local services. Assess to such local services may then influence morbidity and mortality. Finally, community social capital may also influence

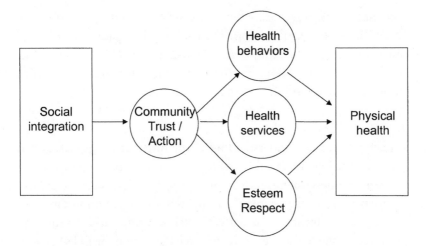

Figure 3.3. Main pathways involved in social capital.

psychosocial processes such as self-esteem and mutual respect that provides the basis for effective social exchanges.

Critiques of Direct Effect Models

Much research is consistent with the benefits predicted by the direct
effect models (Cohen, 1988). However, researchers have also raised a
number of questions about these perspectives.

Inconsistent Research

The direct effect models predict that social integration is related to better
health and well-being. Although most agree that social integration appears beneficial, there is research suggesting that under some circumstances, measures of social integration are related to negative effects on
well-being. The simple existence of relationships sets up the possibility
for conflict that can not only undermine social support but be associated
with significant interpersonal stress in its own right (Coyne and De-
Longis, 1986; Rook and Pietromonaco, 1987). This "dark side" of relationships is suggested by research on violence in marriages and families
as well as interpersonal jealousy, gossiping, dependency, and sexual coer-
cion (see Spitzberg and Cupach, 1998). Social networks can also model

and reinforce negative health behaviors such as smoking and substance abuse (Burg and Seeman, 1994). The data on the negative side of social integration suggest that the prior research on the direct effect model may reveal stronger associations by considering the conditions under which integration can contribute to negative outcomes.

Gaps in Our Understanding

A major gap in our understanding of the direct effect models is that presently little evidence exists on the more specific pathways by which social integration can have effects on health. Identity and social control theorists propose that networks ultimately influence important outcomes via the feeling of control, by self-esteem, and by providing greater meaning to life. Very little research has shown the links between social integration, psychological processes, and relevant outcomes within the same study. For instance, studies on the social control hypothesis have usually not included measures of self-esteem and life meaning to test if they are actually responsible for associations between social integration and better health behaviors. Likewise, little evidence also presently exists on the interesting proposed pathways linking social capital and the loneliness hypothesis to health outcomes. However, these are relatively newer frameworks, and it is probable that critical data on these perspectives are forthcoming. In general, studies that directly include measures of the proposed pathways such as self-esteem or loneliness along with social integration and health measures would be valuable assets to this literature.

In my opinion, social capital provides one of the more intriguing new frameworks based on direct effect models. However, there have been questions raised about the research on social capital and health outcomes that require further clarification (Macinko and Starfield, 2001; Whitehead, 2001). One issue is that social capital has been measured in very different ways depending on the researcher. This problem is magnified by the lack of documentation for the reliability and validity for some of the measures used in current social capital research. A second related issue concerns the extent to which measures of social capital overlap with other more established psychosocial risk factors. One of the key concepts in assessments of social capital includes measures of perceived community trust (Kawachi and Berkman, 2000).

Assessments of community trust may be influenced by personality characteristics such as trait hostility that are known to influence morbidity and mortality (Smith, 1992). Future research is needed to fill in these gaps in understanding the promising concept of social capital.

Processes Not Explicit

In reading much of the research on the direct effect models it is easy to get confused about the measures of social integration that should be related to better health (Glass et al., 1997). In fact, the direct effect models do not typically specify the types of social integration measures that may be related to beneficial health outcomes. This is an important issue because a close examination of more recent data suggests that not all measures of social integration are equally related to well-being. This problem is compounded by the fact that social integration is measured very differently depending on the researcher. Studies in the health domain have used the number of family members, number of group memberships, reciprocity in the network, and marital status as measuring the same general concept of social integration. Some studies have taken the approach of aggregating across these measures to create an overall composite measure of social integration, while others have simply examined the effects of one variable at a time.

What is needed is a more recent perspective on social integration measures that addresses these issues. The material covered in chapter 2 provides a good starting point. For instance, recent research by identity theorists suggests differential effects for social ties or roles that are voluntary or obligatory (Thoits, 1992). Voluntary roles are probably selected to maximize their reward value and thus should be related to better health than obligatory roles (Berbrier and Schulte, 2000; Thoits, 1992). The distinction between strong and weak ties is also interesting and deserves more attention in this literature. Future research will be needed to merge the direct effect models with current thinking in identity and social network research.

Summary and Discussion

There are two broad perspectives linking social support to health: stress-related and direct effect models. Each of these perspectives contains a variety of submodels (for example, matching hypotheses or social control) in an attempt to provide a more specific account of how social support may influence physical health. Each of these conceptual perspectives has its own set of issues to address, and each is in need of more research to provide more comprehensive frameworks for examining how social support influences health outcomes. However, several broader issues warrant discussion regarding these models.

One general issue is the need to further consider these conceptual models in the context of our close relationships (Badr et al., 2001; Gottlieb, 1985). Many studies test these theoretical models by simply assessing general (nonspecific) perceptions of support and relating them to various outcomes. Depending on the researcher's goals or assumptions this can be one approach. There are several reasons, however, why more research might need to focus on specific close relationships (Badr et al.). First, the centrality of these relationships (for example, spouses, confidants) makes them theoretically important for identity-related and social control processes. Second, close relationships are those in which we have more contact, trust, and interdependence that can aid in the seeking, receipt, and provision of support during stress. Finally, a focus on close relationships provides a circumscribed analysis of support processes that can reveal more specific associations as well as complexities that need consideration in these theoretical models and the development of interventions.

Marital ties are one example of a close relationship that would be important to consider within these conceptual models (Badr et al., 2001). Spouses tend to be one of our most important relationships in adulthood and hence may be central to identity and social control processes. Spouses also tend to be a primary source of functional support for married individuals (Brown and Harris, 1978; Coyne and Anderson, 1999). The quality of the marriage, however, appears to be an important factor in how couples interact and interpret the other's behavior. Individuals in poor quality marriages, for instance, tend to have more spousal conflict, which can interfere with the seeking and receipt of effective social support (Coyne and Anderson). In one interesting study, married couples were asked to send various messages to each other (Noller, 1980). Results of this study revealed that couples who had good relationships communicated more clearly than couples who had poorer relationships. This study implies that social support processes may unfold more smoothly and with greater effectiveness in high quality marriages.

One complexity for these theoretical models that emerges when considering support processes in married couples is potential gender differences. Janice Kiecolt-Glaser and Tamara Newton (2001) argue that women may be more sensitive than men are to the quality of the relationship. For instance, when married couples were asked to discuss a problem in their relationship, women tend to show stronger associations between negative behaviors and subsequent stress responses (for example, heightened cortisol) compared to men (Kiecolt-Glaser et al., 1996). One possible explanation for these findings includes gender differences in self-representations (Kiecolt-Glaser and Newton). Women's self-representations are more likely to include information on close and significant others (Acitelli and Young, 1996). Of course, this gender difference has important implications for understanding direct effect and stress-related processes (for example, support seeking) that emerge for women and men.

A second general issue that arose when reviewing these models is the lack of research examining the association between them. Part of this is due not only to differences in the models but also to their associated measurement history. The early review by Cohen and Wills (1985) found that stress-buffering effects were more likely to be found for functional measures, whereas direct effects were more likely for structural measures. Although structural measures of support have traditionally been associated with direct effect models, some research suggests that they are also associated with stress-buffering effects (Barrera, 1988). The same circumstance exists for functional measures of support that under some conditions also appear to be related to direct effects on mental health (Barrera).

The research that exists on these perspectives also suggests that functional and structural measures of support are only modestly related to each other, which some have taken as further evidence for their distinctiveness. However, the modest association between structural and functional measures of support is expected because of differences in their level of analysis (see figure 2.1). Generally speaking, broader constructs such as social integration tap into more processes than specific constructs such as functional support. The result of these differences in level of specificity would be to attenuate any association between them.

An examination of the association between stress-related and direct effect models represents an exciting opportunity to integrate and delineate the boundary conditions of these perspectives. There are at least two ways in which one might approach this issue. One is to examine how measures typically associated with one model may be related to the other set of models. For instance, there are several reasons why structural measures may be related to buffering effects on health. One reason is that social integration provides access to available and received support. This explanation would suggest that functional support measures are important in buffering processes but they need to be considered in combination with the person's larger social network. A second possible explanation for why structural measures predict stress-buffering processes is provided by identity theorists, who argue that social integration is essential for a sense of esteem, feelings of control, and life meaning (Thoits, 1983). Self-esteem and feelings of control are important personal "tools" that can help individuals cope more effectively with stressors in their lives. These processes may also be associated with greater proactive coping that helps a person avoid stressors in the first place (Aspinwall and Taylor, 1997). For instance, someone who has a greater sense of life meaning may be more apt to plan carefully for his or her financial future, which could be an asset for potential problems (for example, job layoff or medical condition).

A second way to examine the association between these models is to conceptualize how stress-buffering effects might lead to direct effects and vice versa. Such an analysis makes salient the importance of extending our view of these models to how they unfold over time. For instance, the seeking and subsequent provision of support during stress can lead to the formation of new relationships (for example, support groups) and organizational ties (for example, the American Cancer Society for cancer patients and their families) and also deepen existing relationships or ties to various organizations (for example, religious groups). These social ties and roles may in turn influence identity processes with subsequent direct effects on health.

The processes discussed at the interface of the direct effect and stress-related models are speculative given the lack of existing integrative research. Nevertheless, the purpose of this discussion is to stimulate plausible thought and research on how these two models may be related instead of pitting the two against each other, as has been more common in past research. Such research may also serve to answer questions about the more dynamic nature of social support processes, which stands in contrast to the more static approach of simply assessing social support at one point in time and relating this to health. Research exploring these issues will ultimately provide the basis for fine tuning our theoretical models linking social support to health outcomes.

4

Social Support and All-Cause Mortality

A number of different theoretical models link social support to health outcomes. These theoretical models are variants of two broad frameworks: stress-related and direct effect models. The main stress-related perspectives include the stress-buffering and stress-prevention models. Of these, the stress-buffering model of support is the most widely researched and predicts that social support should be beneficial primarily for individuals under high levels of life stress (Cohen and Wills, 1985). The direct effect models predict that social support should be generally beneficial across a range of life situations. Major variants of these direct effect models include identity theory and the social control hypothesis, the loneliness hypothesis, and social capital.

Although evidence by and large supports these perspectives, each has been critiqued for data that may be seen as inconsistent with each perspective, gaps in understanding of these models, and processes not explicit in these models. Research has also found that stress-buffering effects are more likely to be shown with functional measures of support and direct effects are more likely to be seen with structural measures of support (Cohen and Wills, 1985). However, research also suggests conditions under which functional measures of support can have direct effects and structural measures of support can have stress-buffering effects (Barrera, 1988). An analysis of the proposed pathways made explicit by these models is consistent with the utility of a more integrative approach that emphasizes the links between the stress-related and direct effect models.

I encourage readers to think about the measurement and conceptual issues raised in chapters 2 and 3 when reading this chapter, keeping in mind a sense of the major perspectives linking social support to health outcomes. In fact most of the research on social support and mortality has not been specifically designed to test these models. Many of these models were developed in parallel with the emerging literature on social support and physical health outcomes, which poses significant conceptual issues that are addressed in this chapter and the chapters that follow. As a result, my review first focuses on the different types of measures linking social support to mortality, and, when possible, I discuss the theoretical processes underlying these effects (as detailed in chapter 3).

It is now time to address the foundation of this book. This book is written with the premise that social support is associated with beneficial effects on physical health. Is there an association between social support and mortality? I examined more than eighty published studies that tested the link between social support and mortality rates. These studies are listed in the reference section with an asterisk and were identified using an electronic search on the databases *Psychinfo* and *Medline*. In addition, the bibliographies of each of these articles as well as those of major reviews of the literature (for example, Berkman, 1995; Leppin and Schwarzer, 1990; Seeman, 1996) were examined for completeness. Although some articles may have been missed, the articles reviewed here are likely representative of the published research on this topic.

I first classified the studies by various sample characteristics (for example, gender or population) and the type of support measure utilized (for example, structural—group memberships; functional—emotional support). I then examined whether the different ways of measuring support predicted mortality rates. Finally, I closely considered any assessed "control factors" (for example, initial health status) or theoretical processes (for example, health behaviors) and how they impacted the study's main results.

I address three major questions based on this analysis.

    1. Is social support related to overall mortality? There are many studies examining this issue, and I attempt to draw some firm conclusions based on the available research.

    2. Is social support the factor influencing mortality? Even if social support predicts mortality it may be a spurious association. The major potential alternative explanations for this link are examined.

    3. Is social support more effective for some than for others? Not all people may benefit equally from social support, and I examine the conditions under which social support appears most effective.

Within these three questions I raise conceptual issues and critiques based on my review of the studies and the larger social support literature covered in chapters 2 and 3. However, I first review the main characteristics of these studies as a preview to these questions.

Characteristics of Studies Linking Social Support to Mortality

The scope of these studies as a whole is impressive. Interest in this topic is also increasing, as evidenced by the publication trends across the decades. In the 1970s only one published study that I found examined the links between social support and mortality. The 1980s were not only a time of wonderful music but of increased interest: there were nineteen studies that directly tested the topic. The 1990s witnessed a large increase in research as about fifty-six studies examined the link between social support and mortality. The years 2000–2001 produced at least ten studies testing this association. The populations for these studies ranged from relatively healthy middle-aged and older adults to medical populations such as cancer and cardiac patients. Of special note is that a fair number of these studies were large population-based studies that literally examined thousands of individuals. Some studies were samples of convenience and included relatively small samples (for

Table 4.1. Most common measures of social support in mortality studies.

Measure of Support	Type of Support
Number of close others, relatives, children, friends, and/or people in household	Social integration
Number of group memberships and/or social activities	Social integration
Contact with close others, relatives, children, and/or friends	Social integration
Perceived emotional, tangible, and/or informational support from close others, family, friends, and/or boss	Functional support
Number of individuals who are sources of emotional, tangible, and/or informational support	Functional support

example, one hundred). Large population-based studies can obtain results that have more generalizability because their participants are more representative of those sampled from some specified area.

As noted in chapter 2, there is considerable variability in the way researchers measure social support. This was also true of the social support and mortality literature. The most common methods of measuring social support in these studies are depicted in table 4.1. Of these different methods of measurement, by and large the most common method was to examine measures of social integration. A fair number of studies examined functional measures of support, whereas a small number of studies examined both structural and functional measures of support. Of the studies that examined social integration measures, some measured multiple components of social integration and then created an overall index of social support. All in all, the diversity of measures and participants in these studies provides a relatively strong basis for asking the questions posed at the beginning of this chapter.

Before we begin to address the questions of interest, let me first describe the typical design features of these studies. Researchers often first identify a sample of interest. In some cases it is a representative sample of a specific geographical area, but in many cases it is a sample of convenience. The sample is also either a relatively healthy group or a specific medical population (for example, cardiovascular patients). Either structural or functional measures of support are then taken at the first visit (time 1), along with other standard risk factors known to influence future health status. These important "control variables" often include initial health status (for example, chronic conditions), age, socioeconomic status (SES), and gender. In more recent studies, measures of current physiological risk are included, such as cholesterol and blood pressure levels. A fair number of studies also include measures of health behaviors (for example, exercise or smoking) known to influence mortality to determine whether social support is an independent predictor of mortality. The study population is then followed for a period of months to years.

Is Social Support Related to All-Cause Mortality?
Overall Evidence

In a majority of studies, mortality from all causes was examined as the major outcome variable. All-cause mortality is usually defined as death from diverse causes, including cancer and cardiovascular diseases. (Some studies did examine social support and mortality from specific causes, and I focus on those smaller sets of studies in chapter 5.) What is the status of studies examining social support and all-cause mortality? Importantly, about 80 percent of the studies I reviewed found an association between either structural or functional measures of support and lower overall mortality rates (Berkman and Syme, 1979; Blazer, 1982; Brummett et al., 2001; Orth-Gomér and Johnson, 1987). These studies show that individuals low in support appear to have, on average, a two to three times greater risk of mortality compared to those high in social support. Thus, the available research provides strong overall evidence that social support is related to lower mortality rates across a variety of diseases. Combined with the voluminous literature on social support and mental health (Cohen, Underwood, and Gottlieb, 2000), it appears that individuals with good social support live both longer *and* happier lives. This does not necessarily mean that the association between social support and mortality is a simple one. In the upcoming sections I highlight some of the main findings and complicating issues that arose from my review.

Evidence and Issues in Linking Structural Support to Overall Mortality

The most impressive evidence for an association between the degree of social integration and all-cause mortality comes from large population-based studies (for example, Berkman and Syme, 1979; House, Robbins, and Metzner, 1982; Orth-Gomér and Johnson, 1987). For instance, researchers in Sweden followed a random sample of more than 17,000 men and women between the ages of 29 and 74 for six years (Orth-Gomér and Johnson). They measured social integration as a composite index of the number and degree of contacts across a wide range of relationships (for example, family, neighbors, coworkers). Results of this large study demonstrated that social integration was associated with lower all-cause mortality rates even after considering the influence of age, gender, education, employment status, smoking, and exercise habits.

The evidence from such studies does not necessarily imply that the association between structural aspects of support and mortality is a simple one. Several trends from this literature caught my attention. A substantial majority of studies that utilized structural measures of social support found an association with lower overall mortality rates. However, researchers who utilized composite structural measures (for example, the social network index) of social integration more consistently found it to predict lower mortality rates (Berkman and Syme, 1979; House, Robbins, and Metzner, 1982; Kaplan et al., 1988). About 85 percent of these studies found aggregate measures of social integration to predict lower mortality rates. Some studies only examined single-item or domain-specific assessments such as the number of relatives or close friends. Although some of these measures also predicted lower mortality, they were not as consistently related to these outcomes as aggregate measures of integration (for example, Dalgard and Håheim, 1998; Hanson et al., 1989; Zuckerman, Kasl, and Ostfeld, 1984).

There are several possible reasons for the consistent association between aggregate measures of social integration and mortality. One possible theoretical reason is provided by identity theorists. Any one structural measure may index only a limited role in a person's life. However, information on multiple relationships or roles provides a more comprehensive assessment of the influence of relationships on identity and well-being. Researchers from the functional perspective of support might also argue that a broad structural assessment better captures the potential supportive capacity of one's social network from a variety of sources.

There is also a simple statistical explanation for a more consistent association between composite measures of social integration and mortality. According to statistical models, related measures that are based on more items are usually more reliable, which increases the measure's sensitivity to detect potential associations. It was difficult to evaluate this possibility in the present set of studies because most did not report the reliabilities associated with their aggregate measures. This possible statistical explanation is not necessarily at odds with the theoretical ones discussed above. A more reliable measure also allows a more sensitive test of theoretical perspectives.

There is, however, one apparent exception to the association between single domain structural assessments and mortality that appears important. The number of social activities (that is, participation in informal and formal group or organizational activities) appears to be a consistent predictor of lower mortality rates (Jylhä and Aro, 1989; Sugisawa, Liang, and Liu, 1994; Welin et al., 1985). Approximately 83 percent of all studies that examined social or group activities found them to predict lower mortality rates. At first it might seem as if social activities may simply be tapping into how generally active or healthy a person is and that these factors are responsible for the reported associations. After all, someone who is less active or in poorer health is less likely to physically participate in social and group activities. However, the association between social activities and mortality often exists even after considering the influence of participants' initial health status and general exercise levels (Dalgard and Håheim, 1998; Irvine et al., 1999; Orth-Gomér and Undén, 1990).

One possible explanation for an association between social activities and lower mortality rates is provided by functional support theorists. These theorists might argue that the number of roles and activities is actually measuring contact and access to supportive behaviors across these social contexts. As a result, individuals might reap the benefits from these sources of support. This argument would have to assume some special access to support in this context because contact with family and friends is not as simple a predictor of lower mortality rates (Frasure-Smith et al., 2000; Hanson et al., 1989; Ganzini et al., 1997). On the other hand, identity theorists provide the most straightforward explanation for these findings: these more voluntary roles are easier to exit if involvement becomes nonrewarding (Berbrier and Schulte, 2000; Thoits, 1992). Such increased social participation in groups is in turn predicted to provide an individual with a more diverse sense of self-identity and worth with subsequent benefits on health (Thoits, 1983).

Of the studies examining structural measures of support and mortality, many included measures of health behaviors such as exercise, alcohol consumption, and smoking (Berkman and Syme, 1979; Orth-Gomér, Rosengren, and Wilhelmsen, 1993; Liu, Hermalin, and Chuang, 1998). These health behaviors may provide evidence for the feasibility of the social control hypothesis. Unfortunately, most studies examined the independent prediction of mortality via social support by statistically controlling for all relevant risk factors at once. This means that the effects of health behaviors were usually included with demographic variables and prior health status. Of the few studies that did examine these control factors in smaller "steps," the effects of social support on all-cause mortality remained reliable even after considering health behaviors such as smoking, physical activity, and alcohol consumption (Seeman et al., 1987; Sugisawa, Liang, and Liu, 1994; Welin et al., 1992).

Although social support proved to predict mortality above and beyond what was predicted by these health behaviors, some of these studies did find that the association between structural measures of support and all-cause mortality was weaker than when these health behaviors were not considered. For instance, the Alameda County Study examined thousands of men and women (Seeman et al., 1987). It was found that the risk associated with a lack of social integration, although significant, was reduced when considering a set of behavioral and psychological risk factors including smoking, exercise, and eating breakfast. Although more research that directly tests this health behavior pathway is needed, these studies suggest that at least a part of the complex association between social integration and all-cause mortality may be due to health behaviors. Such results are consistent with the social control hypothesis, although no research on all-cause mortality has yet provided evidence for the direct or indirect control postulated by this perspective.

Thus far, all of the studies discussed examined structural measures of support at an initial assessment and its association with subsequent mortality. One assumption here is that structural measures of support are relatively stable during the intervening years. Of course, people undergo changes in structural aspects of support such as the formation of new relationships, changes in contact with children, or even the death of friends and family. One interesting new development is an examination of how changes in these structural indices of support predict mortality rates (Cerhan and Wallace, 1997; Lund et al., 2001). For instance, it is possible that individuals with sustained low structural support may be more at risk for early mortality than someone with sustained high structural support or a recent decrease in structural support. Another interesting possibility is that individuals with a recent decrease in structural support may be more at risk than someone with sustained high structural support.

The possible association between changes in structural support and mortality was examined in at least two studies (Cerhan and Wallace, 1997; Lund et al., 2001). These studies examined changes in social integration indices over three- to four-year periods, then related these changes to mortality four to eight years later. One of these studies reported that sustained low structural support over both time periods was associated with the highest mortality after considering age, education, perceived health status, and various health behaviors (Cerhan and Wallace, 1997). Although decreases in social integration over time also predicted higher mortality rates, this effect was nonsignificant when considering the above control factors. The other study on this topic found a more complicated set of findings but did show that low integration over both time points predicted higher mortality in seventy- to seventy-four-year-old women (Lund et al., 2001).

The studies discussed above are unique in this literature because structural aspects of support were conceptualized as a more dynamic process over time. Of course, one potential limitation of these studies modeling changes in social integration is that some additional changes may have occurred over the subsequent follow-up period but went unmeasured. Future research that includes annual assessments may be able to better capture important fluctuations in social integration over time.

There are additional ways of conceptualizing fluctuations in measures of support and their prediction of mortality. More specifically, there may be meaningful fluctuations in these measures (for example, contact) over not just years but perhaps weeks (Lang, Featherman, and Nesselroade, 1997). This argument would be analogous to research on self-esteem that once conceptualized it primarily as a stable process. More recent data suggest that there may also be meaningful short-term fluctuations in self-esteem (Kernis et al., 2000). That is, some individuals may have a relatively consistent pattern of fluctuating self-esteem that may in turn influence well-being. We probably all know of individuals whose lives seem to be in constant upheaval. These people may represent one extreme end of this process.

In one study demonstrating the feasibility of this approach, researchers in the MacArthur Successful Aging Studies examined week-by-week fluctuations in perceived control during a seven-month period (Eizenman et al., 1997). Results revealed that this variability in control was not just a random occurrence but a relatively consistent characteristic for some individuals. Furthermore, individuals with greater fluctuations in control were more at risk for mortality over a subsequent five-year period, whereas overall levels of control did not predict subsequent mortality.

One interesting question raised by this study relates to the factors responsible for the observed fluctuations in perceived control. Functional support and identity theorists might argue that changes in social support may have been partially responsible for these fluctuations over time. To this point, researchers have also examined weekly fluctuations in both relationship availability and how efficacious individuals felt about their social life (Lang et al., 1997). Consistent with the possible role of relationships in self-relevant control, results of this study showed that variations in relationship availability were strongly associated with changes in self-efficacy. Overall, the research on fluctuations in these social processes suggests the promise of a more dynamic approach to studying how both structural and functional measures of support influence all-cause mortality.

One final and surprising aspect of studies examining structural measures of support and all-cause mortality is the lack of diversity in measures. Most focus on the simple presence of a relationship or contact with specific network members. In contrast, social network theory suggests the importance of measures such as network density (that is, linkages among network members), multiplex (that is, number of people with exchanges with person), and clusters (that is, subunits of networks). In the only study I found that provided such a comprehensive assessment, researchers examined elderly individuals using nineteen different network variables. Results revealed that many of these network measures (for example, multiplex or clusters) predicted lower mortality over the subsequent three-year period (Cohen, Teresi, and Holmes, 1987). Although more research is needed on a larger sample, this study suggests the utility of a broader approach using a variety of social network measures (Scott, 2000; Wasserman and Galaskiewicz, 1994). However, conceptual developments that specifically link these less utilized network measures to the health domain will also be necessary to provide greater guidance to researchers.

Evidence and Issues in Linking Functional Support to Overall Mortality

Although relatively less research has examined the association between functional measures of support and its association with all-cause mortality, several conclusions are also possible. It is clear that a majority of these studies found an association between functional aspects of support and lower mortality rates (for example, Blazer, 1982; Berkman, Leo-Summers, and Horwitz, 1992; Brummett et al., 2001). However, as the case with structural measures of support, a closer examination of these studies reveals that these associations are more complex than the models in chapter 3 might predict.

The dominant perspective linking functional support measures to mortality is the stress-buffering model. Although the buffering model would predict functional social support to be health-promoting primarily under conditions of high stress, most of these studies never measured life stress. Thus it must be assumed that over the long term, these functional supports helped buffer the effects of any unmeasured life stress. Of course, this assumption is problematic in the absence of any direct measure of stress.

A few mortality studies did report data on both stress levels and support. Consistent with the buffering model, these studies found that mortality rates were highest for individuals low in support and high in stress (Johnson et al., 1996; Falk et al., 1992; Rosengren et al., 1993). For instance, Falk and colleagues examined the buffering model in a random sample of 621 men (ages 78–79) in Malmo, Sweden. These researchers found that the combination of high job strain and low support was associated with the highest mortality rate over the subsequent seven years. However, not immediately consistent with the stress-buffering hypothesis, this study also found structural measures of support (for example, social participation) to demonstrate buffering effects on mortality (also see Johnson, Hall, and Theorell, 1989).

The fact that stress-buffering effects are seen with both functional and structural measures of support may be seen as inconsistent with the review of Cohen and Wills (1985). However, as discussed in chapter 3, more sophisticated modeling of these data may provide evidence that structural measures provide the larger context by which functional support is provided. In addition, there are a number of direct theoretical ways in which structural measures may have stress-buffering effects via their influence on identity, control, and perhaps proactive coping (see chapter 3). However, at this point in time it remains an empirical question for future studies, and researchers interested in the stress-buffering model should also examine relevant structural measures of support.

It is also important to examine more precisely the role that stress may play in the social support and health link. There are at least two ways that stress may result in negative long-term effects on health: reactivity and exposure (Cacioppo and Berntson, in press). Reactivity refers to the magnitude of the stress response, and individuals who react more strongly to stress may be at greater risk for future health problems. In comparison, some individuals experience more turbulent lives because they are exposed to a greater number of stressful events (for example, low SES). This differential exposure to stress may then increase their risk for health problems. Of course, reactivity and exposure may be related (for example, high stress exposure and reactivity), and other processes may be important (for example, recovery from stress), but most prior research has focused on these distinct pathways. These two explanations of how stress may influence health correspond to the stress-buffering and stress-prevention models, respectively (see chapter 3). Unfortunately, the existing studies on social support and physical health do not allow for a separation of these pathways because total stress scores may represent a combination of these processes. Future research is needed, using more specific measures of stress that link up to these possible pathways (see Cohen, Kessler, and Gordon, 1995).

The matching hypothesis suggests that support should be most beneficial when it meets the particular demands of the stressors. An examination of this hypothesis could not be done with any confidence because of the lack of studies testing this proposition. However, the 1992 study by Falk and associates on job strain did examine different aspects of support, including emotional and informational. Perhaps inconsistent with the matching hypothesis, all aspects of support showed a stress-buffering association with mortality rates. Of course, one problem here is the categorization of job strain as relatively controllable or controllable. Because of the long-term nature of mortality studies, the absence of direct measures of stressor controllability over time may preclude a strong test of the matching hypothesis.

According to some researchers, there are several functional components of support that should be particularly effective because they are useful across a wide variety of life situations (Cohen et al., 1985). The two that have been argued to be most effective are emotional support and informational support because people can typically benefit from useful information and reassurances of their self-worth. Although there are only a few studies that provide a relatively pure assessment of informational support, there are a number of studies that specifically assessed emotional support. Consistent with the importance of emotional support for health, about 70 percent of these studies found it to predict lower mortality rates (Blazer, 1982; Hanson et al.,

1989; Orth-Gomér, Rosengren, and Wilhelmsen, 1993). In one of these studies, researchers examined older men and women who were hospitalized for a heart attack (Berkman, Leo-Summers, and Horwitz, 1992). A unique feature of this study is that measures of emotional support were available before the heart attack. Thus their assessment of emotional support is unlikely to be confounded with the event itself (for example, stress mobilization). After considering the influence of demographic factors and other important clinical indicators of risk (for example, ejection fraction), emotional support measured before the heart attack was associated with lower mortality during the next six months.

A complicated set of issues emerge when examining the effects of received support on mortality rates. As discussed in chapter 2, some researchers have argued that received support may be associated with detrimental influences on mental health. It is interesting in light of these suggestions that about half of the studies examining received support found it to be associated with *higher* subsequent mortality rates (Forster and Stoller, 1992; Krause, 1997; Sabin, 1993). In fact, it is the component of received tangible support that appears to be most consistently related to higher mortality (Forster and Stoller; Kaplan et al., 1994). A simple potential explanation based on the concept of support mobilization is that individuals who are more dependent on receiving support are simply more physically impaired to begin with. However, these studies do not appear to support this explanation because most considered the influence of initial health status (Kaplan et al.; Penninx et al., 1997).

Although it is still possible that studies did not provide a comprehensive enough assessment of impairment, one study is particularly informative because of its measurement strategy. This study examined mortality in older adults and measured activity limitations due to health as well as tangible support with these activities of daily living (Forster and Stoller, 1992). The specificity of these measures makes it a more sensitive test of whether people dependent on received support are simply more physically impaired to begin with. Inconsistent with this proposition is the fact that these researchers found that received tangible support with daily activities predicted higher mortality rates in women, an effect that was evident even after considering the degree of functional impairment with activities (also see Sabin, 1993).

So what is it about receiving support that may be unhealthy? Before I attempt to evaluate several proposed explanations, let me mention that studies examining received support showed the most variability in outcomes (some showed no effect, for example, Avlund, Damsgaard, and Holstein, 1998; Oxman, Freeman, and Manheimer, 1995), and it is unclear whether these effects would be significant if averaged across all studies examining received support. With that caveat, there are several possible explanations for received support not being as healthy as other types of support (for example, social integration or emotional support). One explanation suggests that individuals who received such support take a harmful hit to their self-esteem (Bolger, Zuckerman, and Kessler, 2000) that in turn might be associated with negative health outcomes (see chapter 2). No mortality studies to date have evaluated this possibility. However, one interesting implication here is that these negative effects should be more evident in individualistic cultures in which autonomy and independence is emphasized (Markus and Kitiyama, 1991). Perhaps in collective cultures where such behaviors are more in keeping with the group norms, then the effects of received support should be more beneficial and its absence particularly detrimental.

A second possible explanation for why received support may be harmful is that greater reliance on it may also increase the opportunity for interpersonal conflict. It has been shown in several studies that network members may provide support in a way that does not meet the needs of the individual or demeans the person and their problem (Dakof and Taylor, 1990; Dunkel-Schetter and Bennett, 1990). For instance, cancer patients report that their support networks were unhelpful by occasionally being critical of their response to cancer or expressing too much worry (Dakof and Taylor). Research also suggests that it is not the case that network members do not know how to support individuals (for example, what to say or what is helpful). On the contrary, being a support provider in such situations can be stressful because individuals do not want to say something to upset the individual, or they may be anxious over the person's disease status. Ironically, the anxiety and fear raised by such concerns may interfere with the retrieval of information on how to be a good support provider, and individuals may thus rely on more shallow or impatient ways of responding.

Another possible reason for the apparent detrimental effects of received support may be related to the simplistic modeling of such associations. According to the support deterioration-deterrence model (Norris and Kaniasty, 1996), received support may be important because it prevents deteriorations in perceived available support during stress. This process is particularly important because stressors can have a wide influence on one's support network and decrease their supportive capacity. For instance, researchers from a family systems perspective have argued how coping with a serious illness is a potent stressor that can also induce problems in familial relationships (Ell, 1996). Studies on the support deterioration-deterrence model suggest the feasibility of this model in disaster situations such as adjustments following Hurricane Hugo (Norris and Kaniasty). These data suggest that future researchers would need to test more complex models linking received and available support to mortality in order to appreciate the potential role of received support.

Discussion of Evidence

It is clear that levels of social support assessed as both structural and functional aspects appear to be associated with lower overall mortality rates. However, there were a number of issues that I have tried to highlight from this literature that suggest a reconsideration of the ways in which we think about the health benefits of social support as well as how we study these issues in the future. These more complicated results provide us with the impetus to further develop our theories and models. One aspect that I believe to be particularly interesting is the consistent association between social activities and lower mortality rates. We know very little of why this effect exists, and future research is needed to parse the possible mechanisms based on identity theory or its association with potentially unique functional aspects of support. The other interesting question deals with a consideration of whether fluctuations in both structural and functional social support over time predict mortality. This emphasis on fluctuations in support highlights the dynamic nature of social support that I believe is presently missing in the research literature. However, before we accept as fact the associations between social support and mortality, let's consider in the upcoming section the possibility that social support may not be the "real" factor influencing mortality.

Is Social Support the Factor Influencing Mortality?

At this point it is helpful to make it explicit that many researchers (including me) assume that social support is a causal factor influencing mortality. Of course it is possible that social support is not really the important variable influencing health outcomes. Critics of this research may claim that it is simply correlated with some other variable that is the real factor influencing these outcomes. In this sense, social support may not be causing lower mortality but is simply associated with another variable that is the real hero. To assess these possibilities, researchers use what are called statistical controls for such variables. These statistical controls essentially take out any overlap that the competing variables have with each other in predicting outcomes.

Potential Alternative Explanations for the Social Support and Mortality Link

The initial results of large prospective studies begged the question of whether social support was indeed the factor responsible for these health outcomes. One variable that has received attention is prior health status. We know that past health status is a strong predictor of future health status. According to this alternative explanation, people who are in poor health tend to die faster and also have less social contact because their illness makes them physically less able to socialize. In this sense, higher social support is not influencing mortality but is simply a by-product of people who are healthier. The now classic study of Alameda county residents by Berkman and Syme (1979) was one of the first modern studies to demonstrate an association between social support and mortality. In this study, a random sample of more than 6,000 residents of Alameda county were surveyed in 1965 and followed for nine years. As their measure of social support they used the social network index (see chapter 2) and found that individuals scoring low in social support were between 2.3 to 2.8 times more likely to die during the subsequent nine-year period.

This study is not only a classic because it was one of the first to demonstrate such an association but also because of its careful consideration of alternative explanations. Back in the 1970s, there was little belief among the established medical community that such social factors may influence mortality. Berkman and Syme used a general measure of initial health status and found that the effects for social relationships were found at each level of health status. Thus, these effects were not limited to those in poor health. Although their general measure of health status was not as strong because it lacked more recent biomedical indices, subsequent research has confirmed that the association between social support and health is not explained simply by initial health status. Of the studies that have found an association between social support and mortality, many have also assessed initial health status ranging from self-reports of health status to more well-documented indices (for example, hypertensive status, diabetes, or cholesterol levels), and most have found that these effects are still significant when considering these measures (Brummett et al., 2001; Dalgard and Haheim, 1998; Ruberman et al., 1984).

A second proposed set of alternative explanations for support effects has to do with demonstrating that social support predicts mortality independent of other more established risk factors. One of these factors is SES, which is also a reliable predictor of mortality. SES can be assessed in different ways, but most studies examined household income, occupation, and/or educational status. In the Berkman and Syme study, the possible role of SES was also considered, and the association between social support and mortality was evident across all levels of income and education. Thus, social support appeared to influence health independent of SES. Subsequent studies have again confirmed this initial finding (Kaplan et al., 1988; Roy, FitzGibbon, and Haug, 1996).

There has also been some attempt to establish that social support effects are not related to health behaviors such as smoking and exercise because these factors have been shown to predict mortality in their own right. As noted earlier, many studies assessed health behaviors but simply considered them together with other alternative explanations (for example, SES) in an attempt to demonstrate the unique effects of social support. These studies suggest that social support effects are still significant when considering these health behaviors (Ceria et al., 2001; Kaplan et al., 1994; Penninx et al., 1997). Of course, social control theorists do not conceptualize health behaviors as alternative explanations, and research does suggest that at least some of the association between social integration and mortality may be due to such health practices. Although the prior research has treated health behaviors as alternative explanations, it is equally appropriate to conceptualize them as pathways postulated by this existing theoretical model. In fact, the same argument might be extended to most of these "alternative explanations," and a reconsideration of each will be examined in the next section.

There are at least two other "control" variables that have been standard practice in social support and mortality research. These relate to the basic demographic factors of age and gender. It is well established that both of these factors predict mortality. For instance, men are at a higher risk for coronary artery disease (CAD) than women, and older individuals are at greater risk for CAD than younger individuals (American Heart Association, 2001). As a result, prior researchers have attempted to establish that social support effects on mortality were not simply due to possible overlaps with age and gender. Again, Berkman and Syme (1979) found that the effects of social support on mortality was independent of age and also held for both men and women. Most of the prior research also suggests that these factors are not responsible for the association between social support and mortality (Liu, Hermalin, and Chuang, 1998; Seeman et al., 1987; Williams et al., 1992).

A Reconsideration of "Alternative Explanations"

Although it is important to consider alternative explanations such as those provided by initial health status, it is always useful to ask the question of what exactly is being considered. Measures of initial health status can include diagnosed disorders such as hypertension and physiological indices such as lipid levels. This may be problematic because it ignores the possibility that individuals with strong social support may be less likely to develop certain chronic conditions such as high blood pressure (Lepore, 1998) and that social support may operate through such health-relevant physiological processes (Uchino, Cacioppo, and Kiecolt-Glaser, 1996). When framed in this light, the results linking social support to all-cause mortality may be even stronger than they appear due to the stringent set of medical controls used in past research. Although such controls were necessary in the earlier studies, future research will need to carefully consider recent advances in how social support may influence more intermediate health end points (Uchino et al.). This will also entail the formulation of more complicated models that provide a clearer picture of how social support can lead to the development of certain diseases such as CAD.

As is the case for initial health status, there are other ways of conceptualizing the role of SES on the social support and mortality link. If one views SES as a chronically stressful condition (Gallo and Matthews, 1999), then the stress-buffering perspective would predict that social support should be especially beneficial. One can then start to model more complex associations between social support and health instead of simply viewing SES as a nuisance variable to be controlled in our research. Again, this highlights the importance of thinking carefully about how such variables may actually be part of the phenomenon. In one study that directly addressed this issue, Krause (1997) examined a survey of more than 2,250 men and women in the United States. He found that available support was a strong predictor of lower mortality over the next eleven years, especially for individuals in the *high SES group*. Although these results are not immediately consistent with the stress-buffering model, they suggest that these variables are not independent but interact in important ways to predict mortality rates. They further suggest that an examination of "positive profiles" (for example, high social support or high SES) may be useful in future research.

As already mentioned, there are good reasons to not conceptualize health behaviors as simple alternative explanations. As you might guess, there are also important issues to consider when statistically controlling for age and gender. For instance, in controlling for age we ignore the possibility that social support may have a cumulative effect over time. For instance, Rowe and Kahn (1987) argued that factors such as social support and feelings of control might actually slow the biological aging process. Assuming that social support remains stable, this important paper suggests that differences between individuals low and high in support may grow larger as time passes. Thus, by "controlling" for age, we may be taking out part of the cumulative effect of support over the years.

Discussion of Evidence

Prior research has clearly demonstrated that social support appears to be the important factor influencing all-cause mortality. This association is not explainable solely in terms of differences in initial health status, SES, health behaviors, age, and gender. I have also argued that although prior research has utilized these "control variables" to examine the independent influence of social support on mortality, there are perspectives that suggest more complex ways to model these variables. Nonetheless, the way these variables have been treated in prior research would only serve to decrease our ability to demonstrate that social support influences mortality. In this sense, the consistent effects observed in prior research are even more impressive.

Where does this discussion of alternative explanations take us? On the one hand, researchers who want to demonstrate an independent effect of social support may argue that the literature is not sufficiently developed to recommend alternative modeling of these data. I am sympathetic to this argument because the social support literature has seen little theoretical development during the past ten years. However, an examination of the existing theoretical frameworks described in chapter 3 suggest many more complex ways to conceptualize these variables than has presently been the case in these social support and mortality studies. Some researchers (like me) will probably decide to do two sets of analyses, one the traditional way and the other with more complex modeling. Such analyses will help to replicate prior research and also aid in the development of expanded theoretical models on how to conceptualize social support effects. At a later point in this book, I hope to facilitate alternative modeling by developing revised models to explain how social support influences health based on this review of the literature.

Is Social Support More Effective for Some than for Others?

A third important question concerns the conditions under which social support is most effective. In fact, this question overlaps with the prior section because it starts to address more complex associations that may exist between social support and mortality. The question of the conditions under which social support is most effective is generally referred to as *moderational* analyses. The stress-buffering model is a good example of moderation because it predicts that social support is most effective for individuals under high life stress but has little effect for individuals under low life stress. Thus, the level of stress moderates the association between social support and mortality. Although it is not possible to discuss all possible moderators in this chapter, the three considered in this section are gender, sociocultural factors, and personality. All of these variables have received limited attention in the social support and mortality literature but may help specify the conditions under which social support is most effective.

Gender

One potential moderating factor is the gender of the support recipient (Shumaker and Hill, 1991). Early on, several of these mortality studies found that the health effects of social support appeared stronger for men than women (House, Robbins, and Metzner, 1982; Kaplan et al., 1988). Before accepting this possibility, I should mention that some researchers have argued we must pay careful attention to the age ranges in these studies (Seeman, 1996). Women live longer than men on average, so the findings in some studies may be obscured by the lower mortality rates in women. This possibility was difficult to evaluate because most studies simply treat gender as a control variable and not a moderating factor. However, in a few studies that have examined gender differences and included older samples (older than sixty-five), social support predicted lower mortality in both men and women (Jylhä and Aro, 1989; Seeman et al., 1993).

Nevertheless, there are good conceptual reasons to suspect that the association between social support and mortality might be stronger for men than women. Explanations for these potential gender differences do not dispute the fact that social support is beneficial but argue that structural measures of support can tell us as much about the overload or conflict potential of the network as its support potential. We know that the social networks of women are larger than men, and women are often called upon to be the support providers in our society (Shumaker and Hill, 1991). Both of these factors can be associated with increased interpersonal stress that might effectively cancel out at least some of the benefits of social support (Shumaker and Hill; Seeman, 1996). Combined with evidence suggesting that women tend to be more relationship oriented (Taylor et al., 2000), we can see how women might be more adversely affected by overload or conflict in their social networks. In fact, in a large review of the marital literature, researchers concluded that wives tend to be more sensitive to the negative qualities of the marriage compared to husbands (Kiecolt-Glaser and Newton, 2001). This is important because spouses tend to be an important source of support, and the presence of negativity in the marriage may have a differential impact on support processes (for example, seeking support) for women compared to men.

Sociocultural Differences

Another potentially important moderating factor is the sociocultural context of the support recipient. One possible important factor here is an individual's SES. Individuals low in SES face more stressful lives than their high SES counterparts, with stress that ranges from financial to personal safety issues (Gallo and Matthews, 1999). According to the buffering model, social support should be particularly effective for individuals with major life stress. The studies on social support buffering the negative effects of stressors such as job strain and life events on mortality are consistent with this possibility (for example, Rosengren et al., 1993). Although the one study examining the role of SES on the social support and mortality link did not find immediate evidence for such a buffering effect (Krause, 1997), recent data on SES, support, and more intermediate health outcomes suggest some evidence to this point (Vitaliano et al., 2001). In one study researchers found that the availability of emotional support was associated with better cardiovascular and immune profiles, but only for individuals who had low income.

Another sociocultural variable of potential importance is the cultural background of the individual. Early on it was suggested by Lisa Berkman (1986) that social support effects might be weaker in more integrated societies, presumably because of the higher level of social support available. Such integrated societies tend be more collective cultures (for example, Eastern or Latin American cultures) that emphasize the importance of the group over the individual (Markus and Ki-tiyama, 1991). Although less research exists, it is important to note that there have been a handful of studies in collective cultures (Ho, 1991; Liu, Hermalin, and Chuang, 1998; Sugisawa, Liang, and Liu, 1994). These studies indicate that structural measures of support predict mortality in surprisingly similar ways to studies conducted in more individualistic cultures. For instance, one study examined 2,200 elderly individuals in Japan from a representative national sample (ages sixty or older). The researchers found that social participation was a significant predictor of lower mortality over the next three years (Sugisawa et al.). A recent publication from the Honolulu Heart Study replicated these findings in more than 3,450 Japanese American men in Hawaii with a composite index of both structural and functional measures of support (Ceria et al., 2001).

In one informative study that compared Mexican Americans and nonethnic whites, researchers examined heart attack patients from the Corpus Cristi Heart Project (Farmer et al., 1996). This study addresses the questions raised by Berkman (1986) because Mexican Americans are considered to have a more collective cultural orientation than nonethnic whites. This social support study is also unique in the sense that it directly compared two different cultural orientations and their links to mortality. Researchers found that during the next 3.5 years, a composite index of structural and informational support predicted lower mortality in these cardiac patients. However, Mexican Americans actually benefited more than nonethnic whites from social support as shown by subsequent lower mortality rates. As I speculated earlier, it is possible that people in more individualistic cultures may be particularly sensitive to the negative connotations of some forms of support (for example, threats to autonomy and control), which may explain part of this observed cultural difference. Nevertheless, future research will be needed to determine whether the theoretical mechanisms postulated by existing models (see chapter 3) work in similar ways for more collective cultures.

Personality Differences

Prior research also gives us good reason to suspect that social support may be more beneficial for some personality types than others (Smith

and Gallo, 2001). In particular, the stress-buffering model would predict that personalities characterized by increased stress or strain may
benefit most from social support. One such personality factor is the
Type A profile, which consists of high levels of achievement striving,
hostility, and aggression. This personality dimension rose to prominence in the late 1970s when the Western Collaborative Group Study
reported that Type A individuals had a two to three times greater mortality rate than their more relaxed Type B counterparts (Rosenman et
al., 1975). Consistent with the importance of social support for such
individuals, researchers found that the frequency of social activities
was a strong predictor of lower mortality over the next ten years, especially for Type A men (Orth-Gomér and Undén, 1990).

Because of mixed findings linking the Type A personality to
health, researchers have more recently focused on the specific dimension of hostility as particularly health damaging (Smith, 1992). Hostile
individuals are characterized by a general cynicism and mistrust for
others. A number of studies have found hostile persons to have higher
mortality rates than their less hostile counterparts (Miller et al., 1996).
Although no study that I am aware of has examined whether social
support influences mortality rates in hostile individuals, research from
the National Heart, Lung, and Blood Institute Family Heart Study is
consistent with this possibility. In this large study of low and high risk
individuals, researchers found that the combination of low support
and high hostility was associated with a greater history of coronary
disease as well as greater carotid artery atherosclerosis as measured via
ultrasound techniques (Knox et al., 1998; Knox et al., 2000).

Although the above study suggests that individuals high in hostility and low in support may be most at risk, other research suggests
the importance of examining whether hostile individuals indeed benefit as much as low hostile individuals from social support. There are
good reasons to suspect that hostile individuals' distrust of others may
limit any benefits they could potentially receive from social support.
One way is through lower levels of support seeking in the first place.
One study found that hostile individuals appeared more stressed
(higher blood pressure levels) when disclosing a negative personal
event (Christensen and Smith, 1993). Of course, self-disclosure is one
important way that individuals seek support.

Another way that hostile individuals may be limited in their receipt of social support is that their mistrustful nature may cause them to question the motives behind a supportive statement or behavior (for example, "I wonder what that person wants in return"). These thought processes may effectively cancel out any benefits of social support. To test this possibility, researchers examined whether hostile persons would benefit from emotional support provided in a laboratory setting (Lepore, 1995). Results of this study demonstrated that low hostile individuals benefited from emotional support as shown by their lower levels of blood pressure reactivity during a stressful task. On the other hand, hostile individuals' cardiovascular reactivity during stress was not lowered by the provided emotional support. These data are consistent with the notion that social support effects may depend, in part, on relevant personality processes.

Discussion of Evidence

Prior research has demonstrated that social support effects may be stronger for some individuals than others. In particular, gender, SES, culture, and personality have received some limited attention as moderators of the social support and mortality link. It is understandable that less research has examined this issue because it might be seen as a "second generation" issue of study once we know that social support is important in the first place. I now think that we have enough data to conclude that social support has effects on all-cause mortality. Future researchers should strongly consider first modeling basic social support effects, and then testing more complex moderational models to determine the conditions under which social support is most (or least) effective.

Of these questions, how conceptually relevant personality factors interface with social support may be particularly important (Smith and Gallo, 2001). In the past, personality has been seen by some as a variable that needs to be separated from support effects to demonstrate the independent effects of social relationships. However, personality processes may be important to consider because they can influence one's selection into and interpretation of various situations. For instance, although shy individuals tend to avoid social gatherings, if at a party they might interpret ambiguous social information (for example, a person with whom they are talking wants to get a drink) as signs that they are boring to others (Henderson and Zimbardo, 2001). By guiding such thoughts, personality may also influence how others view us. The shy person in the above scenario may later avoid the person who went to get a drink and thus appear to be less sociable.

Extending this thinking to social support research, relevant personality factors can influence how and when people seek support as well as the benefits they receive from support transactions (Pierce et al., 1997). Our social network members' view of our personality may also influence whether they spontaneously provide us with support or how they react to our support mobilization attempts. The questions at the interface between personality and support take on added importance in light of research indicating that certain personality processes predict mortality rates (Miller et al., 1996; Smith and Gallo, 2001). The next generation of studies examining factors such as personality that may influence the effectiveness of social support will be critical for us to build more comprehensive and accurate models.

Summary and Discussion

In my opinion the available research has answered the important question posed at the beginning of this chapter: social support does predict all-cause mortality. This association is evident using both structural and functional measures, with some measures (for example, composite indices, social activities, or emotional support) showing more consistent associations than other measures. In addition, social support predicts all-cause mortality after considering standard factors such as age, initial health status, gender, and SES, suggesting that it is the variable associated with mortality. An examination of moderators of the social support and physical health link is just beginning, but initial mortality studies and the larger social support and mental health literature suggest the utility of such approaches.

Is social support a "magic bullet" against disease? I would characterize it more as one of the many pellets that seem to influence mortality. Several issues are worth highlighting. First, the effects of social support on mortality are typically not large. Social support studies often require hundreds, if not thousands, of participants to find an effect. This is not surprising given the myriad other factors that influence mortality rates. Nevertheless, I would agree with researchers who have compared the strength of the association between social support and mortality as being similar to many standard risk factors, including exercise and blood pressure (House, Landis, and Umberson, 1988). Second, it would be a mistake to consider social support apart from more traditional medical risk factors. Social support may have some of its effects through risk factors such as exercise, blood pressure, and initial health status. An important challenge for future research is to incorporate these traditional medical risk factors into social support theories and resist the tendency to treat social support as an exclusively "social science" phenomenon.

Although the initial evidence linking social support to lower mortality is quite impressive, there are ways in which we can do our research better. There were several general issues running through the literature that are appropriately discussed at a broader level. One has to do with the measurement of both structural and functional measures of support in these studies. A fair number of these studies include single-item measures of social support. As noted earlier, single-item assessments are usually characterized by more limited sensitivity in detecting potential associations. To complicate matters, the assessment of social support sometimes involved questionnaires with limited or no prior validation. The process of validating a questionnaire is important to determine whether it is actually measuring much of what it intends to measure. The lack of validating evidence in some studies hinders our ability to understand more fully the nature of the association between social support and mortality (for example, pathways or alternative explanations).

In one sense, the fact that the evidence linking social support to mortality is so consistent, despite these measurement issues, attests to the strength of these findings. However, the next generation of social support and mortality studies will need to test specific theoretical models, moderating factors, and more precise mechanisms given the overall evidence to date. Addressing these issues will require more sensitive and valid measures of social support. Unless given more attention in future research, the measurement issues discussed above will dramatically hinder the progress of researchers wishing to accurately model more complex associations between social support and mortality.

Similar measurement issues pertain to the assessment of the more common "control" factors in existing social support and mortality studies. Of these, the measurement of health behaviors should receive particular attention given its theoretical role in the social control model. However, many of the studies examining health behaviors used single-item self-report measures of behavior (for example, exercise, smoking, or alcohol consumption). These assessments represent one of the weaker ways to assess health behaviors because of the limited reliability and hence sensitivity of these assessments (Smith and Ruiz, 1999). In future research it will be particularly important to have valid and reliable measures of pathways such as health behaviors that also include non-self-reported data (for example, aerobic capacity). As noted earlier, testing more complex models requires more sensitive measures.

Despite the above issues, the available research appears to have answered a crucial question about social support and its links to mortality. Other important questions remain. We have yet to cover data on the specificity of social support effects on mortality. For instance, is social support related in similar ways to cardiovascular and cancer mortality? Within specific health problems, such as cardiovascular disease, at what point in the disease process does social support operate? Does it play a role in the development of cardiovascular disease or have a major impact only after someone is clinically diagnosed? These questions and others are examined in chapter 5.

5

Social Support and Mortality from Specific Diseases

Social support appears to be a robust predictor of all-cause mortality. In chapter 4 I discussed my examination of more than eighty studies published during the past twenty-two years and concluded that both structural and functional measures of support predicted lower all-cause mortality rates. In particular, composite measures of social integration and participation in social activities were consistent predictors of lower mortality rates. Likewise, stress-buffering effects of support on mortality were evident, and research suggested that emotional support may be one particularly beneficial type of social support. The associations between social support and all-cause mortality were apparent even after considering initial health status and controlling for more traditional medical risk factors. Emerging research in this area also suggests the importance of examining potential pathways and the conditions under which social support is most protective (for example, personality processes).

Even though it now appears that social support is associated with all-cause mortality, another important set of questions remains to be considered. All-cause mortality is an important end point, but is social support protective against each major cause of disease? Cardiovascular diseases are the leading cause of death in most industrialized countries, so it is possible that the results reviewed in chapter 4 simply reflect this specific end point. We do not yet know whether social support is more effective for some diseases than others. In this chapter I attempt to answer this question by examining studies that have looked at mortality from specific diseases such as cardiovascular disease, cancer, and acquired immunodeficiency syndrome (AIDS), caused by human immunodeficiency virus (HIV). This information is critically important in the focused development of interventions that seek to utilize social support to promote better health outcomes.

Another closely related question considered in this chapter is the stage of disease in which social support plays a role. Does social support actually influence the development of disease, or is it primarily effective after the medical diagnosis of disease when individuals are in direct need of support? As an example, can social support influence cardiovascular diseases that take decades to become clinically significant? Or is social support mostly effective after one is diagnosed with cardiovascular disease and faced with life-changing (diet, exercise) and stressful (mortality salience) circumstances? This information would again be extremely important in the design of social support interventions.

There are several important issues to keep in mind when asking these specific questions of the social support literature. Only a handful of studies allow for an examination of specific diseases, so firm conclusions are often not possible. An even smaller number of studies provide information on the stage of disease that social support may influence, so appropriate caution is further warranted. In an attempt to supplement these studies I present research that also provides indirect evidence for a theoretical association between social support and specific diseases as well as the stage of disease that might be impacted.

Important methodological issues should be kept in mind when reviewing studies linking social support to specific diseases. One particularly important issue is the base rate of the disease. For instance, although HIV/AIDS is a significant health end point, relatively fewer people have this disease compared to those with cardiovascular disease, and this can impact our ability to detect associations with social support. Another important consideration is the age of the sample and the length of the follow-up period. It may be harder to detect associations in younger populations over short periods of time because of the relatively low base rate of certain diseases in young to middle-aged populations.

Each major disease also has a unique natural progression that ultimately compromises physical health. Therefore, I start each section in this chapter with a basic introduction to the specific disease under consideration. Because of the smaller set of studies under consideration for each disease, links to larger conceptual perspectives covered in chapter 3 will not be performed at this point.

Social Support and Cardiovascular Diseases

Cardiovascular disease is a broad term used to cover several diseases of the cardiovascular system, including coronary artery disease (CAD) and hypertension. It is the leading cause of death in the United States and most industrialized countries. In 1998, cardiovascular diseases claimed almost 950,000 lives, 41 percent of all deaths during that year (American Heart Association, 2001). In fact, each year it claims over 10,000 more lives than the next six leading causes of death combined. It is estimated that if all major forms of cardiovascular disease were eliminated, life expectancy would be raised by about seven years. This stands in comparison to a life expectancy gain of three years if all forms of cancers were eliminated (American Heart Association).

Coronary artery disease is a condition in which the coronary arteries become narrowed, ultimately resulting in decreased blood flow to the heart. The heart, like any other muscle in the body, needs oxygen and other nutrients from the blood to function. Its function is crucial because it distributes oxygen and nutrients in blood to the rest of the body and helps dispose of waste products and carbon dioxide. Narrowing of coronary arteries can lead to clinical conditions that significantly compromise the ability of the heart to perform its life-sustaining function.

The pathological change in the coronary arteries is the result of atherosclerosis, which is a progressive buildup of fatty deposits within the arterial wall. This buildup does not appear to be a passive process that simply occurs with the passage of time. Recent research suggests that inflammation (for example, macrophage activity or cytokine release) may play a key role in the progression of CAD (Libby, Ridker, and Maseri, 2002; Ross, 1999). The end result of this process is a loss of elasticity and narrowing of the arteries. The narrowing artery increases the chance that a blood clot will form, thereby increasing the risk of blocking the arterial passage. Although most people think of CAD as occurring in older adults, it is important to note that the atherogenic process starts very early. For instance, the beginnings of arterial plaque can be found in children, and young adults can have advanced lesions. Of course, only when the disease is in its later stages (as is often the case with older adults) does it result in clinical symptoms. Thus, CAD is generally considered a disease with a long-term developmental history.

Coronary artery disease has a complex etiology, including genetic, biochemical, and lifestyle factors (for example, family history, inflammation, or diet). One perspective on atherosclerosis is the response to injury hypothesis (Ross, 1999; Ross and Glomset, 1976). According to this hypothesis, the beginnings of the atherosclerotic process can be traced to factors that cause injury to the inner layer of the coronary arteries. An initial injury may heal, but repeated or chronic injury can result in inflammatory processes (for example, migration of monocytes to area of injury) that start the atherosclerotic process. As an example, bifurcations in coronary arteries are often the sites for atherosclerotic lesions. These sites may be particularly vulnerable because they are subject to differing sheer stress, which can lead to repeated injury over time.

As atherosclerosis progresses to a clinically significant problem, angina may result. Angina is characterized by chest pains caused by an imbalance in the oxygen supply and demand to the heart. During a physically demanding task, the heart works harder and thus requires more oxygen. However, the diminished circulation caused by narrowing of the coronary arteries may not be able to adequately supply the necessary oxygen, and angina can result. If obstruction of the coronary artery occurs, a myocardial infarction (MI) can result. MI (heart attack) is a condition in which cardiac muscles die from lack of oxygen. If enough cardiac muscle dies, death can occur in a short period of time.

Hypertension, another leading cardiovascular disorder, is a condition of elevated blood pressure (systolic blood pressure [SBP], 140 mm Hg or more; diastolic blood pressure [DBP], 90 mm Hg or more). In about 5 to 10 percent of patients, the cause of the heightened blood pressure can be determined, and the hypertension is thus labeled secondary. For instance, problems in kidney function can raise blood pressure because of the kidney's influence on regulating blood volume. However, in the vast majority of patients the cause of elevated blood pressure is unknown, and the hypertension is thus labeled essential or primary. Because of the heightened workload within the cardiovascular system as well as the increased pressure in various organ systems, the consequences of hypertension include kidney damage and increased risk of MI, stroke, and heart failure.

Several recent trends in the hypertension literature are worth mentioning because of their implications for the social support literature. First, traditionally DBP has been emphasized as an important predictor of future cardiovascular disease. In fact, studies suggest that the risk for disease increases even for levels of DBP below that considered hypertensive (MacMahon et al., 1990). However, there is increasing appreciation for the prognostic importance of SBP (Lloyd-Jones et al., 1999), especially in older individuals. In isolated systolic hypertension, SBP is 160 mm Hg or higher in the presence of DBP lower than 90 mm Hg. In the elderly, isolated systolic hypertension predominates and is a leading risk factor for cardiovascular disease.

A second important trend is the increasing appreciation in general for the health relevance of blood pressure formerly considered normal. In the well-known Framingham Heart Study, Vasan and colleagues (2001) followed more than 6,800 participants who were initially free of cardiovascular disease. They classified individuals as in the "high-normal" range if SBP was between 130 and 139 mm Hg or DBP was between 85 and 89 mm Hg. Results over a ten-year period revealed that the risk for the development of cardiovascular disease was significantly greater for both men and women with high-normal blood pressure readings. Although the clinical implications of these findings are sure to be debated (for example, whether drugs that lower blood pressure should be used in such populations), the main message is that blood pressure levels below those normally considered hypertensive may place individuals at elevated risk for subsequent cardiovascular disease.

Research Linking Social Support to Cardiovascular Diseases

Given that cardiovascular diseases are the leading cause of death in industrialized counties, it's probably the case that the data linking social support to overall mortality include a large proportion of deaths from this category of disease. An adequate number of studies have separated cardiovascular deaths from other causes of mortality. These studies overall strongly suggest that social support is associated with lower cardiovascular mortality using both structural (Case et al., 1992; Farmer et al., 1996; Kaplan et al., 1988; Orth-Gomér and Johnson, 1987; Welin et al., 1992) and functional (Berkman, Leo-Summers, and Horwitz, 1992; Farmer et al., 1996; Frasure-Smith et al., 2000; Brummett et al., 2001; Orth-Gomér, Rosengren, and Wilhelmsen, 1993; Williams et al., 1992) measures of support.

One important issue based on these data is the stage(s) in which social support has an influence on cardiovascular outcomes. There are at least two ways in which social support may be related to cardiovascular mortality. Social support may influence the development of disease or play a role after the medical diagnoses of cardiovascular disease. It is possible that social support may play a role in both of these processes. This is an important issue because the optimal design of interventions should focus on the relevant stages of disease that are impacted by social support.

There is at least one clear conclusion based on this literature: social support appears beneficial for individuals after the clinical diagnosis of cardiovascular disease (Berkman, Leo-Summers, and Horwitz, 1992; Brummett et al., 2001; Oxman, Freeman, and Manheimer, 1995). Furthermore, the beneficial effects of social support on mortality in patients with cardiovascular disease appear for both structural (Orth-Gomér and Undén, 1990; Ruberman et al., 1984) and functional measures (Berkman et al.; Brummett et al.; Coyne et al., 2001) of support. For instance, in a recent study researchers followed for more than six years hundreds of men and women with CAD (Brummett et al.). Results showed that contact with people who provided support was a strong predictor of lower subsequent mortality even after considering the influence of income, smoking, and disease severity.

There was also at least one trend in this area of research that was consistent with the larger literature examining social support and all-cause mortality. Again, measures of social activities were consistently related to lower mortality in cardiac patients (Irvine et al., 1999; Orth-Gomér and Undén, 1990; Oxman, Freeman, and Manheimer, 1995).

In one study, researchers found that MI patients who participated in more social activities had a lower risk over the next two years of dying from sudden cardiac death (Irvine et al.). The beneficial effects of social activities were not found for the more common structural measures of network contact. The study suggests that there may be something particularly beneficial about engagement in social activities.

These studies also suggest the utility of examining social support in combination with other psychosocial risk factors. For instance, the mortality risk associated with low social support appears greater for Type A patients (Orth-Gomér and Undén, 1990), depressed patients (Frasure-Smith et al., 2000), and highly stressed patients (Ruberman et al., 1984). Although these studies capture different psychosocial processes, what they have in common is an increase in life strain or stress. Thus, these results might be seen as consistent with the buffering hypothesis of support, although it should be noted that two of the three studies used more structural measures of support in their study.

Given that social support appears to predict survival in people who already have clinically significant cardiovascular disease, the next question relates to whether social support also influences the development of cardiovascular disorders. Indeed, it would be extremely impressive if this proved to be the case given the complicated and long-term nature of cardiovascular disease. Several studies to date have examined whether social support predicted the incidence of cardiovascular disease. Disease incidence refers specifically to the number of new cases. Thus, depending on how initially healthy the study population is, these studies can provide varying degrees of confirming evidence on whether social support influences the development of cardiovascular disease. This is a particularly important point to keep in mind because conditions such as CAD and hypertension develop slowly over time, with many people unaware they are walking around with clinically significant cardiovascular disease (American Heart Association, 2001).

To date, the research linking social support to the development of cardiovascular disease is inconclusive. In one study consistent with the risks of low social support, researchers in Sweden examined hundreds of men for six years (Orth-Gomér, Rosengren, and Wilhelmsen, 1993). They found that emotional support was related to a lower incidence of both fatal and nonfatal cardiac events (also see Vogt et al., 1992). However, researchers in Hawaii following participants for about eight years did not find structural measures of support to predict the incidence of cardiovascular disease (Reed et al., 1983). Finally, a large study of more than 32,000 male health professionals also found little evidence for the possibility that social support predicted the incidence of cardiovascular disease over a four-year period (Kawachi et al., 1996). It should be noted that most of these studies examined only men, which places limitations on their generalizability.

One recent study did examine functional support in women over a nine-year period and found evidence consistent with the role of social support in the development of hypertension (Raikkonen, Matthews, and Kuller, 2001). In this research, 541 participants from the Healthy Women Study were followed for an average of nine years. Results of this study showed that changes in functional support over the study predicted the development of hypertension. Interestingly, social support measured at the beginning of the study did not predict the development of hypertension. Instead, declines in social support over the years predicted a rise in blood pressure. These data are consistent with research covered in chapter 4 on the importance of modeling changes in support over time and their association with morbidity and mortality.

The results of the study by Raikkonen and colleagues notwithstanding, the overall mixed pattern for this question may be related to the difficulties in examining this issue. Remember that the development of CAD is a long-term process that takes decades for clinical symptoms to arise. Ideally, studies testing this proposition would have long-term data, including social support measured at several different points in time to determine such effects. Such long-term studies are rare and expensive, so recent developments in cardiovascular imaging of underlying CAD may be able to provide an important "intermediate" end point to address this question. For instance, researchers can perform computed tomography scans of coronary arteries to determine the degree of calcium deposits. The degree of coronary calcification is correlated with underlying CAD and a robust predictor of future coronary risk (Rumberger et al., 1999). To date, several studies have shown that social support predicts less underlying CAD as indexed by various imaging techniques (Knox et al., 2000; Seeman and Syme, 1987). In one prospective study, researchers followed CAD patients over a twenty-four-month period. Individuals with low emotional support had a greater progression of CAD over the next two years as indexed by angiography (Angerer et al., 2000).

Although more direct evidence is needed on whether social support predicts the development of cardiovascular disease, indirect sources of evidence on other "intermediate" outcomes suggest the feasibility of this proposed link. In one study, three hundred healthy representative women from the Stockholm area were studied in regard to their cardiovascular risk profile (Horsten et al., 1999). One risk profile of interest is the metabolic syndrome, which consists of hypertension, central obesity, dyslipidemia, and hyperglycemia. Each of these factors in isolation predicts cardiovascular risk but together this syndrome is an even more potent predictor of future cardiovascular morbidity and mortality (Kaplan, 1989). Importantly, results of this study showed that women scoring lower in functional support were more likely to have components of the metabolic syndrome (Horsten et al.).

One model linking social support to long-term disease processes is the reactivity hypothesis (Kamarck, Manuck, and Jennings, 1990). According to this perspective, social support may buffer the adverse effects of cardiovascular reactivity that place individuals at risk for future cardiovascular problems. The reactivity hypothesis may be linked to subsequent cardiovascular problems because it provides one mechanism by which the inner layer of the coronary arteries can be injured and the atherosclerotic process initiated and maintained (see the earlier discussion on the response to injury hypothesis). Although more evidence is needed, preliminary evidence suggests that exaggerated cardiovascular reactivity during stressful circumstances may lead to subsequent increases in blood pressure and greater atherosclerotic buildup in the arterial walls (Kamarck et al., 1997; Light et al., 1992).

To test this developmental reactivity hypothesis of social support and cardiovascular disease, many laboratory studies have been conducted to examine whether the provision of support reduces cardiovascular reactivity to stressful tasks (Lepore, 1998; Uchino, Cacioppo, and Kiecolt-Glaser, 1996). In these studies, the participant is typically asked to perform a stressful task (for example, an impromptu speech task) while a friend or experimenter provides some form of support. The most common form of support provided was emotional support. Overall, these studies using friends, strangers, and the experimenter to provide social support reveal buffering effects on cardiovascular reactivity during stress (Lepore, Allen, and Evan, 1993; Christenfeld et al., 1997).

Several important assumptions in these laboratory reactivity studies of social support deserve mention. These studies assume that this buffering process would occur outside of the laboratory over relatively long periods of time, to reduce the potentially harmful increases in cardiovascular reactivity associated with stressful life events. If these assumptions are correct, then we would expect for the effects of social support to be more evident in older individuals because of the possibly cumulative influence of social support across the years. We have provided evidence in several studies showing that social support is associated with lower resting blood pressure primarily in older adults (Uchino et al., 1995; Uchino et al., 1999).

As noted in the beginning of this chapter, resting blood pressure is a strong predictor of future cardiovascular disease. Recently, researchers have also begun to emphasize the prognostic importance of blood pressure obtained during everyday life. Blood pressure readings can be easily recorded via ambulatory blood pressure monitors worn during the course of the day or night. They can be programmed to take readings at random times during the day to get a representative sample of blood pressure during daily activities. Studies examining the importance of ambulatory blood pressure are numerous and suggest that it predicts future cardiovascular problems above and beyond that predicted by conventional blood pressure readings (Prisant et al., 1990; Perloff, Sokolow, and Cowan, 1983).

Several studies have examined the influence of social support on ambulatory blood pressure (Gump et al., 2001; Spitzer et al., 1992; Steptoe, Lundwall, and Cropley, 2000). In these studies, participants filled out a diary sheet after the ambulatory blood pressure reading. This methodology allowed researchers to link up the blood pressure readings with more specific aspects of the environment. In one study examining blood pressure during more structural aspects of social interactions, it was found that ambulatory blood pressure was lowest when interacting with family members than when alone or interacting with strangers (Spitzer et al., 1992). A similar finding of lowered blood pressure was obtained when examining interactions with spouses than when alone (Gump et al.). Finally, one study found that women with high levels of available support showed the lowest average ambulatory blood pressure during the course of the day (Linden et al., 1993). Overall, these studies are consistent with the role of social support as a risk-reducing factor in the development of cardiovascular disease.

In summary, the main question in this section concerns whether social support influences mortality from cardiovascular diseases. Consistent evidence links social support to lower cardiovascular mortality. Social support may influence particular stages of cardiovascular disease. There is relatively strong evidence that social support predicts survival in cardiac patients. However, whether social support predicts the development of cardiovascular disease is inconclusive, although recent research on more intermediate outcomes such as cardiovascular reactivity and ambulatory blood pressure suggests the viability of this proposal. More longitudinal studies that examine both structural and functional measures of support over longer periods of time are needed. In addition, these studies should provide multiple assessments of social support and cardiovascular risk. The incorporation of more intermediate outcomes would also be useful to model the pathways by which social support ultimately influences cardiovascular morbidity and mortality.

Social Support and Cancer

Although cardiovascular diseases are the leading cause of death in the United States and most industrialized countries, perhaps no diagnosis strikes more fear in people than that of cancer. Cancer is the second leading cause of death in the United States, and more than one million new cancer cases are expected to be diagnosed in 2001 (American Cancer Society, 2001). It is estimated that one of every three individuals will have cancer at some point in their lives. Despite these statistics, it should be highlighted that modern medicine has made strides in both the detection and treatment of cancer. Educational campaigns have also been helpful over the past twenty years to increase awareness and

screening for the warning signs of cancer. This has been important because the prognosis and five-year survival rate for most cancers are
much more favorable the earlier the stage of disease (Tamparo and
Lewis, 1995).

Cancer is actually a generic term to describe many different diseases that are characterized by the uncontrolled growth and spread of
abnormal cells (Abbas, Lichtman, and Pober, 1997). A key to cancer
appears to lie in the DNA of cells, which contains the genetic code that
directs cell development and growth. DNA controls the characteristics
of tissues and organs because normal cells reproduce in an orderly fashion with a specified time course. In some cases, however, damage to
cells may cause a change in their DNA. In many cases, the body is able
to repair such damages to DNA or the cell dies off before it replicates.
However, in the case of cancer, uncontrolled replication of such cells
leads to tumors that can ultimately result in death if not detected and
treated.

Tumors can be of two types. Benign tumors are made of cells
much like the original cells and are usually confined to a specific area
and slow spreading. Removing such tumors is often necessary, but they
are less dangerous than malignant or cancerous tumors. Cancerous tumors are different from the cells around them and proliferate relatively
quickly. Even more important is the fact that they can grow and spread
to other parts of the body (metastasize), spreading cancerous cells
throughout the body via blood or lymph.

There is no one cause of cancer, and many factors seem to play a
role in its initial development and progression. Recent research suggests the importance of genetics in the risk for some forms of cancer
(for example, *BRCA1*, a gene for breast cancer). Also important are
carcinogens that include chemical factors and some forms of radiation
that may damage cells and increase cancer risk (for example, high exposure to x-rays). However, some of the main factors implicated in the
development of cancer are behavioral or lifestyle in nature, including
smoking, excessive alcohol consumption, diet, and sun exposure. In
fact, several types of cancer could be almost completely eliminated
(lung cancer caused by smoking) or significantly reduced (skin cancer
caused by sun overexposure) just by altering one's behavior (American
Cancer Society, 2001).

Fortunately, the body is not defenseless against cancer (Abbas, Lichtman, and Pober, 1997). According to the concept of immunosurveillance, the immune system plays an important role in destroying abnormal cells before they become tumors, and the immune system may kill tumors in the body once they are formed. It is assumed that transformed tumor cells express molecules on their cell surfaces that are recognized as foreign and thus stimulate an immune response. A number of specific immune cells have been implicated in playing a role in immunosurveillance. For instance, natural killer cells have the ability to nonspecifically kill certain tumor cell lines. It should be noted that immunosurveillance is not perfect because cancers may arise in people with normal functioning immune systems. Tumors have also evolved evasion mechanisms that may protect them from detection via the immune system (for example, secretion of products that suppress antitumor responses).

Research Linking Social Support to Cancer

The number of studies linking social support to cancer specific mortality is not large. However, there are at least two ways in which this question has been examined. Some studies have investigated whether naturally occurring social support (family, friends, social activities) predicts cancer specific mortality. Other studies have examined whether interventions aimed at increasing social support among cancer patients result in longer survival.

The results from studies of naturally occurring social support provide preliminary evidence that social support may predict lower cancer mortality (Ell et al., 1992; Hibbard and Pope, 1993; Welin et al., 1992). For instance, one study examined advanced cancer patients who completed the social network index (SNI) (Cassileth et al., 1985). Follow-up several years later showed that the SNI did not predict survival in these cancer patients. However, a longer follow-up period of up to eight years revealed that those who were more socially integrated did indeed live longer than those less integrated (Cassileth, Walsh, and Lusk, 1988).

In another study, researchers examined cancer patients with both localized and disseminated tumors (Ell et al., 1992). Follow-up several years later revealed that emotional support predicted longer survival in patients with localized tumors. It appears that social support had more of an influence earlier in the stage of the disease; no measure of support predicted survival in patients with disseminated tumors. Researchers also examined nearly a thousand men in Sweden for twelve years (Welin et al., 1992). This study found that the number of social activities and people in the household predicted lower cardiovascular and cancer mortality. However, the effect for cancer mortality was no longer significant after controlling for age, smoking status, perceived health, and other aspects of social ties. This finding could reflect evidence for the social control hypothesis because smoking status was one of the strongest predictors of cancer mortality in this study. Unfortunately, the inclusion of both structural measures of support in the analyses at the same time may have resulted in a more conservative test of social support effects because these measures were significantly correlated with one another.

Although the number of studies was small, I should point out that there were some notable ones that failed to find an association between naturally occurring social support and cancer mortality. For instance, in one large study researchers examined professional men over a four-year period. Although they found that the SNI predicted lower cardiovascular mortality, no effect was found for cancer mortality (Kawachi et al., 1996). Another study done by these researchers found that per capita social activities aggregated at the state level were a significant predictor of lower cancer mortality, even after controlling for poverty levels (Kawachi et al., 1997).

Despite the overall evidence observed in these studies examining naturally occurring social support networks, several methodological issues should be highlighted. These methodological issues can hopefully serve as a guide for future research. As noted in the beginning of this chapter, some diseases have different base rates in the population—cancer mortality rates are still much lower than cardiovascular mortality rates—and this can make it more difficult to find associations with social support. In addition, several of these studies used relatively shorter follow-up periods, which would result in even lower mortality base rates for cancer. Overall, both of these issues need to be considered in future studies examining the association between social support and cancer mortality.

Some forms of cancer are much more deadly than others. For instance, the five-year survival rate for pancreatic cancer is only 4 percent, compared to 85 percent for breast cancer and 93 percent for prostate cancer (American Cancer Society, 2001). It is likely that the pathophysiology of the deadlier forms of cancer (for example, pancreatic or liver) makes them much less susceptible to psychosocial influences. Future research may have to separate out morbidity and mortality from more specific sources of cancer by using larger samples and following them over significant periods of time.

None of these studies separated the positive aspects of social ties from their potentially negative qualities. As covered in chapter 2, one of the problems with both structural and functional measures of support is that they ignore the negative qualities of social relationships (Uchino et al., 2001). This problem may be even more serious in cancer studies because recent research still indicates that cancer patients experience negative interactions with their support network members, and these negative interactions are related to poorer coping and greater psychological distress (Manne et al., 1999; Manne and Glassman, 2000). Future research should attempt to separate these negative qualities of social relationships because they may offset or interfere with positive support effects (Coyne and DeLongis, 1986).

Other studies on social support and cancer have examined the efficacy of providing support to cancer patients via group therapy (support groups). Although the number of studies is not large, much of this research was spearheaded by the well-known effects of a support group intervention published by David Spiegel and colleagues (1989). These researchers randomly assigned eighty-six breast cancer patients to a support group or a group given routine oncological care. In the support intervention group, patients met weekly for ninety minutes to discuss their thoughts and feelings on how to cope with cancer. Results of this landmark study found that breast cancer patients provided with the support group intervention lived about eighteen months longer than individuals given standard oncological care. According to Spiegel and colleagues, their social support intervention may have been effective because it "countered the social alienation that often divides cancer patients from their well-meaning but anxious family and friends" (p. 91). In other words, support interventions may offset the potential negative effects of interactions with family and friends.

There have been several attempts to replicate the support group results found by Spiegel and colleagues. One of these was a recent study that examined a large sample of metastatic breast cancer patients (Goodwin et al., 2001). Patients were randomly assigned to a control condition or an intervention group that fostered support among group members and encouraged open emotional expression. Although the study found beneficial effects of the intervention on their quality of life, it did not find differences in survival between the support group and control condition. In an accompanying editorial, David Spiegel (2001) acknowledged that the current literature is mixed, but that the current climate for cancer patients is much different than in the late 1970s when the first study was conducted. As he noted in his earlier paper, the stigma that surrounded cancer in earlier years may have resulted in some degree of social isolation. Today, more emotional support is available to cancer patients as a result of the increased availability of support groups and attempts to destigmatize the disease. As a result, it may be harder to detect survival differences between support group interventions than has been the case in the past.

It is clear that the questions surrounding support groups and their potential links to cancer survival are not settled (Helgeson and Cohen, 1996; Spiegel, 2001). Support groups clearly influence the quality of life for cancer patients and thus may play a theoretical role in survival. As argued by other researchers, future studies may need to take into account the possibility that all individuals do not benefit equally from support groups (Helgeson and Cohen). For instance, according to the stress-buffering model, social support should be most effective for individuals under greater levels of distress so those individuals may benefit more from support group interventions. The argument by David Spiegel (2001) also suggests that a focus on socially isolated individuals may be particularly effective.

Resolution of this question may also involve the deconstruction of support groups to determine the aspects that are most beneficial for participants. Functional support theorists suggest that different aspects of social support may be exchanged during support group interactions (for example, emotional support or informational support) and that some types of support may be more beneficial than others (Bolger, Zuckerman, and Kessler, 2000; Cohen, 1988). Although a time-intensive task, examining these issues can be addressed via complex behavioral coding of interactions in these support groups (see Benjamin, 1996, for one theoretically derived coding system). Support groups can also provide new structural forms of support (for example, friendships within the group or seeking ties with other organizations) that can help in identity issues that appear salient with cancer patients. Detailed ancillary measures of changes in both functional and structural support as a result of the intervention would also be needed to address effects that occur outside of the support group context.

There is some evidence of beneficial effects of general psychosocial interventions in cancer patients who included as part of their treatment a social support intervention (Fawzy et al., 1993; Shrock, Palmer, and Taylor, 1999). Fawzy and colleagues (1993) evaluated the effects of a six-week structured group intervention that provided education, problem-solving skills, stress management, and social support to cancer patients. Importantly, a six-year follow-up revealed that only 9 percent of individuals in the structured group intervention had died compared to 29 percent of individuals in the no intervention condition. It is interesting to speculate that these general interventions may be conceived of as the provision of information support (problem-solving or stress management skills) from medical professionals. These interventions suggest that the combination of social support with other coping skills may be particularly beneficial.

It is premature to conclude what stage of cancer may be influenced by social support. One study found that lower satisfaction with social contact was associated with a biological index of prostate malignancy (prostate-specific antigen) in a community screening program (Stone et al., 1999). Research on more "intermediate outcomes" such as immune function in healthy populations and in cancer patients may help clarify these issues (Baron et al., 1990; Levy et al., 1990; Uchino, Cacioppo, and Kiecolt-Glaser, 1996). If the immune system plays a role in immunosurveillance, then evidence that social support is associated with better immune function in otherwise healthy individuals would suggest a theoretical role for social support in the development and progression of cancer.

To address this point, we reviewed the literature on social support and immune function in humans (Uchino, Cacioppo, and Kiecolt-

Glaser, 1996). Researchers in this area typically examine various in vitro measures of immunity by sampling blood and performing tests on cells of the immune system (for example, lymphocytes). One popular measure includes an assay called natural killer cell activity. In this assay, natural killer cells are cultured with a susceptible tumor cell line, and the ability of these cells to kill the tumor is determined. There is strong evidence that such measures are correlated with increased resistance to tumors (Whiteside and Herberman, 1994). We found in our review of the literature that social support was associated with better immune function in healthy individuals (for example, greater natural killer cell activity), especially in older adults (Uchino, Cacioppo, and Kiecolt-Glaser, 1996). This link between social support and better immunity in older adults may be particularly informative because the risk for developing cancer increases with age (American Cancer Society, 2001).

There are also several studies examining social support and various indicators of endocrine and immune function in cancer patients (Levy et al., 1990; Turner-Cobb et al., 2000). Hormones play a potentially important role in cancer because they have been shown to influence aspects of immune function. Cortisol may be particularly important because it tends to be elevated during more chronic stress, and it has well-documented immunosuppressive effects (Uchino, Kiecolt-Glaser, and Glaser, 2000). Importantly, a recent study reported that social support predicted lower overall cortisol levels in breast cancer patients (Turner-Cobb et al.).

To directly explore the effects of social support on immune function in cancer patients, Levy and colleagues (1990) studied sixty-one stage 1 and 2 breast cancer participants. An interesting and unique aspect of this study is that emotional support from several sources was measured, including the spouse, physician, friends, and nurses. They found that only emotional support from the spouse and physician predicted stronger natural killer cell activity in these patients. These findings suggest that social support from significant relationships may indeed influence cancer outcomes via its influence on the immune system. In addition, the specific dimension of emotional support may have particularly strong effects on immunity in both healthy and cancer populations and needs to be examined more fully in future research (Levy et al., 1990; Uchino, Cacioppo, and Kiecolt-Glaser, 1996).

Any preliminary conclusions about the role of social support on cancer incidence or survival needs to be considered in light of the relatively small number of existing studies. The strongest evidence for a role of social support on cancer mortality comes from studies of naturally occurring social support as well as studies using more intermediate outcomes such as immune function. The evidence is most mixed when examining the role of support groups on cancer mortality. Future research that investigates support group and cancer survival may need to identify individuals who benefit more from support as well as what happens within and outside of the support group as a result of these interventions. More generally, the larger literature on social support and cancer mortality will need to consider the relatively low base rate of cancer mortality compared to cardiovascular disease and the specific types of cancer that may be more susceptible to support influences. The potential negative interactions that occur in cancer patients' social networks also need attention. Therefore, longer-term research that examines positive and negative qualities of relationships and more specific cancers in larger samples should be a priority.

Social Support and HIV/AIDS

The first cases of AIDS in the United States were identified in 1981. According to recent statistics, more than 20 million people have died worldwide since the start of the epidemic, and an additional 40 million individuals are now living with HIV/AIDS (UNAIDS/WHO, 2001). With no known cure, HIV/AIDS continues to be a significant worldwide health problem.

AIDS is a condition in which the body's immune system eventually loses its ability to fight off foreign invaders (Abbas, Lichtman, and Pober, 1997). As a result, the person is at risk for morbidity and mortality from pathogens that a healthy person would normally have no trouble fighting off. In fact, it was the occurrence of several deaths from rare infectious diseases, particularly Kaposi's sarcoma, a rare form of cancer, that initially alerted health professionals to AIDS.

AIDS is caused by HIV. Although HIV can be detected in different bodily fluids, it is found in larger quantities in blood, semen, and vaginal fluids. Upon entering the body, it infects cells with specific

surface molecules (for example, helper T-cells or macrophages). Ultimately, HIV infection can result in the destruction of the infected
cells.

One of the important cells infected and destroyed by HIV is the
helper T-cell. One good way of thinking about the function of helper
T-cells is to view the immune system as an army that defends the body.
Helper T-cells are essentially the commanding generals of this impressive force. Moreover, these generals are irreplaceable. The helper T-cells
are absolutely essential to coordinate the different aspects of the immune response. By depleting helper T-cells, HIV cuts off the ability of
the immune system to effectively fight against foreign invaders.

Initial reactions to HIV infection in some individuals consist of
an acute syndrome with flu-like symptoms (Abbas, Lichtman, and
Pober, 1997). Although the body mounts a vigorous immune response,
the virus can reside in a "latent stage" that can last for years. During
this phase, HIV may be diminished in blood but disease progression
continues in lymphoid organs. Clinically, there are stages of increasingly serious conditions associated with HIV infection that can end in
death. One is chronic swelling of the lymph glands that can last for several years. This is testament to the body's attempt to fight off the disease, but as helper T-cells are destroyed the body starts losing the battle
and some individuals may develop AIDS-related complex (with symptoms that include diarrhea, fevers, fatigue, night sweats, etc.). At later
stages of the disease when helper T-cell counts are low, the person is at
risk for opportunistic infectious pathogens.

Although no cure is presently available, recent biomedical research has been extremely successful in extending the lives of individuals infected with HIV (Kelly et al., 1998). Medical interventions view
HIV infection as more of a chronic condition to be managed (like diabetes) until a cure can be found. Medications such as protease inhibitors act by inhibiting the replication of HIV and can significantly
reduce overall viral load in the blood. These medications are significantly extending the lives of patients living with HIV. And although
they are effective, in some individuals they can have serious side effects,
and the monetary costs associated with the strict regimen can be substantial. These problems are magnified in less economically developed
countries in which HIV infection has become one of the most serious

health threats in recent history. Vaccines against HIV are now being evaluated in several large clinical trials, and the results should be forthcoming.

Research Linking Social Support to HIV/AIDS

Research on social support and the progression of HIV infection is in its infancy, partly because of the understandable emphasis on first mapping the pathophysiology of HIV/AIDS. I distinctly remember being at an interdisciplinary meeting on HIV/AIDS in the early 1990s and being surprised at the lack of psychosocially oriented research. This was even clearer to me at the poster session in which I presented research linking social support to better immune system function. Only one person (of hundreds) stopped at my poster to discuss my research with me. I could have used some social support myself! However, the emerging paradigm of HIV as a more chronic condition has resulted in a need for more psychosocially oriented research (Kelly et al., 1998). This is only a recent trend, however, and compared to other diseases there is presently little research on whether social support influences HIV mortality. Given the small number of studies no firm conclusions are possible.

A few studies have reported that social support predicted longer survival in HIV patients (Lee and Rotheram-Borus, 2001; Patterson et al., 1996). Consistent with the potential benefits of social support, it was found that patients in advanced stages of HIV infection survived longer if they had larger social networks and greater emotional support (Patterson et al.). Other researchers examined parents with advanced-stage HIV infection for up to 53 months (Lee and Rotheram-Borus). During this time, 44 percent of the parents died. The analyses revealed that the factors predicting longer survival were the number of children, presence of a partner, and coping with the illness by seeking support. This study provides evidence for identity and social control theorists who argue that the presence of close others provides a sense of responsibility and additional incentives to live. This enhanced meaning to life may motivate individuals to adhere more closely to their lifesaving medical regimens. The finding that coping with the illness by seeking support was related to longer survival is also consistent with functional support theorists who argue that the provision of support is stress buffering and health promoting.

There are some studies that did not find social support to predict HIV mortality (for example, Blomkvist et al., 1994), and one found that larger social networks predicted faster progression to AIDS symptoms (Patterson et al., 1996). The study by Patterson and colleagues is particularly informative because besides the findings reported above with advanced-stage HIV patients, they also found that larger social networks predicted a faster progression to AIDS-defining symptoms in early-stage HIV patients. This suggests that the stage of disease may be particularly important to consider in future social support and HIV studies (Miller and Cole, 1998).

There are several potential explanations for the surprising finding that in some cases larger social networks were associated with faster disease progression (Miller and Cole, 1998). One explanation includes the possibility that larger networks may be associated with risky behaviors and sexual activity due to unhealthy norms. Other links focus on the possibility that larger social networks may be associated with greater stress in HIV patients because they could result in higher exposure to AIDS-related caregiving and bereavement. If validated by further research, these explanations again highlight the suggestion in chapter 2 on the importance of a simultaneous consideration of the positive and negative qualities of social relationships.

There is at least one more explanation for these findings based on the larger social support literature that can incorporate the potentially harmful effects seen early in the course of the disease and the beneficial effects seen in more advanced-stage HIV patients. Although speculative, perhaps larger networks can be significant sources of stress early in the course of disease. There continues to be considerable stigma associated with HIV, so network members may not know how to react to the diagnosis or may be naive about its implications for themselves (for example, catching HIV). Consider the circumstances that led to the retirement of basketball great Earvin "Magic" Johnson. These negative network interactions may result in a (selective) reliance by patients later in the stage of disease on network members who are primarily supportive and understanding. Longitudinal studies that track changes in patient's networks over time would be needed to test this possibility.

A number of studies have examined social support and the progression of HIV infection as measured by more intermediate outcomes such as immune function. Several have failed to find a significant association between social support and aspects of immune function in HIV-positive men (Goodkin et al., 1992; Perry et al., 1992). However, several other studies have reported an association between social support and helper T-cell counts (a marker of disease progression) in HIV-positive men (Persson et al., 1994; Theorell et al., 1995). The state of this literature makes firm conclusions difficult at present.

One of the more long-term studies on this issue to date examined the association between social support and changes in helper T-cells across a five-year period (Theorell et al., 1995). This study was also unique in that it examined a representative sample of Swedish HIV-positive hemophiliac men. Results of this study showed that the availability of social support did indeed predict helper T-cells in this sample. However, high and low social support groups did not differ in helper T-cell counts during the early years of the study. Social support became a more powerful predictor of helper T-cells as time progressed (years four and five). For instance, during year five of the study, individuals with high social support showed a 37 percent reduction in helper T-cells from the first year of the study. In contrast, individuals with low social support showed a 64 percent reduction in helper T-cells from year one.

There are at least two important implications of this study. First, only at later points in time did the effect for social support emerge in HIV patients. These findings are consistent with the notion that there may be a cumulative effect of social support over time. Second, because the effects of social support on helper T-cells only occurred later in time, if researchers were to only examine the association between social support and helper T-cells later in the stage of disease, information on the longer length of time that individuals high in social support took to get to that stage would be lost. This point highlights the importance of longitudinal data examining social support throughout the full course of the disease.

Although I know of no large-scale studies that have linked social support to the incidence of HIV infections, there are studies suggesting its importance on risk behaviors that are linked to infection (Kelly et al., 1993). For instance, appropriate social norms and support from an individual's network members can reinforce less risky behaviors and potentially reduce the probability of HIV infection (Kelly et al.). A number of general psychosocial interventions have been guided by this premise and have used principles of social support to initiate and maintain behavioral change in at-risk populations. For instance, one intervention attempted to reduce AIDS risk in single inner city women (Hobfoll et al., 1994). Women in this study were trained in assertiveness, negotiation, and planning skills related to risky behaviors (for example, unprotected sex). The researchers also emphasized the importance of these behavioral changes in light of their important network members such as their family. Results of the intervention revealed positive behavioral changes on measures such as condom purchases that were maintained during the six-month postintervention period.

In summary, there have been only a small number of studies examining the association between social support and mortality from HIV/AIDS. Studies suggest that social support may influence factors that place individuals at risk for contracting HIV. There is some evidence that social support may play a larger role in survival later in the course of the disease. The studies examining more intermediate outcomes of immune function in HIV patients were mixed, but hint at the possibility that social support influences the progression of disease if followed for longer periods of time. However, because the number of studies is small and some data are conflicting, caution is warranted before making any conclusions. Future research will need to examine the possibility that social support is important at different stages of the disease by identifying participants early in the course of infection and following them for significant periods of time.

The real importance of these studies lies in the promise that social support may be playing a role in one of our most serious public health challenges. No doubt these studies can serve as the impetus for future research on social support and HIV mortality. For instance, one important future research agenda would be to model more completely the influence of structural measures of support to HIV/AIDS outcomes given their potential positive and negative effects on survival (Miller and Cole, 1998). As argued by others, the presence of a social network can often have a negative influence on health by encouraging or modeling risky behaviors (Suh et al., 1997). In contrast, there are also important pathways by which structural measures of support may influence longer survival. For example, social control theorists would predict that social integration can be associated with greater adherence to medical regimens and less risky behaviors. Given the particular importance of cooperation with medical regimens for patients with HIV infection, social control theorists can provide a focused test of their proposed pathways linking integration to better outcomes and also help in the design of appropriate interventions.

Summary and Discussion

This chapter examined the status of the research linking social support to specific diseases: cardiovascular disease, cancer, and HIV/AIDS. An ancillary aim was to determine whether there is a particular stage of disease in which social support may have positive health effects. There is relatively strong evidence linking both structural and functional measures of support to cardiovascular mortality. Although studies linking social support to the incidence of cardiovascular disease are more limited, the strongest evidence to date shows the benefits of social support on mortality in patients who are diagnosed with cardiovascular disease. The number of studies linking social support to cancer and HIV/AIDS mortality is relatively small, so conclusions are difficult. Nevertheless, the existing studies are provocative enough to suggest the promise of future investigations.

Although some of the issues linking social support to outcomes are disease specific, several general recommendations for future research can be made. More studies need to include both structural and functional measures of support in predicting disease specific mortality. Both structural and functional measures were clearly predictive of all-cause mortality, which suggests their importance in these specific disease processes. A more comprehensive assessment of support would also allow researchers to model how structural and functional measures of support may work in combination to predict these specific disease states. For instance, it is possible that social integration provides the important context by which functional support is made available. This conceptually driven modeling is more warranted than simply adding all social support measures into the equation predicting mortality rates, which has been the case in some studies. The examination of specific models also provides a more sensitive test of the health effects of social relationships. This may be particularly important because diseases such as cancer and HIV infection are characterized by lower base rates.

More longitudinal studies are also necessary to link social support, intermediate outcomes such as immune function, and disease-specific mortality. Consistent evidence links social support to more intermediate physiological processes that are implicated in each of these diseases (Uchino, Cacioppo, and Kiecolt-Glaser, 1996). This would mean that future studies should consider conceptualizing these physiological measures as mechanisms by which social support has its effect on mortality. Future research that includes repeated assessments of social support and such intermediate outcomes can help researchers determine the plausibility of these more complex links relating social support to disease-specific incidence and outcomes.

The examination of social support and each of these diseases provides an excellent opportunity to test the proposed theoretical pathways covered in chapter 3 because of the well-specified disease context. For instance, biomedical researchers have identified specific health behaviors that influence cardiovascular mortality, and this research could lead to a more sensitive test of pathways than simply examining health behaviors and all-cause mortality. However, the research examining social support and disease-specific mortality has not yet addressed such mechanistic questions. To be fair I should mention that this is a general characteristic of the social support and mortality literature and represents our attempts to simply demonstrate that social support influences all-cause and disease specific mortality. An over-reliance on this practice, however, hinders our general understanding of the phenomena and makes the interpretation of conflicting data problematic. Given the expense and long-term nature of these questions we can and should be doing both. To facilitate the examination of specific pathways, in chapter 6 I attempt to extrapolate information from the studies covered in chapters 4 and 5 that bears on the theoretical models covered in chapter 3. This information will be used to revise the existing model on how social support may ultimately influence mortality.

6
Pathways Linking Social Support to Health Outcomes

> On the surface, the incredibly varied ways people can live together might seem to make the task of understanding the precise connections between living together and health totally helpless. . . . And yet, in spite of all the potential factors that could have hidden the connection between living together and health, the data presented here stand as a mute testimonial to its power.
> —James Lynch, *The Broken Heart*

In his book appropriately titled *The Broken Heart,* James Lynch (1977) reviewed early laboratory and clinical evidence linking loneliness or a lack of social connections to cardiovascular disease. The analogy of a "broken heart" by James Lynch more than twenty-five years ago is on strong ground. In chapter 5, more recent research was reviewed suggesting that social support is a protective factor for cardiovascular morbidity and mortality. These studies also suggest the potential role of social support on other diseases. Preliminary evidence found links between social support and cancer and HIV progression, although less research exists on these questions and more complex associations were evident. This research also suggests the importance of future studies that examine the stage(s) of disease on which social support has an influence by incorporating more intermediate health-related outcomes (for example, blood pressure or coronary calcification).

In order to use this research to benefit people, it is crucial that clear theoretical models on how social support ultimately affects physical health be developed. In chapter 3, the major models linking social support to health outcomes were covered. However, much of the social support and mortality literature was not designed specifically to test the theoretical models covered earlier but to provide important data on their independent association with mortality. As a result, there has been little theoretical development in the social support and physical health literature during the past ten years.

Due to the lack of mortality studies directly testing these theoretical models, the main goals of this chapter are twofold. One goal is to fine-tune the existing models linking social support to physical health outcomes. These models provide a good starting point because they are specific enough to allow tests of their theoretical predictions as well as guide interventions. I first start with an evaluation of the processes suggested by the theoretical models discussed in chapter 3 based on the existing physical health studies. These models are then fine-tuned to reflect the evidence available from these morbidity and mortality studies.

The second goal of this chapter is to formulate a broader theoretical model that places these more specific models in a larger context. In the second part of this chapter, I examine data linking social support to health at multiple levels of analysis in order to complement the analysis of the existing theoretical models. Such a multilevel approach makes explicit the levels of analysis that are most likely to be informative for the phenomenon of interest (Cacioppo and Berntson, 1992). I will examine the complementary sociocultural, behavioral, psychological, and physiological levels of analysis that may inform research linking social support to mortality. The purpose of this model is to help make connections with other areas and guide broad future research relevant to social support.

Evaluation of Existing Conceptual Models
Pathways Highlighted by Stress-Related Models

Of the stress-related models, the buffering model has received prior attention in social support and mortality studies. At its broadest level, the stress-buffering model suggests that social support should influence health outcomes primarily for individuals under high levels of life stress. This model postulates that social support is beneficial because it protects individuals from the deleterious effects of stress in peoples' lives. The studies that have measured life stress with social support are consistent with this proposition and suggest that the link between life stress and mortality is stronger for individuals with low support. This stress-buffering effect has been found using both structural and functional measures of support (Falk et al., 1992; Rosengren et al., 1993). It should be noted, however, that stress may operate via differential reactivity and/or differential exposure (Cacioppo and Berntson, in press), and existing studies do not allow us to differentiate these processes (see chapter 4).

Although a review of the evidence linking stress to health outcomes is beyond the scope of this book, let me point out a few key aspects of this literature. Not all stress is unhealthy, and long-term, uncontrollable stress is more likely to be linked to negative health outcomes (Cohen et al., 1998; Kiecolt-Glaser and Glaser, 1995). However, even acute stressors can have negative effects in unhealthy populations. Research suggests that acute psychological stress can induce silent myocardial ischemia in patients with existing heart disease (Rozanski et al., 1988). In fact, ischemia due to mental stress can occur at a lower heart rate than is seen during exercise-induced ischemia and may predict future mortality in cardiac patients (Rozanski et al.; Sheps et al., 2002). Thus, there may be a role for social support in reducing the harmful effects of both chronic and short-term stress, depending on the context and population of interest.

The fact that stress-buffering effects are seen with both functional and structural measures of support presents an opportunity to evaluate the role of both types of measures on the stress-buffering processes. As noted in chapter 2, structural aspects of support such as network size and group membership provide the social context for support. Friends can provide us with emotional support, and group activities can provide a sense of belonging support. Therefore, structural aspects of support might be related to greater stress buffering via an indirect path because social networks and activities provide access to functional support (Bloom et al., 2001).

There are also potentially important alternative pathways by which structural measures of support may have stress-buffering effects. As highlighted by identity theorists, social relationships, roles, and activities may be related to increased self-esteem and feelings of control (Thoits, 1983). Self-esteem or perceptions of control in turn appear to be important coping resources that help individuals adjust successfully to various life stressors (Aspinwall and Taylor, 1997; Hobfoll, 1989). Structural measures of support may thus be related to stress buffering, independent of any functional support being provided. In such cases it is the internalization of our social world via identity processes that can ultimately influence our efficacy in coping with stressful life events.

A variant of the stress-buffering model is the matching hypothesis (Cohen and Wills, 1985; Cutrona and Russell, 1990). The matching hypothesis postulates that stress-buffering effects should be more evident when the type of support matches the needs of the stressors. For instance, informational support should be most effective for stressors that are more controllable. The information provided can help an individual regain control over a situation. Although there is some research consistent with the matching hypothesis when examining psychological adjustment, there is little evidence for such a process in research examining mortality rates. Of course, the number of studies were small, so future research may indeed reveal evidence for the matching hypothesis.

In many circumstances, the complexity of life stressors will make a clean test of the matching hypothesis difficult (Barrera, 2000). Many stressors have aspects that are more controllable than others, and the controllability of the stressor can change over time. For example, for many people a major source of stress is related to their work. However, stress with a boss may be uncontrollable whereas stress related to performance may be more controllable (for example, via adequate preparation). These situations can vary over time due to changes in management or workload. Future studies that include assessments of stressor controllability would be useful in the evaluation of this model.

Proponents of the stress-buffering model have also suggested that there are components of support that may be associated with beneficial effects across a wide range of life stressors (Cohen et al., 1985). Of these, emotional and informational support have been highlighted because it is assumed that people can always benefit from useful information or reassurances of their worth. The research reviewed earlier does suggest that the component of emotional support may be associated with lower mortality rates (Berkman, Leo-Summers, and Horwitz, 1992; Penninx et al., 1997). These data highlight the importance of perceived or actual social interactions that provide the individual with messages of caring and concern. According to the stress-buffering model, these expressions of concern may lift one's mood and also influence self-esteem or efficacy in dealing with life stressors (Krause, 1987b). This research thus highlights the pathways involved in at least one specific functional dimension of support in the stress-buffering process.

In contrast to studies suggesting the benefits of available support on mortality, research examining the influence of received support suggested some potentially negative effects. More specifically, some studies found that receiving more tangible or instrumental support was associated with increased mortality rates (Kaplan et al., 1994; Penninx et al., 1997). One possible explanation for this increased mortality risk suggests the role of diminished self-esteem and efficacy on subsequent health (Bolger, Zuckerman, and Kessler, 2000). For instance, research on what is termed "invisible support" suggests the benefits of support provisions that are not noticed by the receiver (Bolger et al.). In such a case, a person can benefit from the received support but not experience the diminished self-esteem that can come with having to rely on support. Another explanation suggests that received support may increase the opportunity for interpersonal conflict if it is not provided in a warm and nurturant manner. Currently, there is no evidence in the mortality studies to confirm any one of these pathways, and it is possible that both may be at work. Nevertheless, these studies on the negative effects of received support again highlight the potential importance of esteem and stress (interpersonal) on mortality, pathways that are also implicated in the positive effects of support and health.

Other researchers have emphasized that received support may be indirectly beneficial because it protects individuals from declines in perceived available support during stress (Norris and Kaniasty, 1996). This position is predicated on the notion that under some conditions stressors can erode perceptions of available support. Studies that have examined the association between received and perceived available support within a defined context (for example, in response to disasters) tend to support this notion as well as the role of received support in preventing such stress-induced decreases in perceived support (Norris and Kaniasty). This research suggests that the effects of stressors on social support processes need further consideration in the stress-related models of support.

As was the case for psychological outcomes, little research has examined the stress prevention aspect of support on mortality. No study that I reviewed on social support and mortality appeared to have examined this intriguing model. Research linking structural and functional measures of support to lower mortality may in theory reflect such a stress-prevention process via processes such as proactive coping. Research is needed, however, to directly examine whether social support predicts lower exposure to stressful events, which in turn predicts lower mortality rates.

A "Retuned" Model of Social Support, Stress, and Physical Health

The findings described in the previous section provide an opportunity to reexamine the role of social support in stress-relevant health outcomes. The main components and pathways of this retuned model as highlighted by physical health studies are depicted in figure 6.1. The top portion of the model covers the role of stress on health via differential exposure or reactivity. An important modification of this model centers on the more precise links between social support and stress-related processes. As covered earlier, stressors that are chronic, uncontrollable, or present in unhealthy populations are thought to ultimately influence health via an appraisal process. However, as depicted in the middle boxes, stressors can also result in a mobilization of received support or a deterioration of available support over time. In some cases, received support can prevent the deterioration of perceived support with favorable influences on esteem, control, and other coping processes. These beneficial effects of functional support may ultimately influence the association between stress and health in at least two ways: functional support can prevent stress from occurring in the first place (path 1—stress prevention) or it can dampen the stress response once it occurs (path 2—stress buffering). Finally, social integration provides the access to functional support and may independently influence processes such as esteem that are related to better health outcomes in the face of potential stress.

There are several aspects of this revised model that I would like to highlight. First, in this model there is an increased emphasis on the

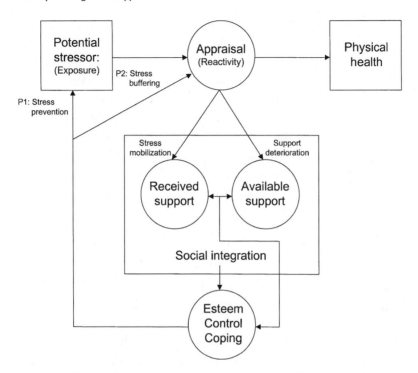

Figure 6.1. "Retuned" stress-related models of support highlighting the pathways made salient by prior models and existing studies on physical health outcomes. P1=Pathway 1, P2=Pathway 2.

conceptual links between stress, support, and health. As noted earlier, stress can influence support-related processes, and this may have implications for the effectiveness of social support over time. Stress may also influence health via at least two pathways (Cacioppo and Berntson, in press), and these pathways need to be made explicit in current support models. As discussed in chapter 4, one pathway involves greater exposure to stressful circumstances. Social support may counteract this process via the stress-prevention pathway; initial evidence suggests that support is associated with decreases in daily hassles (Russell and Cutrona, 1991). The other important stress-related pathway is how reactive individuals are to any given stressor. Social support appears to help individuals reduce the magnitude of stress responses, as revealed by laboratory studies (Lepore, 1998).

I should also emphasize that this model represents a best-case scenario highlighting *only* the beneficial influences of support. As covered earlier, received tangible support under some circumstances may be linked to increased mortality via lower levels of esteem and decreases in control. Although studies as a whole indicate that social integration is associated with lower mortality, it may also be linked to negative processes (for example, social conflict or burden of support provider) that can weaken links between social networks and mortality (Shumaker and Hill, 1991). Researchers wishing to test or utilize this revised model would be well advised to keep these caveats in mind. If negative effects do occur, researchers testing this model would be able to understand them better by measuring the proposed variables in the model (for example, received tangible support possibly lowering self-esteem). Further explication of the detrimental effects of social relationships will require more detailed measures of the negative qualities of relationships, such as insensitivity, conflict, and neglect (Rook and Pietromonaco, 1987).

This model is also admittedly based primarily on the theoretical implications of the types of support measures that have been linked to physical health. No study that I am aware of has directly examined these more specific psychological pathways (for example, appraisals or esteem) possibly linking social support to mortality. These processes do appear to represent key common pathways by which both structural and functional support measures can influence stress-related disease outcomes. It may also be useful in helping better understand how the negative qualities of relationships may exacerbate stress-related outcomes. The strength of this revised model is in the main processes that are made explicit for researchers to evaluate.

Pathways Highlighted by the Direct Effect Models

One of the main pathways implicated by direct effect models is the influence of social roles and ties on identity formation (Thoits, 1983, 2001). This identity formation includes the development of self-esteem, feelings of efficacy or control, and life meaning. Although no study to date has examined these processes as mediators of the influence of social integration on mortality, some studies do suggest that perceptions of control are related to better health (Rodin, 1986; Rowe and Kahn, 1987). For instance, research from the MacArthur studies of successful aging showed that variations in perceived control were related to mortality rates five years later (Eizenman et al., 1997).

The studies reviewed in this book suggest that both structural and functional measures of support may have direct effects on mortality (Blazer, 1982; House, Robbins, and Metzner, 1982). Of course it is possible that these measures of support are having buffering effects, but the studies simply did not measure life stress. Nevertheless, this does challenge us to think about how functional measures of support can also have effects consistent with direct effect models. Current conceptualizations of functional support highlight the social support components that are provided when an individual is under stress. However, functional support exchanges can occur independently of stress, which provides the basis for examining its direct effect on health. As an example, think about how many times you tell your children or spouse you love them independent of any stress in their lives. Therefore, one possible way in which emotional support can have direct effects on health is related to its potential influence on positive affect and esteem-related processes.

It is easy to remember the people who have been there for you through the toughest of times. However, because social support can be provided in the absence of stress, there may be much more social support operating in our lives than what we actually encode as supportive. For instance, mentors can give important social support by providing feedback to students on projects. These supportive exchanges can include praise for a job well done (emotional support), constructive comments (informational support), and help writing up aspects of their project (tangible support). Not all of these circumstances may be perceived by the student as supportive, although they indeed meet the functional definitions of support. As another example, take the simple case of a person who prepares both breakfast and lunch for his or her spouse during the course of the work week. This simple practice clearly results in an easier life for the spouse (sleep in later, fewer time pressures), but it is unclear if this practice would be actually encoded by the receiving spouse as being supportive. Consistent with these examples, researchers found that many acts performed with supportive intentions may not be noticed as such by the recipient (Bolger, Zuckerman, and Kessler, 2000). This research suggests that social integration not only provides the access to functional support during stress but also during a wider range of social contexts and interactions.

The social control hypothesis also highlights the importance of identity-related processes on health outcomes (Umberson, 1987). However, it makes the further prediction that social support may have effects on health via social control of important health behaviors such as smoking, exercise, and diet. Although no mortality study that I reviewed examined either direct or indirect social control in relation to social support, many studies have examined the role of health behaviors (Cerhan and Wallace, 1997; Seeman et al., 1987). Unfortunately, these studies were usually not attempting to test the social control hypothesis but instead conceptualized health behaviors as risk factors. This meant that they often lump these health behaviors with other risk factors such as baseline health status in their analysis. Thus, these studies provide at best a partial test of the role of health behaviors on the social support and mortality associations.

In evaluating the role of health behaviors on the social support and mortality link, researchers will often statistically take out the effects of these risk factors on mortality. These studies suggest that social support continues to predict mortality when statistically controlling for these health behaviors and standard risk factors (Berkman, 1995; House, Landis, and Umberson, 1988). However, there are studies that looked at the effects of social support on mortality with and without statistically removing the risk factors that included health behaviors. Many of these studies show that the effect of social support on mortality, although still significant, is reduced when considering these risk factors (Ceria et al., 2001; Kaplan et al., 1994; Kawachi et al., 1996). In one study it was found that statistical adjustments for risk factors including smoking, alcohol intake, coffee intake, physical activity, body mass, lipoprotein levels, and income reduced the mortality risk for low organizational activities by about 16 percent (Kaplan et al.). This reduction in explanation when controlling for these health behaviors is consistent with at least partial mediation of the social support and mortality link.

The social control hypothesis is not entirely unique in its prediction of healthier behaviors. You can probably recall times in which you received health advice from people in your social network. This informal network is often called upon for health-relevant information (Croyle and Hunt, 1991). Functional support theorists would argue that informational support in the form of health advice may also influence health behaviors (O'Reilly and Thomas, 1989). In addition, emotional support can be important in helping individuals initiate and maintain healthy behavioral change (O'Reilly and Thomas; Watson and Tharp, 1997). Stress is also related to poorer health habits, so proponents of the stress-buffering model might claim that the effect of health behaviors on the support and mortality link is consistent with the buffering model (Uchino, Uno, and Holt-Lunstad, 1999). What is unique about the social control hypothesis is the proposed direct social control and indirect internalization of social control as pathways influencing health behaviors. Presently, no data are available on these mechanisms in studies examining social support and mortality risk, so separating these pathways are difficult at this point in time.

The loneliness model is a recent perspective on how social integration can have direct effects on health (Stroebe and Stroebe, 1996). Loneliness is usually defined as a subjective discrepancy between desired and actual social connections (Russell, Peplau, and Cutrona, 1980). Loneliness has also been linked to poorer health habits such as sleep difficulties and increased peripheral resistance in the arteries that may in turn influence health outcomes (Cacioppo et al., 2002; Cacioppo et al., in press). In fact, loneliness may be viewed as a chronically stressful situation with concomitant physiological alterations because lonely individuals tend to feel more threatened during the course of their daily lives (Cacioppo et al., 2002; Hawkley et al., 2003). Consistent with this perspective, loneliness has been linked to higher mortality rates (Penninx et al., 1997). Given the reliable connection between social support and loneliness (Green et al., 2001; Pinquart and Sorensen, 2001), the viability of integrating loneliness into our thinking of social support and health outcomes is clear. However, no studies that I know of have directly examined loneliness as a direct pathway by which social integration may influence mortality.

Future researchers interested in the loneliness model should distinguish between social and emotional loneliness because they are related to different measures of social integration (Stroebe and Stroebe, 1996; Weiss, 1973). Social loneliness is a result of a general lack of social interactions and connections. It should thus be more highly related to social activities and general measures of network contact, size, and density. In comparison, emotional loneliness is a result of the lack of close relationships such as a confidant or significant other and should be related to the presence of absence of such relationships (Green et al., 2001; Stroebe et al., 1996). The fact that many types of social integration measures predict mortality suggests that both social and emotional loneliness may be important pathways. Future research will also be needed to evaluate this model using functional measures of support because studies indicate that such measures are associated with lower social loneliness (Pinquart and Sorensen, 2001; Stroebe et al.).

The concept of social capital is one of the more recent perspectives highlighting the health-relevant pathways of the direct effects model. The potential unique contribution of social capital is in its level of analysis. Social capital emphasizes the importance of community level integration and trust that can be used for the larger social good. As such, it highlights the importance of community level pathways such as access to health services, community norms favoring healthier behaviors, and collective efficacy (Kawachi and Berkman, 2000). There are only two studies that I know of that have examined social capital and mortality rates (Kawachi et al., 1997; Kennedy, Kawachi, and Brainerd, 1998). These studies demonstrated that social capital at the state or regional level predicted lower mortality rates even after considering poverty levels.

Because social capital theory has only recently been applied to the health domain, there is presently little direct evidence on the pathways by which social capital may influence mortality. Researchers in this area have proposed the importance of social capital in fostering community norms that favor healthier behaviors. In addition, the increased community trust associated with social capital may be associated with a collective efficacy that can have direct positive effects on health as well as indirect effects via better control of relevant health policies and community access to health services (Kawachi and Berkman, 2000). One of the few studies that examined the health correlates of social capital in Spain found that regions with higher social capital are able to obtain more health funding and implement health reforms (Rico, Fraile, and Gonzalez, 1999). The simultaneous analyses of these pathways in research examining social capital and disease outcomes would be important contributions to this perspective. Concerns about the different ways that social capital has been measured and the validity of these assessments as reflecting more than individual level processes (for example, social integration or hostility) are also important future research topics (Macinko and Starfield, 2001; Whitehead, 2001; see chapter 3). Although promising and provocative, the research applying social capital to health is at its beginning, and the upcoming years will clarify its links to health and mortality. Readers are again referred to figure 3.3 for a review of this model.

A "Retuned" Direct Effect Model

Based on the present review of pathways, a revised direct effects model is depicted in figure 6.2. The top half of the model contains the pathways highlighted by social identity, social control, and functional support theorists because both structural and functional measures appear to have direct effects on mortality. As highlighted by these theorists, support effects may be mediated via levels of esteem, meaning, and control that have a direct effect on health or through the control of health behaviors. Functional support is also postulated to have a direct effect on these processes as well via the provision of emotional, informational, and belonging support. In comparison, the bottom half of the model highlights the pathways made salient by the loneliness model. This addition to the model is perhaps the most speculative given the absence of studies directly linking social integration to health via feelings of loneliness. Nevertheless, evidence suggests that loneliness may influence health via behaviors such as poorer sleep or various psychological processes such as appraisals of threat, esteem, or control (Cacioppo et al., 2002; Hawkley et al., 2003).

There are several points worth highlighting about this revised model. First, the links between both structural and functional measures of support, health behaviors, and mortality are the key aspect of the model that appear to receive direct support. The rest of the model represents plausible pathways based on the theoretical positions cov-

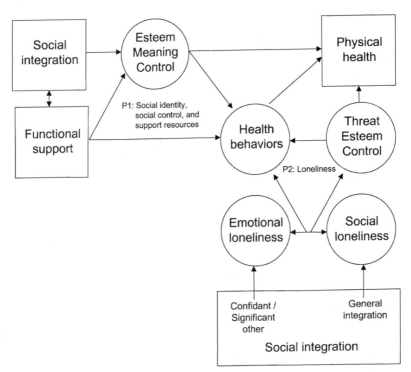

Figure 6.2. "Retuned" direct effect models of support highlighting the pathways made salient by prior models and existing studies on physical health outcomes. P1 = Pathway 1, P2 = Pathway 2.

ered in chapter 3. As a result, this model is meant to make explicit the pathways to be assessed in future studies. Second, as in the other revised model, this represents the best-case scenario in that both social integration and functional support can have negative effects on these theoretical pathways (for example, decreased esteem or encouragement of unhealthy behaviors). These negative effects need serious consideration when evaluating this revised direct effect model.

As noted above, the social capital model in theory extends the direct effects model to a broader level of analysis. Therefore, the merging of this revised model with the more traditional direct effect model would require extending the level of analysis from the individual to the broader community level of analysis (Kawachi and Berkman, 2000). Future research will be needed to determine the usefulness of this broader approach as well as its links to more traditional measures and pathways highlighted by social support research.

General Discussion of Models

It is my intention that the retuned stress-related and direct effect models be used as conceptual guides for future research. Based on the available social support and mortality literature, these are plausible models linking social support to mortality that incorporates the prior corpus of research as well as more recent data and concepts. An advantage of these revised models is the formalization of pathways that are specific enough to allow for test of their proposed effects.

There are several general issues that I would like to highlight as part of these models. Unlike prior theoretical perspectives covered in chapter 3, these models highlight the role of both structural and functional measures of support in the stress-related and direct effect models. In my opinion, the research on mortality justifies an expanded view of these measures that have in the past been treated as relating to different outcomes. Although there may indeed be conditions in which structural and functional support are related to unique effects, an expanded analysis of the common links between these measures is a neglected and potentially important avenue for future research.

It is also clear that testing these revised models will require a convergence of interdisciplinary perspectives. Sociologists are more closely tied to social identity perspectives whereas psychologists and medical professionals are more closely allied to the functional support view. Because there is evidence that both of these perspectives are important, studies that incorporate both pathways are sorely needed. This can most easily be done via collaborative research programs that focus on more integrative and dynamic models linking social integration with functional measures of support and its associations to health outcomes.

I would again like to repeat my caution that these models represent best-case scenarios of the support process. Both social integration and functional support can lead to negative effects on health. For instance, integration into a group that encourages unhealthy behaviors or the receipt of bad informational support can have detrimental effects. An evaluation of the models depicted would be sufficient to demonstrate if indeed some aspects of support are associated with negative effects on health. As an example, if there is deviant social control operating then it should be reflected in the measurement of health-related behaviors. However, more specificity may be gained by the simultaneous measurement of negative aspects of relationships described more fully in chapter 2.

One salient disadvantage of these revised models is that they do not highlight the larger issues that may complicate their validity and application. For instance, there may be cultural differences in social support processes that make a straightforward application of these models challenging (Dressler, 1995). These models are also based primarily on the implications of the social support and mortality literature and thus are more limited in their examination of additional processes. In the next section of this chapter, I attempt to address both of these limitations. More specifically, I examine the larger context for support effects as well as more specific processes that were not highlighted in the social support and mortality studies. This approach is meant to illustrate the breadth and complexity of social support effects and is not meant to be an exhaustive review.

A Broader Perspective on Social Support and Mortality

There are several ways to attempt to formulate a broader perspective on social support and mortality. One broad framework for examining complex, multiply determined phenomena such as the association between social support and mortality is integrative multilevel analyses (Cacioppo and Berntson, 1992). As shown in figure 6.3 these levels of analysis can range from the broad sociocultural context to the more micro physiological concomitants of social support. In some cases we have already covered the theoretically emphasized processes at these levels of analyses. For instance, identity theorists highlight the importance of self-esteem (personologic level factor), whereas social control theorists highlight the importance of health behaviors (behavioral level factor). Functional support theorists, on the other hand, have emphasized the role of stress appraisals (psychological level factor) on buffer-

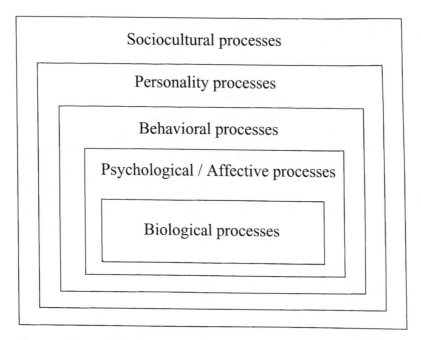

Figure 6.3. Potential levels of analyses linking social support to physical health outcomes.

ing processes. What I would like to do is highlight processes that are not explicit in the models covered thus far. In doing so, I will draw from the larger literature examining basic support processes as well as research linking social support to mental health outcomes. The goal here is to underscore a broader perspective on social support that can place support in its proper context and be used as a guide for future research.

Sociocultural Processes

One of the limitations of present social support research is a lack of emphasis on the larger sociocultural context in which support processes unfold. In theory, there are several factors at this level of analysis that might influence how social support works. At a broad cultural level is the distinction between more collective and individualistic cultures (Markus and Kitiyama, 1991). These distinctions are best considered as general tendencies that emerge when the members of the culture are considered as a whole. Within any given culture there is significant variability in how strongly these tendencies are expressed.

Generally speaking, in the United States (as well as most Western societies) we operate primarily in a more individualistic culture, where we are socialized that the main goal of our development is to be relatively independent. This independence goal stresses the importance of attending to the self, appreciation of one's differences from others, and the importance of asserting oneself. In contrast, many Eastern, Latin, and African cultures view the self as part of a larger social whole. This view emphasizes the self as interdependent with the surrounding context, and it is the self in relation to others that is most important (Markus and Kitiyama, 1991).

To make this point more salient, in Japanese culture there is a concept known as "enryo" that serves as an implicit guide to social interactions. Enryo literally means "distance-consideration" and refers to culturally transmitted sets of behavior that deemphasize the self as an object of attention and instead convey respect in interactions (Johnson and Johnson, 1975). Often this may result in sacrificing one's own needs in order to maintain harmonious relationships. This can lead to situations that can seem strange to individuals not privy to such culturally determined patterns. A not too uncommon exchange among my Japanese friends and family is to keep insisting that the other person take the last piece of food on the table even though all of us are still hungry! Friends of mine who are not Japanese simply shake their heads in disbelief when these interactions take place for what seems to them an inordinate period of time.

There are several ways in which cultural variables such as individualism-collectivism may influence the association between social support and mortality. One way is by influencing access to social support. Early on, researchers hypothesized that it may be more difficult to find associations in more integrated or collective cultures presumably because of the greater level of support available (Berkman, 1986). This greater level of support would make it more difficult to differentiate between individuals within such a culture. My review indicates that collective cultures seem to similarly benefit from certain aspects of support. However, because of the small number of studies and the lack of research comparing different cultural groups a definitive answer to this issue is not possible.

One of the most basic questions at the sociocultural level of analysis is whether cultures varying on individualism-collectivism might differ in levels of social support. If this link is demonstrated then it is plausible that culture may play a role in association between social support and mortality. In this research it is unclear whether these cultural orientations influence overall social support (Dilworth-Anderson and Marshall, 1996; Fijneman, Willemsen, and Poortinga, 1996). However, one clear conclusion is that these cultural orientations influence the types of relationships that serve as primary sources of support (Dilworth-Anderson and Marshall; Dressler, 1994).

One challenge posed by this conclusion is to identify aspects of relationships within a culture that are most important and thus potentially health relevant. In this sense, the most direct way in which cultural orientations may influence the association between social support and mortality is by modifying the types of relationships and forms of support that are seen as culturally appropriate (Dressler, 1994). If not culturally appropriate, supportive behaviors may actually be a source of stress. It might be awkward if your boss asked you for job-related social support! This means that researchers need to be sensitive to viewing support in its proper cultural context in order to examine its beneficial effects (Dressler; Janes and Pawson, 1986). For instance, familial sources of social support may be more directly relied upon and hence more important than friend support in many collective cultures (Dilworth-Anderson and Marshall, 1996).

The evidence for the importance of a culturally sensitive assessment of support in health research has been demonstrated in a sustained program of research by William Dressler and colleagues (for example, Dressler, 1994). These researchers have been able to identify important sources of support by examining the sociocultural history of specific ethnic groups. Their program of research revealed that culturally appropriate forms of social support were associated with lower blood pressure in Mexican (Dressler et al., 1986), Brazilian (Dressler, Dos Santos, and Viteri, 1986), and African American cultures (Dressler, 1991). This research is also notable because it illustrates the importance of considering culture within societies that are considered more collective in nature.

A more recent approach to examining cultural processes linking social support to health is that of cultural consonance (Dressler, Balieiro, and Dos Santos, 1997). There seems to be some agreement among individuals within ethnic groups about who would be the proper sources of support for certain problems such as financial difficulties or marital problems (Dressler and Bindon, 2000). Cultural consonance is high to the extent that an individual's reported access to support is consistent with present cultural models of appropriate support (Dressler et al.). Consistent with the importance of such an approach, it was found that higher levels of cultural consonance were associated with better psychological well-being and lower blood pressure in a Brazilian sample (Dressler et al., 1997). Besides its focus on cultural influences on support, a unique strength of this approach is it allows one to link the individual and cultural levels of analysis in social support research.

The research on culture and social support also makes salient the importance of considering the sociocultural context of the group. For instance, different cultural groups face varied sources of stress that can include prejudice, economic difficulties, and violence that can lead to isolation or a reliance on in-group support processes (Dilworth-Anderson and Marshall, 1996). In addition, immigration can isolate cultural groups that have formerly relied on families as a major source of support. These issues would argue for an examination of the challenges faced by specific cultural groups in considering how social support fosters adjustment to stressful events.

Another sociocultural variable that may influence the association between social support and mortality is that of socioeconomic status (SES). In earlier chapters, low SES was primarily examined as a source of life stress with relevance for the stress-buffering model of support. However, it may be important to examine whether SES is associated with more basic social support processes. It may be a particularly important sociocultural factor to consider because a large body of research suggests that lower SES is related to higher morbidity and mortality from a wide variety of diseases (Adler et al., 1994).

The literature examining the association between SES and social support is not large (Krause, 2001; Taylor and Seeman, 1999). However, these studies do address the fundamental issue of whether SES is associated with difference in social support. In one study, researchers surveyed a random sample of older adults from the Health Care Finance Administration list and found that lower SES was related to less contact with friends and family as well as less satisfaction with the support they received (Krause and Borawski-Clark, 1995). Other studies have similarly found that lower SES is related to lower overall perceptions of support (Cohen, Kaplan, and Salonen, 1999).

A consideration of the social context of individuals varying in SES also suggests additional insights into why low SES may be related to lower social support and the implications for health. One interesting observation is that social networks are normally composed of individuals with a similar SES background (Lin, 1982). As a result, the broader social networks of individuals low in SES may be similarly taxed and thus be a limited source of support (Krause, 2001). Perhaps more significantly, even close sources of support may have difficulties in providing support. For instance, spouses tends to be a strong source of support for married individuals, and many of the problems faced by individuals low in SES affect the entire family. This may limit the ability of the individuals closest to the person to provide support during times of need.

Personologic Level of Analysis

The personologic level of analysis refers to personality or individual difference factors that may be associated with social support. There are at least three ways in which such personologic factors may be important (Pierce et al., 1997). First, personologic factors may serve as guides that direct the conditions under which one seeks support. Second, they can influence how one might view the availability or receipt of social support. Finally, they can influence whether network members spontaneously provide support or how members react to a person's seeking of support. This may be related to network members' expectations of that person's potential reaction to support (for example, comfort level). Although a complete review of how all relevant personologic factors may influence support is not possible here, there is one particularly relevant factor that has not been addressed in earlier chapters. This relates to the variable of attachment style.

The concept of attachment has its roots in the writings of John Bowlby (1982). He argued for the existence of an organized behavioral attachment system that mediates infant responses to threat or distress. Because of the dependency of the infant, adult caretakers become a symbolic "safety net" that the infant relies on during times of distress. This attachment process develops over time and is based on repeated interactions with the primary caretaker. If these interactions are positive, infants can come to rely on the caretaker as a reliable source of protection and support and hence develop a secure attachment style. However, if these interactions are inconsistent or negative, infants may develop more ambivalent or avoidant attachment systems (Ainsworth et al., 1978).

The concept of infant attachment has been widely applied to the adult literature on close interpersonal relationships (Cassidy and Shaver, 1999; Diamond, 2001). It is thought that these infant-caretaker attachment processes provide the basis for adult expectations regarding their social relationships. More specifically, it is proposed that early infant-caretaker interactions provide the basis for the development of working models of relationships as trustworthy and dependable (Hazan and Shaver, 1987). These interactions can shape one's self-identity as well as one's expectation of the dependability of others. Although the categorization of attachment styles in adults differ somewhat, one popular model is based on whether a person has internalized a positive or negative mental model of the self and others (Bartholomew, 1990).

The mental model approach gives rise to four categorizations of attachment styles. If all goes well between the infant and caretaker, the secure attachment style arises, which is characterized by a positive model of self and positive model of others (Bartholomew, 1990). The other categorizations are more insecurely attached and differ in the specifics underlying the insecure attachment. For instance, the ambivalent style has a negative model of self but positive model of others. This results in an individual that values relationships with others but is afraid or anxious about rejection. The dismissive attachment style is characterized by the opposing issues. This individual has a positive model of self but negative model of others. As a result this individual tends to value independence over relationship goals. Finally, the fearful attachment style has both a negative model of self and others, which results in social avoidance.

Attachment processes have been noted as the possible basis of perceived available support. Is there evidence that early familial experiences or perceptions may be associated with social support? Studies suggest that individual's perceptions of their early childhood experiences are related to their perceptions of support (Flaherty and Richman, 1986; Sarason et al., 1986). In one such study, participants completed ratings of their emotional closeness to their parents while in medical school (Graves et al., 1998). A follow-up of these individuals found that these initial ratings of parental closeness were associated with a greater number of close contacts providing social support thirty years later. Although this study relies on retrospective reports of parental warmth, it suggests that these relationship-based mental structures can have consequences over a long period of time.

There are several ways in which attachment styles may influence social support processes. As noted earlier, the first possibility is that attachment styles can affect the extent to which individuals seek support during times of need (Ognibene and Collins, 1998). That is, individuals with less secure attachment styles may be less likely to seek support in the first place. In one study, researchers placed participants in an anxiety-provoking situation with their romantic partners and examined their behavior during a "waiting" period (Simpson, Rholes, and Nelligan, 1992). The participant's behavior was then coded for anxiety and support-seeking behaviors during this period. Individuals with secure attachment styles were more likely to seek support from their partners as their anxiety levels increased.

A second way in which attachment styles can influence support processes is by affecting the perceived quality of social support. That is, insecure individuals may be less likely to benefit from received support or perceive it to be available. Consistent with this possibility, individuals with more insecure attachment styles report less satisfaction with the support they receive (Kobak and Sceery, 1988). This may especially be the case for the dismissive attachment style that is built on feelings of independence from others. In this case, social support could be perceived as threatening one's sense of independence. Researchers studying adolescents found that the dismissive attachment style was associated with difficulty in getting assistance from peers and instructors (Larose and Bernier, 2001).

A person's attachment style may also influence whether social network members spontaneously provide support or how they react to that person's support-seeking behaviors. That is, individuals differing in attachment styles may behave in ways that influence how receptive others view them to support. Although much less research exists on this possibility, an early study examined how individuals perceived an interaction partner who was low or high in social support (Sarason et al., 1985). Results of this study found that people high in social support were viewed by others as more likable and greater in social skills than people low in social support. Given research linking attachment styles to differing levels of social support, these findings suggest that securely attached individuals are more likely to be viewed positively and hence "receptive" to support.

Another interesting finding from attachment research is that secure individuals are more likely to provide support in response to their partner's stress. In one study, researchers examined the interactions between couples where one person disclosed a personal problem (Collins and Feeney, 2000). Each participant's attachment style was measured and their interactions videotaped and coded for their supportive statements. Results of this study demonstrated that individuals with a secure attachment style provided more support regardless of whether the partner was clear about their support needs. This finding highlights the importance of examining how personality may influence an individual's willingness to provide support to others in the first place.

Although individuals with less secure attachment styles seem to have smaller social networks (Anders and Tucker, 2000), presently most attachment research has focused on the link between attachment style and functional measures of support. Very little attention has examined whether attachment style is associated with more structural measures of support. Of these structural measures, links to formal groups and social activities may be particularly important in light of the findings in this book. It is possible that one's model of the trustworthiness of others may be linked to lower trust at the group or community level of analysis, as highlighted by social capital theorists. This suggests that securely attached individuals may be more likely to get involved in groups and organizations. In a study discussed earlier (Graves et al., 1998), researchers found that ratings of emotional closeness between parents and child were associated with greater group participation approximately thirty years later. These data suggest the importance of examining how attachment history might cast long shadows on many aspects of one's subsequent social life.

Behavioral Level of Analysis

The behavioral level of analysis examines the behaviors of individuals and how they might explain associations between social support and mortality. The most salient factor at this level of analysis is the role of health behaviors in explaining the social support and mortality link. This pathway has been discussed previously, and research suggests that health behaviors may explain part of the link between social support and health outcomes (see chapter 4). A second related behavioral pathway not yet discussed in detail is adherence to medical regimens. Adherence is usually defined as cooperation with the advice and treatment given by healthcare professionals (Ley, 1977). This pathway may be especially important in populations with chronic diseases such as diabetes and cardiovascular disease because adherence predicts better health outcomes (O'Brien, Petrie, and Raeburn, 1992).

According to social control and identity theorists, social support may promote greater cooperation with medical regimens through direct or indirect social control of a person's behavior with subsequent effects on health. Functional support theorists also highlight how emotional support may help initiate and maintain healthy behavioral change. In one study, researchers in the Multiple Risk Factor Intervention Trial (MRFIT) included a comprehensive assessment of both structural and functional measures of social support (O'Reilly and Thomas, 1989). MRFIT was a national study aimed at examining the effects of risk factor reduction on mortality rates. This particular study involved a subset of individuals from the MRFIT project and examined the differences between individuals who lowered their risk and those who did not during a re-screening three years after the project ended. Results of this study showed that informational, emotional, and available support for risk reduction predicted a more healthy profile. Moreover, individuals reducing their risk had larger networks (especially familial network ties), which explained the differences in risk due to more functional measures of support. It is also interesting that individuals who reduced their risk reported higher levels of conflict within their network. This may be seen as consistent with the social control hypothesis that predicts beneficial effects of social control on physical health, but increased psychological distress due to social control efforts (Lewis and Rook, 1999).

Social support effects on cooperation with medical regimens should be especially evident in chronic disease populations because the health risks are especially salient to them as well as their support network. As an example of this process, researchers examined the factors that predicted greater adherence to antiviral medication in patients infected with human immunodeficiency virus (HIV) (Catz et al., 2000). These researchers found much variability in adherence—nearly 33 percent of patients missed one dose within the prior five days. Predictably, lower adherence was associated with higher viral loads. More important for our discussion is that perceived emotional support was a significant predictor of greater adherence to antiviral medication in these HIV patients. These results are consistent with a host of studies that showed social support predicts greater adherence in patients with various chronic diseases, including diabetic patients (Burroughs et al., 1997); transplantation patients (Teichman et al., 2000), and coronary patients (Toobert et al., 1998).

Psychological Level of Analysis

The psychological level of analysis addresses the psychological or mental processes by which social support may ultimately influence mortality. This is a particularly important level of analysis as many researchers postulate psychological mediation of social support effects (Cohen, 1988). For instance, the stress-buffering model suggests that psychological appraisals of stress are important pathways by which social support has its health effects. To the extent that support is available, then stress appraisals should be lower due to the presence of a coping option (Lazarus and Folkman, 1984). As a result, social support should be able to modify these appraisals and decrease unhealthy stress reactions.

Presently there is little direct evidence on the psychological pathways linking social support to health outcomes (House, 2001). This is surprising given the centrality of appraisals in the stress-buffering model. Laboratory studies examining the influence of received support on cardiovascular reactivity would be an ideal paradigm to examine these processes because of the well-defined context. However, to date few of these laboratory studies have been able to elucidate the more specific psychological processes responsible for social support effects.

Stress and coping studies suggest a link between certain appraisals and the tendency to seek social support (Dunkel-Schetter, Folkman, and Lazarus, 1987; Folkman and Lazarus, 1985). In one study, researchers examined this idea in middle-aged participants (Dunkel-Schetter et al.). They found that more support was provided when there were perceived threats to health, but less tangible support was provided when there was a perceived threat to a person's self-esteem. Clearly, the link between appraisals and support are complex, but the lack of research on this topic makes speculation about this central psychological mechanism problematic. These findings, however, do suggest a certain degree of specificity in appraisal patterns and support seeking.

There are other psychological processes that may influence the social support and mortality link. The potential role of perceived loneliness in social support effects was already discussed. Social support is also associated with lower levels of depression, perceived stress, and greater satisfaction with life (Sarason, Sarason, and Pierce, 1990). These psychological processes may either influence the development of disease or exacerbate disease in unhealthy populations (Smith and Gallo, 2001). Very few studies have examined whether these psychological processes were responsible for the link between social support and health outcomes.

In one recent study we examined whether these psychological processes could explain the increased blood pressure seen in older adults characterized by low social support (Uchino et al., 1999). Contrary to our expectation, we found that the measures of depression, satisfaction with life, and perceived stress did not appear to be responsible for the association between social support and lower blood pressure in older adults. However, given the complexity of the pathways by which social support may influence health outcomes, it is unlikely that evidence will be found for a single dominant pathway. Although beyond the scope of this book, ultimately more sophisticated statistical procedures may be necessary to minimize measurement error and examine whether the aggregation of pathways can explain social support effects (see MacKinnon et al., 2001).

One factor that does appear to be an important psychological mediator of some social support effects is perceived control. Social support may be associated with greater perceptions of control because it potentially provides the resources that are important in coping with stressors or life more generally. Consistent with this possibility, social support was found to be related to increased perceptions of control in response to daily life stressors (Atienza, Collins, and King, 2001). Moreover, social support buffered the effects of daily stressors on negative moods. This study also found strong evidence for perceived control as an important psychological pathway because subsequent analyses showed that this stress-buffering effect of support was due to variations in perceived control. More studies like this are needed in the social support and physical health literature to examine whether variations in psychological processes can explain the links found in this book.

Physiological Level of Analysis

Social support may ultimately influence health via relevant physiological processes. After all, the body is the final common pathway by which environmental factors influence health, and research is consistent with the role of multiple physiological systems in social support effects (Uchino et al., 1996). In contrast, many of the studies on social support and mortality "control" for basic physiological risk factors such as blood pressure to examine whether social support is an independent predictor of mortality. As covered in earlier chapters, there is evidence that social support predicts physiological processes in healthy individuals (Uchino et al.). These data force us to rethink the role of standard physiological factors in social support research.

An important question relates to what biological systems may be influenced by social support. Given the link between social support and all-cause mortality, one might expect that social support could have beneficial effects across many different physiological systems. Depending on the initial health of the participants, this research could shed light on the role of social support in the development or exacerbation of disease. In fact, evidence on the link between social support and health-relevant biological processes suggests that social support may be operating in both circumstances. However, to address this question we reviewed the evidence linking social support to aspects of the cardiovascular, endocrine, and immune systems (Uchino et al., 1996).

By far most of the studies had examined whether social support predicted measures of cardiovascular function. The studies that we reviewed showed that social support was reliably related to lower resting blood pressure in healthy individuals. Furthermore, the association between social support and resting blood pressure may be more evident in older individuals (Uchino et al., 1995). The results are important because resting blood pressure predicts cardiovascular risk even at levels below that normally considered hypertensive (Vasan et al., 2001). More recent studies also suggest links between social support and lower ambulatory blood pressure that may be health relevant (Gump et al., 2001; Steptoe, Lundwall, and Cropley, 2000).

Studies have also examined whether altering social support in intervention studies was associated with better cardiovascular regulation in hypertensive individuals. Such studies are important in that they can directly demonstrate a beneficial health effect of social support in cardiovascular patients. In one early study, researchers identified four hundred hypertensive patients and assigned them to various interventions or a control condition (Levine et al., 1979). One of these intervention groups was a family support condition in which patients were asked to identify a target individual with whom they had frequent contact (typically a spouse). The target individuals were then trained to increase understanding, support, and reinforcement regarding positive management of the patient's hypertensive state. Results revealed that family support alone decreased diastolic blood pressure (DBP) (that is, DBP below the hypertensive limits for their particular age group) by 11 percent at an eighteen-month follow-up assessment. Subsequent follow-ups of this project sample revealed reliable long-term effects of the social support component on blood pressure regulation (Morisky et al., 1983; Morisky et al., 1985).

We also examined evidence linking social support to neuroendocrine function. Hormones and neurotransmitters are potentially important physiological end points due to their role in stress-related disorders (Chrousos and Gold, 1992) and the aging process more generally (Sapolsky, Krey, and McEwen, 1986; Seeman and Robbins, 1994). Neuroendocrine processes also mediate aspects of cardiovascular and immune function (Ader, Felton, and Cohen, 2001) and thus may shed light on how these diverse physiological systems are coordinated as a function of social support. In our review there was some evidence that social support was associated with lower catecholamine levels (Fleming et al., 1982; Seeman et al., 1994), which is consistent with the beneficial effects of social support on cardiovascular function.

Another important hormone implicated in disease processes is cortisol, which has well-documented immunosuppressive effects (Greenspan and Baxter, 1994). There presently exists little research that directly examines the links between social support and cortisol levels. At the time of the Uchino et al. review, the small number of inconsistent findings prevent any firm conclusions. We argued that advances in the measurement of cortisol will likely clarify the association between social support and cortisol levels. For instance, an examination of cortisol obtained during the course of an entire day may be a better indicator of cortisol levels in everyday life rather than an assessment at one point in time. It is thus promising that a recent study that measured cortisol over the course of three days showed that social support predicted lower overall cortisol levels in breast cancer patients (Turner-Cobb et al., 2000). Nevertheless, more research is still needed to reliably document this association.

One neuroendocrine hormone with promising and largely unexplored links to social support is oxytocin (Knox and Uvnas-Moberg, 1998; Taylor et al., 2000). Oxytocin is a hypothalamic hormone that is best known for its role in milk ejection during breastfeeding and uterine contractions accompanying labor. However, oxytocin also appears to vary according to various social stimuli (for example, touch or massage) and has antistress effects in both the brain and more peripheral physiological systems (Taylor et al.). For instance, oxytocin release is associated with decreases in cortisol levels, blood pressure, sympathetic activity, and increases in parasympathetic activity (Uvnas-Moberg, 1998). It also appears that the antistress effects of oxytocin stimulation become more pronounced over time; thus individuals in stable, fulfilling relationships or social groups should experience the greatest benefits.

At present little research exists on oxytocin responses in humans and their potential link to social support. There are several ways in which oxytocin release may be related to social support. Both structural and functional types of support may be associated with the situations that elicit an oxytocin response (for example, touching or hugging). Over time, these oxytocin responses may become conditioned to these social stimuli such that mental schemas or memories may trigger its release in the absence of direct social interactions (Uvnas-Moberg, 1998). It has also been proposed that oxytocin may be a primary pathway regulating stress-buffering effects via its influences on other physiological systems (Knox and Uvnas-Moberg, 1998). Due to the recency of these proposed links, however, little direct research presently exists. Future research will no doubt clarify the potentially exciting links between social support processes and oxytocin.

A final physiological pathway by which social support may influence mortality is via the immune system. Indeed, some of the strongest associations we found in our review were for a link between social support and better immune function, especially in older adults (Uchino et al., 1996). This association in older adults was particularly noteworthy because the risk of cancer increases with age, and infectious diseases are a leading cause of death in older individuals (Effros and Walford, 1987). Research further suggests the biological significance of these immune differences in social support. For instance, in one study researchers found that individuals lower in support were less likely to clinically seroconvert to a hepatitis B vaccination (Glaser et al., 1992). In another research study, investigators examined whether social support predicted susceptibility to infection from the common cold virus. In this study, consenting participants were directly exposed to common cold viruses (via nasal drops) and quarantined for five days (Cohen et al., 1997). Individuals who had more diverse social networks (relationships from a variety of domains such as work, home, or church) were less likely to develop clinical colds.

Although most research linking social support to immune processes has emphasized its potential role in cancer, HIV, and other infectious diseases, it may also have important implications for cardiovascular disease. There is increased emphasis on how immune processes may influence the atherosclerotic processes (Ross, 1999). For instance, immune cells (for example, macrophages) can accumulate at the site of cholesterol deposits and release hormones that contribute to the formation, development, and subsequent rupturing of plaques in the arterial walls (Libby, Ridker, and Maseri, 2002). Given the association between social support and lower cardiovascular mortality, the role of immune-related processes in explaining this link should be given more attention in future research.

Discussion of Pathways Highlighted by a Broad Model

An examination of additional potential pathways at different levels of analysis suggests the importance of a broad but integrative approach to studying the links between social support and mortality. Results of this multilevel analysis suggest the importance of sociocultural, personologic, psychological, behavioral, and physiological processes in explaining the research links covered in this book. These broader pathways are more speculative given the lack of direct research examining their plausibility in a health context. Nevertheless, it places this research in a broader context and can provide the basis for a more integrative agenda over the next generation of research on social support and health outcomes. Readers are also referred to the excellent models proposed by Sheldon Cohen (1988) and Lisa Berkman and colleagues (2000).

A broad model linking social support to mortality is depicted in figure 6.4. The innermost boxes represent the more micro and mid-level factors that may explain the links between social support and morbidity and/or mortality. Accordingly, structural and functional measures of support may ultimately influence morbidity and mortality through two distinct but not necessarily independent pathways. One pathway involves behavioral processes as outlined by social control and social identity theorists. The other involves more psychological processes that are linked to appraisals, emotions or moods (for exam-

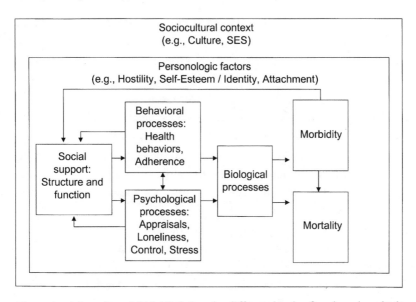

Figure 6.4. A broad model highlighting the different levels of analyses by which social support may influence physical health outcomes.

ple, depression), and feelings of control. Note that the behavioral and psychological levels are linked as each has been shown to exert an influence over the other. For instance, feelings of stress can adversely impact on the practice of health behaviors (Grunberg and Baum, 1985), whereas health behaviors such as exercise can have beneficial effects on feelings of stress (Rejeski et al., 1992). Finally, these psychological and behavioral pathways may also have reciprocal influence on social support processes. For instance, psychological distress may influence perceptions of support and contribute to negative social interactions (Alferi et al., 2001; Coyne, 1976). These cyclical links between support, behavior, and psychological processes may provide an important basis for understanding both the development and exacerbation of disease for people low in social support.

An important aspect of the innermost boxes is that the behavioral and psychological pathways ultimately influence mortality through relevant physiological changes such as cardiovascular, neuroendocrine, and immune function. For instance, health behaviors such as exercise influence cardiovascular disease via changes in blood pressure and cholesterol profiles (U.S. Department of Health and Human Services, 1996). This link makes salient an important point: future research will need to conceptualize how these physiological mechanisms play a role in the links between social support and health outcomes. Researchers collecting information on social support and health-relevant physiological processes will be able to determine the more precise conceptual links between social support and these biological pathways. In fact, these physiological measures can be assessed as more "intermediate" health end points, although ultimately an evaluation of the full model with its links to morbidity and mortality would be necessary.

An additionally important aspect of figure 6.4 concerns the proposed links to and from disease morbidity. This makes salient two significant aspects of this broad model. First, the links with morbidity highlight the potential role of social support in the development of certain diseases. Research reviewed in chapter 5 suggests that social support may influence diseases with a long-term etiology (for example, cardiovascular disorders). The studies linking social support to biological processes were consistent with this premise, although more longitudinal data are needed to directly test these links. Second, the feedback loop between morbidity and social support highlights the unique challenges faced by individuals diagnosed with disease that can impact their social network. Close network members are often called upon as sources of support after the diagnosis of disease. However, in some cases the strain placed upon network members in dealing with the person's illness may be considerable. For instance, the person may be threatened by the potential loss of the close relationship or having to bear witness to their loved ones' distress. This may result in network members withdrawing in an attempt to cope with an overwhelming situation (Bolger et al., 1996).

The mid- and outer-level boxes represent the more macro-level processes that include relevant personologic and sociocultural variables. The figure highlights that the more micro-level processes are embedded within a larger set of personologic and sociocultural issues. These more macro processes can be viewed as "conditioning" factors that influence the strength of the pathways depicted in figure 6.4. The most obvious links are those that influence the social support box. For instance, cultural processes may determine the type and function of relationships that are most important for health (Dressler, 1995). Not so obvious but also important is the role of these factors on other aspects of the model. As an example, ethnic groups differ in their susceptibility to different diseases (for example, African Americans and hypertension), which would impact on the more specific physiological pathways and disease outcomes that are influenced by social support.

There are a number of general issues that I would like to discuss that bear on this broader model. First, each of the models covered in chapter 3 and revised in this chapter are essentially submodels in this broader approach. This model essentially places social support in a larger context and makes salient the "bigger picture." Second, this broad perspective may have implications for the study of more macro-level processes in their own right. Researchers examining why SES differences appear for mortality have suggested that social support may be an important pathway (Cohen, Kaplan, and Salonen, et al., 1999). In fact many broad psychosocial risk factors (for example, hostility) posit social support as an important process to consider. As a result, this broad model can be linked up to other models and highlight the pathways made salient by social support research.

There are also at least two important conceptual implications of data linking social support to disease-relevant physiological processes. First, the association between social support and mortality may actually be stronger than previously demonstrated because prior research has typically taken out part of the phenomena by controlling for these physiological processes. Second, if these basic physiological variables were dominant pathways, then one would expect that they would significantly weaken the association between social support and mortality after they have been controlled (Baron and Kenny, 1986). Despite these controls, associations between social support and mortality still exist, which suggests the importance of modeling a broader, more complex set of physiological pathways. In most studies only basic physiological factors such as resting blood pressure have been examined, although other biological processes are relevant but largely untapped (for example, cytokine profiles). It will also be necessary to examine physiological end points that are more closely linked to morbidity and mortality, such as the degree of coronary calcification.

The processes outlined in this broad model will need to be considered in the context of specific disease states. The etiology of cardiovascular disease is of course not the same as HIV, and these differences will influence the specifics of the model. In such cases, different behavioral (for example, health behaviors) and physiological processes are salient. The psychosocial processes triggered by the diagnosis of these diseases may also be different. For instance, individuals with HIV face substantially more social stigma than cardiovascular patients, and the outlook for those with HIV is less certain (Davison, Pennebaker, and Dickerson, 2000). These factors may contribute to further adjustment problems and less available social support at a time of great need.

Even within specific diseases one will need to take into account the particular stage of disease. The disease-specific factors that weighed heavily in the development of disease will need to be considered along with the challenges faced when one is diagnosed with a medical condition. The diagnosis and treatment associated with diseases raise a number of adjustment issues over time. These adjustment issues can include dealing with (1) stress and depression, (2) cooperation with medical regimens, and (3) medication side effects, to name a few.

I would like to make a parting comment about the models covered in this chapter. I believe that we are no longer at the stage in which social support researchers can simply measure support and document an association with physical health. We are at the stage in which we need to understand why these existing effects occur. This will entail testing specific pathways as well as an appreciation of larger contextual factors that shape and guide health-relevant support processes. In the absence of this understanding, interventions may be misguided, and the results of those who "get it right" will seem at odds with others who do not. This means that each aspect of the models gets tested on as solid a ground as social support itself. We should do as good a job of thinking about and measuring the process end of the model (for example, health behaviors or physiological function) as we do social support.

7

Intervention Implications

The greatest handicap of applied psychology has been the fact that, without proper theoretical help, it had to follow the costly, inefficient, and limited method of trial and error. . . . There is nothing so practical as a good theory.
—Kurt Lewin, *Field Theory in Social Science*

The classic quote by Kurt Lewin, a prominent social psychologist, serves to remind us about the dynamic interplay between theory and practice. He strongly believed that a good theory could serve as the backbone of relevant interventions. He further argued that practical applications could serve as a stringent test of theory and thus inform researchers on the usefulness of their existing frameworks (Lewin, 1951). Of course, this premise needed to be balanced with the fact that attempts to apply our knowledge prematurely may result in ineffective interventions that decrease the credibility of the social sciences, or may even end up placing participants at risk.

One of the problems faced by researchers seeking to apply social support findings is that there is no single coherent framework that can explain the diversity of research findings in this literature (Gottlieb, 1988). In chapter 6 I attempted to specify the pathways responsible for the links between social support and health by integrating existing social support models with the morbidity and mortality studies reviewed in chapters 4 and 5. This preliminary analysis suggests that both structural and functional measures of social support play important roles in the stress-related and direct effect models. Each of these models in turn highlighted the pathways made explicit by current conceptual perspectives on functional support and social integration. For instance, identity and functional support theorists specify the psychological and personologic level pathways of self-esteem, life meaning, stress appraisals, and control. Social control theorists argue for the importance of some of these pathways, but also highlight the role of health behaviors as crucial mediators of associations between social support and health. Finally, an integrative multilevel analysis of social support effects revealed a broader perspective on this complex phenomenon. This analysis highlighted the larger sociocultural variables that may influence support as well as the more micro physiological processes by which social support may influence the development or progression of specific diseases.

Although the literature has not yet directly demonstrated that the revised social support and health models work via these proposed pathways, there are a number of broader findings that might be used to guide effective interventions. Epidemiological evidence strongly points to the role of both structural and functional supports on lower mortality rates. Of these measures, involvement in social or group activities, aggregate measures of social integration, and emotional support appear to be particularly consistent predictors of lower mortality. There was also some evidence that received tangible support predicted higher mortality rates.

Certainly one can argue about whether we yet know enough, especially in terms of mechanisms, to apply this knowledge effectively to design relevant interventions. The reality here is that support interventions have already been one of the most widespread psychosocial interventions in the mental health and medical systems. Literally hundreds of attempts at support interventions have been done to examine their purported beneficial effects on a variety of outcomes (Hogan, Linden, and Najarian, 2002). These interventions address a real need to mobilize the strengths of our social bonds to address personal and community-wide health issues.

In this chapter I explore the more applied implications of the links between social support and mortality. I address two main points that bear on the application of these research findings. First, I review some of the ways in which social support interventions have been conducted in the past. This overview is not comprehensive but is an attempt to provide a general sense of the different intervention approaches and their effectiveness (see Cohen, Underwood, and Gottlieb, 2000 for a comprehensive and practical review). Second, I attempt to form some common links between the theoretical and applied literatures on social support and health. More specifically, the connections between these intervention approaches and the models presented in chapters 3 and 6 are discussed.

Social Support Interventions

There have been numerous attempts to design support interventions to promote well-being, behavioral change, and physical health. According to one comprehensive review, literally hundreds of support interventions have been conducted (Hogan, Linden, and Najarian, 2002). These existing intervention studies are not without problems. For instance, many of these studies have not provided direct evidence that the intervention even modified social support levels (Hogan et al.). Such issues are discussed at length at the end of this chapter. Interventions also differ dramatically in their approach and orientation. The question is how best to categorize these diverse support intervention studies.

One widely used categorization scheme was proposed by Benjamin Gottlieb (1988). He argued that support interventions can be categorized along two dimensions based on the provider of support. The first dimension has to do with the nature of the relationship between the support provider and participant. Is the support provider a newly formed relationship (for example, practitioner or peers) or does the support involve already established relationships from a person's existing support network? The second dimension focuses on the unit of support. Is support provided in a one-on-one setting or is it provided in a group setting? Based on this typology, I provide a select overview of support interventions based on the type of relationship that the intervention focuses on (professional, peer, and existing network sources of support). Within these types of support interventions, the unit of support is discussed when relevant. These intervention approaches are then discussed based on the larger social support and physical health literatures covered in chapters 4 to 6.

Support from Professionals

Social support interventions have used a variety of sources to provide support to the person in need. One approach has been to use professional sources of support to facilitate coping or to promote healthy behavioral change. These professionals can range from physicians, nurses, psychologists, social workers, and paraprofessionals trained to facilitate support. Often these professionals provide various aspects of informational support as well as some forms of emotional support. For instance, home visitation or contact with professionals has been used to try and increase social support to reduce preterm delivery or the potential negative developmental outcomes of preterm deliveries (Olds and Kitzman, 1993).

One intervention strategy using professional sources of support was based on evidence suggesting that individuals with low social support have more negative birth outcomes (Feldman et al., 2000; Nuckolls, Cassel, and Kaplan, 1972). In one intriguing study, researchers designed an intervention to test whether support from a professional during labor could act similarly to positively influence birth outcomes (Kennell et al., 1991). The support provider met the woman from the time of admission and stayed with her during delivery. The person was specifically trained to provide emotional support (for example, encouragement) and informational support (for example, what was to be expected). Continuously provided support to the mother during birth was associated with significantly better outcomes such as reduced rates of cesarean section and epidural anesthesia compared to outcomes in women not provided with such support. However, the results of a subsequent clinical trial did not reveal beneficial effects of a support intervention on pregnancy outcomes (Villar et al., 1992). It is noteworthy that a more recent support intervention in this area suggests that the effects of support interventions on birth outcomes were stronger for individuals lacking natural support resources (Norbeck, Dejoseph, and Smith, 1996). This finding is consistent with the notion that introducing a new supportive relationship as an intervention strategy may be primarily effective for those who have existing deficits in their support networks (Gottlieb, 2000).

Other studies have compared the effectiveness of professional sources of support for patients with various chronic health conditions. These studies are often conducted under the stress-buffering framework. Patients diagnosed with a chronic condition may need help coping with the accompanying feelings of uncertainty and loss of control. In addition, adjustment to chronic diseases often requires lifestyle changes and, in some conditions, help with activities of daily living. In one such intervention, researchers kept track of more than four hundred male patients who had a heart attack. When the cardiac patient became too stressed or if they were rehospitalized, researchers arranged visits from trained nurses, who provided informational support to the patient (Frasure-Smith and Prince, 1985). Results of this one-year intervention revealed lowered stress in the intervention group as well as fewer deaths during the study. A subsequent intervention from these researchers, however, that included a larger sample of both men and women failed to replicate these findings (Frasure-Smith et al., 1997). The reasons behind these discrepancies were not clear, although the researchers suggested that decreases in cardiac mortality due to medical advances and the potential of the intervention to increase stress in some patients (for example, reminding them of their cardiac condition) may have been contributing factors.

One of the interesting applications of interventions that utilize professional forms of support is to vary the mode of support. Several studies have examined the use of telephone calls as a cost-effective medium to provide support (Green et al., 2002; Lando et al., 1996). These interventions are appealing because they can be less intimidating than face-to-face contact and can also reach individuals who may not be able to travel as easily due to physical or financial limitations. In one study, telephone support was provided by professionals to encourage quitting smoking (Lando et al., 1996). This support was provided three, nine, and twenty-one months after a smoking cessation program; individuals were also given the option to request up to nine more calls. During these calls, professionals provided emotional support to increase the participants' sense of efficacy and circumvent potential discouragement. Results over a two-year follow-up showed that the intervention did not influence relapse, but there was a trend for individuals in the intervention to be more likely to resume abstinence after a relapse.

One of the most common support interventions from professionals is some form of educational intervention by physicians, dieticians, and physical therapists (Helgeson and Cohen, 1996). Such educational interventions serve as a form of informational support and provide the patient with information regarding the disease, its symptoms, and subsequent treatment. A recent review of such interventions suggests that educational interventions were effective in increasing patient knowledge and fostering adjustment to cancer. In fact, such interventions appear at least as effective as peer support groups (Helgeson and Cohen). The beneficial effects of such educational interventions with professional sources of support have also been demonstrated with specific health behaviors, including exercise patterns in at-risk populations (Writing Group for the Activity Counseling Trial Research Group, 2001).

Although in some cases the overall evidence for the efficacy of professional sources of support is mixed, there appears to be more consistent evidence for the positive effects of such interventions in reducing distress and improving some outcomes in cardiac patients (Hogan, Linden, and Najarian, 2002). Informational support from professionals also appears effective in enhancing adjustment in cancer patients (Helgeson et al., 2000). However, in general the patient populations and outcomes examined have been diverse and have included depressed adolescents, pregnant women, patients infected with human immunodeficiency virus (HIV), and mentally ill patients. Many studies have also not examined whether social support levels were modified by the intervention (Hogan et al.). Thus, more systematic studies would be needed in these different areas to build up a corpus of intervention studies that can inform some inconsistencies in past research.

The use of professional sources of support involves the introduction of a new relationship. The introduction of new network ties may be optimal only under certain conditions (Gottlieb, 2000). One of these is when specialized knowledge or expert opinion is required, as is often the case with patients dealing with chronic conditions. In fact, this is what is unique about professional sources of support. A salient strength of such sources of support, therefore, is expertise and credibility in the health domain, which should translate into a trusted source of informational support. This informational support may be useful to provide direction, increase cooperation with medical regimens, and help individuals gain a sense of control over the disease. This conclusion is consistent with the generally positive effects of educational interventions with professionals (Helgeson and Cohen, 1996).

Although most studies have examined informational support from professionals, I would also like to emphasize the potential importance of emotional support in this context. The importance of emotional support is highlighted by the research reviewed in chapter 4 suggesting reliable links to lower mortality rates. In fact, some of these intervention studies using professional forms of support do attempt to provide forms of emotional support. Emotional support may be important because it can influence the quality of the relationship between the patient and practitioner, which in turn is an important predictor of better treatment cooperation (Sherbourne et al., 1992).

Another important aspect of emotional support in such interventions may lie in its interaction with other support dimensions. Basic research on social support processes suggests that emotional support can facilitate the provision of other forms of support. Some researchers have argued that in order for support to work, stressed individuals must first feel that their views are recognized and that they are valued and accepted as a person (Burleson and Goldsmith, 1998). Emotional support therefore may pave the way for informational support to be especially beneficial in this professional context.

Most of these studies have also looked at the importance of professionals providing functional forms of support. However, the research linking social integration measures to mortality also highlight the need for interventions that promote active participation in groups. One straightforward way in which these data can be implemented into these intervention studies is for medical professionals to provide information on different organizations that might benefit individuals in coping with their particular situation (for example, support groups or agencies that provide information, such as the American Cancer Society). In theory, participation in groups and organizations should increase feelings of esteem, self-worth, and control that should be associated with beneficial effects on adjustment and health. It may also be important here to teach individuals the social skills necessary to make these group experiences positive if they are currently not involved in such social activities or organizations.

It may be the case, however, that some individuals may not be comfortable receiving professional support in more public settings. This may especially be the case for individuals who are more socially isolated. Earlier, the use of the telephone as a mode of support was discussed. This has the benefits of being less intimidating and of being able to reach individuals who may have various travel limitations (for example, physical). Another mode of support to consider in this context may be the use of the Internet, such as chat rooms that are run by professionals. The use of the Internet for discussion of medical problems is a fast-growing alternative (Davison, Pennebaker, and Dickerson, 2000). Part of the appeal here is that questions can be raised in a less intimidating setting. Of course, there are numerous issues that emerge as a result of this technology (for example, advice that may not be based on accurate or complete knowledge of a person's condition or unequal access to this resource). Nevertheless, it remains a possible alternative to reach individuals who may not be comfortable or able to receive professional support in more public settings.

There are several limitations of professional sources of support that should be mentioned. One limitation is that they are usually not as accessible as a person's natural support networks. This may place constraints on the discussion of issues that come up on an everyday basis or on timely support to resolve problems as they arise. In addition, practically speaking, professional forms of support are probably limited to informational and emotional support. Thus, they do not in most cases become a more general source of support as in the case of natural network members (for example, belonging and tangible support).

Support from Peers

Another approach to support interventions has been to use peer groups as a source of support. These interventions in some cases utilize a similar other as a source of one-on-one support to facilitate adjustment. More commonly, these interventions take the form of support groups such as Alcoholics Anonymous or the support group interventions with cancer patients described in earlier chapters. A key aspect of these interventions is to match similar others. However, these interventions differ in terms of the dimensions of similarity that are often implicitly used to guide the matching process.

In one intervention, researchers sought to alleviate the loneliness that can exist among some older adults. They examined older adult women who reported some degree of isolation and provided them with telephone calls from a staff member and calls subsequently from other peers in the study in order to facilitate the formation of supportive ties (Heller et al., 1991). Compared to an assessment-only group, individuals provided with these sources of support did not show changes in well-being. Exploratory analyses, however, showed that individuals who continued their friendships with their peer had more friends to begin with and were less physically impaired.

Although this intervention with older adult women was unsuccessful in altering social support and well-being, the last set of findings regarding the formation of friendship dyads was informative. It suggests that some individuals may have benefited and longer term effects of the friendships may indeed be evident. As the case with most negative findings, however, it is difficult to pinpoint exactly why the intervention did not have the intended effect. It is important to note that this peer intervention was built on the assumption that similar-other peers (older women) would be adequate supportive network ties. However, the relevant dimensions of similarity that are important can be complex. Just think about your own friendships. You probably have friends that are similar to you in basic demographic factors such as age, gender, and ethnicity. However, you probably also have friends who are dissimilar to you on these dimensions but similar to you in terms of hobbies and interests.

Recent research suggests that experiential similarity may be an important factor in seeking social support and helping individuals adjust to different life events (Thoits, 1986; Suitor, Pillemer, and Keeton, 1995). Such experiential similarity has more to do with having common experiences that can help in the friendship formation process and the communication of emphatic emotional support. For instance,

caregivers of patients with Alzheimer's disease are under high levels of
stress due to the many physical and emotional demands of caregiving
(Kiecolt-Glaser et al., 1991; Schulz and Beach, 1999). These caregivers
may believe that individuals in their social network do not understand
the many problems associated with caregiving and that it would be en-
lightening for other family and friends to "walk a mile in their shoes"
(Suitor et al.). However, individuals who share experiential similarity
on this dimension do understand the stress of caregiving and may be a
useful source of emotional and informational support under some circumstances (Bourgeois, Schulz, and Burgio, 1996).

Consistent with the experiential similarity hypothesis, research
suggests that postsurgery recovery in cardiac patients was facilitated by
the presence of a roommate also about to go through cardiac surgery
(Kulik, Mahler, and Moore, 1996). One recent intervention directly
tested this experiential similarity hypothesis by examining patients
about to undergo coronary bypass surgery (Thoits et al., 2000). In this
study, patients were assigned to receive visits from a similar other (vol-
unteer patient who had already had coronary bypass). Unexpectedly,
the results of this study found that the intervention was not associated
with better adjustment compared to a group of patients not provided
with experiential similar-other support. Subsequent analyses did reveal, however, that patients in both the intervention and control
groups spontaneously talked with fellow patients in their ward, and
this predicted better postsurgery adjustment.

Why exactly these natural contacts with fellow patients had more
positive effects than the contact with intervention volunteers is not
known. It may have been that the intervention contacts were not
viewed as positively, but analyses indicated that many participants saw
the intervention person as friendly and helpful (Thoits et al., 2000).
One other possibility is related to the complex process of seeking support. It may be that individuals prefer to seek out their own source of
support when they are ready. At other times it may mostly serve to remind them of the stressful event they are about to experience.

In some circumstances if the need is high enough, similar others
may be less important as a dimension of support. Simply having a
skilled other to listen and lend a helping hand may make a big difference. A friend of mine who works for a large company told me that

some clients will call not about their accounts, but simply to talk to someone. These calls tend to increase in frequency around the holidays, especially during Thanksgiving and Christmas.

One group of individuals with a high need is depressed individuals who usually have low levels of social support (Harris, Brown, and Robinson, 1999). In one intervention researchers examined the application of what they called "befriending" to chronically depressed individuals (Harris et al.). Researchers recruited volunteers to meet and talk with the participants for at least one hour per week. They were trained and encouraged to listen and be there for the participant as well as participate in outside activities and give practical advice. Consistent with the importance of such social support, results of this randomized control trial revealed that remission rates for depression were 39 percent in the control group but 65 percent in the befriended group. The researchers also specifically noted that an important aspect of this intervention was the fact that participants knew these were volunteers who cared enough to provide support, be flexible in their scheduling, and foster an equitable relationship. It is also important to note that this intervention provided many different dimensions of support, including emotional, informational, and belonging support.

A final peer intervention is related to the often-mentioned support group. These support groups are now an established part of how many patients attempt to maintain behavioral change or cope with diverse medical conditions (Davison, Pennebaker, and Dickerson, 2000). It has been estimated that 3 to 4 percent of the population over any one-year period is involved in some form of support or self-help group in the United States (Kessler, Mickelson, and Zhao, 1997). Although many support groups are facilitated by professionals (for example, making sure everyone shares their experiences), the primary emphasis is on what the peer group experience can bring to each individual. In one survey of four major metropolitan areas, researchers found that support groups were available for cardiac patients, HIV patients, alcoholic patients, depressed individuals, and cancer patients (Davison et al.). However, support groups were much more common for conditions or diseases that were stigmatizing, embarrassing, or disfiguring. For instance, HIV patients were found to be 250 times more likely to participate in support groups than were hypertension patients. As noted by the authors, this may reflect the possibility that existing network members may not be providing adequate support.

These peer support groups may be effective because those with experiential similarity are often sought as sources of support. In theory, these individuals should be effective sources of support because they understand the issues that the person is going through. Thus, one strength of support groups is that they bring together individuals who share a common problem such as adjustment to breast cancer or living with HIV. Such support groups with peers can serve multiple functions such as reassurances of the person's worth (emotional support), sharing of useful information (informational support), and a place to go and be themselves (belonging support).

Interventions examining peer sources of support in such groups suggest beneficial effects on adjustment and well-being (Hogan, Linden, and Najarian, 2002). In addition, many of these studies documented that the intervention was successful in altering participants' levels of support. These positive findings have been observed with older adults (Andersson, 1985), HIV patients (Kelly et al., 1993), and breast cancer patients (Goodwin et al., 2001). Many of these studies examined cancer patients and generally found that support groups had beneficial effects (Hogan et al.). In one recent intervention, patients with metastatic breast cancer were randomly assigned to a control condition or an intervention group that fostered support among group members and encouraged open emotional expression (Goodwin et al.). Consistent with other studies, there were beneficial effects of the intervention on their quality of life. Although this study found no differences in survival between the support group and control condition (see chapter 5), we should not neglect the influence of support groups on psychological well-being.

All in all, the studies examining peers as sources of support are again promising. One of the important guiding premises of these interventions is that of matching similar others. However, the dimension of similarity that may be important can be complicated and likely contributes to some of the mixed findings. Nevertheless the strength of this approach includes the formation of networks with increased understanding due to their similarity, an effect that may be particularly important for individuals who have existing conflicts in their social networks or lack supportive ties (Gottlieb, 2000).

There are several important issues to discuss about peer support interventions based on the larger social support literature. An important consideration for facilitating peer sources of support is the degree of contact and the comprehensiveness of the intervention. More circumscribed contact with the support provider is less likely to foster the type of friendship that can serve as a useful source of support across a variety of domains. For instance, the intervention using telephone sources of peer support may have been too circumscribed as an intervention strategy. Interventions that focus on telephone contact and participation in outside activities for informal contact may be more effective because they mimic the natural relationship formation process (Harris, Brown, and Robinson, 1999). Such an emphasis on the friendship formation process can in turn aid in the provision of emotional support because the quality of the relationship can influence the effectiveness of such behaviors (Uno, Uchino, and Smith, 2002). Of course, evaluations of the quality of the support should be built into such interventions to guard against the possibility of negative effects.

Another important factor to consider is that the beginnings of friendship are characterized by some degree of equity (Clark and Mills, 1993). However, the emphasis on the provision of support in one-on-one peer interventions may impede the friendship formation process by fueling feelings of inequity. In order to make these interactions more equitable, interventions may need to foster give and take, not simply emphasizing the provision of support. In fact, the research on received support and mortality suggest some negative effects of only receiving tangible support. Researchers have argued that one mechanism here may be related to the hit our self-esteem takes as autonomous individuals to have to rely on others for support (Bolger, Zuckerman, and Kessler, 2000). The emphasis on greater equity, especially in the friendship formation process, may provide a means by which the potential negative effects of received tangible support are negated. For instance, a person receiving tangible support may not be as threatened if they know that they are also contributing to the other person's well-being by providing emotional or informational support.

For support groups, an emphasis on the friendship formation process may be equally important. Researchers have found that participation in support groups seem to influence the size and composition of one's social network. For instance, studies of individuals with substance abuse problems suggest that self-help groups result in decreased contact with drug-using network members and increased contact with support group friends (Humphreys and Noke, 1997). These network members then become crucial sources of support in offering advice and guidance to help individuals remain abstinent (Humphreys et al., 1999).

One potential concern with support groups is that not all individuals may benefit from such interventions. For instance, individuals who are uncomfortable sharing their concerns or who are less distressed to begin with may not benefit as much. Researchers have argued that we need to take these individual preferences into account in designing such support interventions (Helgeson and Cohen, 1996). In one study researchers examined the effectiveness of peer support groups for breast cancer patients (Helgeson et al., 2000). They found that support groups helped adjustment for individuals who lacked support from their partner. However, for individuals who already had support from their partner, support groups were actually associated with more functional declines over time. The authors suggest that for individuals who started with supportive ties, the peer discussion may have been associated with a reevaluation of the "supportiveness" of their network as others provided feedback on different behaviors. It was also possible that the support groups encouraged these participants to discuss their problems more at home, which led to increases in negative interactions. Future research will determine the potential reasons for these findings. Nevertheless, these findings highlight the fact that individuals bring different personalities, coping styles, and social assets to these groups, which may need to be taken into account when designing such interventions (Goodwin et al., 2001; also see chapter 6).

Support from Existing Network Members

One of most accessible and seemingly straightforward support interventions involves the mobilization of existing network members as a source of support (Cutrona and Cole, 2000). These interventions can include the spouse, other immediate family members, and friends. In some cases the reason that someone may lack support despite an established social network is clear. For instance, individuals may be hesitant to seek support regarding a stigmatizing disease because they may be afraid of the network members' reaction to such information. In other cases it is not so obvious. At its most basic level, the interventions seeking to mobilize existing network members attempt to ask the question of why the individual lacks support in the first place. These interventions take several different approaches but usually center on the following strategies: (1) teaching participants the skills to acquire support from their network, (2) teaching social network members how to be supportive, or (3) simply bringing a significant network member to treatment to help in the adjustment process.

One approach is teaching individuals the skills to elicit support from their network. Overall, this appears to be a promising strategy, and successful interventions have been conducted with adolescents, psychiatric patients, and individuals with chronic diseases (Cutrona and Cole, 2000; Hogan, Linden, and Najarian, 2002). In one intervention, adolescents were assigned to enroll in a semester-long course that focused on friendship development and positive peer and teacher relationships (Eggert et al., 1994). Students also learned how to elicit support regarding personal problems. The results of the intervention were impressive. Compared to adolescents not provided with the intervention, individuals with social skills training showed a trend toward less drug use, a decrease in drug-related problems, and an increase in their grade point average. Results of this intervention also found that individuals in the intervention had an increase in their friendships and in self-esteem.

In some cases, interventions with existing network members need to reach out and directly mobilize the person's network. The challenge here is providing the network members with the understanding and skills to be supportive. This may be especially important when the network members lack experience with the particular condition or have maladaptive beliefs about the course of adjustment (for example, believing that a person just needs to stop dwelling on his or her problems).

In many cases, network members have the proper knowledge to

be effective support providers. However, in some circumstances anxiety over interacting with a vulnerable person and the fear of upsetting them further may interfere with the retrieval of support skills. We can all recall times when we were a bit anxious and said something "silly" as a result. In a study of bereaved participants it was found that many individuals had proper beliefs about what was supportive to these individuals (Lehman, Ellard, and Wortman, 1986). Nevertheless, there were many occasions when bereaved individuals reported unhelpful support attempts from their network. Due to the anxiety about interacting with a distressed person, network members may be a source of indifference or at worst an additional cause of stress in that person's life. If anxiety is indeed the important mechanism at work here, then it may be worthwhile to teach network members anxiety-reduction techniques (for example, progressive muscle relaxation) so that they may be more effective support providers (Gottlieb, 1988).

The "training" of network members to provide support in many cases focuses on family members, and more specifically the spouse. This makes sense because the spouse is usually an important source of support for married individuals. Early interventions with hypertensive patients utilized this approach by helping the spouse increase their understanding of hypertension and reinforce the management of the patient's condition (Levine et al., 1979). Results of these studies suggest that such support training had beneficial influences on the patient's subsequent management of their hypertension.

One implicit model underlying some of these spousal interventions is the social control hypothesis. In such cases, the spouse is the one immediately available to provide the person with feedback regarding attempts to cope or behaviorally manage his or her condition. These interventions, however, may need to recognize the complexity of such strategies in that attempts at social control may be resented or viewed as a source of stress (Lewis and Rook, 1999). Nevertheless, some of these interventions have proven successful depending on the outcome of interest. For instance, interventions focusing on support during weight loss appear more effective than attempts at quitting smoking (Cutrona and Cole, 2000).

Other studies suggest that the inclusion of friends in interventions may be particularly important as an additional source of support.

In one study researchers contrasted a support intervention with standard behavioral treatment (SBT) to help individuals achieve weight loss (Wing and Jeffery, 1999). Participants either came alone or were asked to bring three friends who were interested in weight loss. Participants who arrived alone were either given SBT or provided with a group support intervention (with three other participants) that included structured exercises to increase support. For instance, individuals were asked to call the others to provide support, engage in problem-solving activities regarding weight loss, and dine and exercise outside with the other people in the study. Individuals who arrived with three friends were either given SBT or participated in the support intervention with their friends. Weight loss and completion rates for the program were then monitored after four and ten months.

Results of this study suggest the utility of getting friends directly involved in support interventions. Individuals who participated in the support intervention with friends were more likely to complete the program and maintain their weight loss over the ten-month period. Results further suggested the importance of support more generally because perceived support from others in the group (regardless of whether they were with existing friends) also predicted greater weight loss. One interesting aspect of this study was the finding that individuals who recruited three friends for the study were less likely to have participated in prior organized weight loss programs. These data suggest an additional benefit of recruitment with friends because it may increase participation for individuals who may not wish to go alone.

Overall, interventions with the goal of involving existing network members appear to be a complex but viable support intervention (Cutrona and Cole, 2000). This approach has numerous strengths. First, existing network members already have a substantial social and emotional connection with the participants, which can provide the basis for effective social support. Second, the stability of these relationships can serve as the basis for long-term social support. These interventions, however, will have to be careful in providing individuals with the right skills to mobilize or provide effective support to avoid significant stress that can result from unhelpful support exchanges.

One of the key aspects for interventions that utilize existing networks is to recognize the fact that interventions are dealing at a minimum with a dyad. This point makes several issues salient. One is that being a support provider can be stressful in some circumstances (Coyne, Wortman, and Lehman, 1988). Imagine the stress you might experience if a friend disclosed a very personal problem to you, such as HIV infection or childhood abuse. In addition, providing effective support takes time and work. This can overburden even the most well-intentioned individuals if they are not careful. Interventions that focus on existing network ties may need to carefully train the person to not overburden support providers. Likewise, interventions that make the support providers aware of their stress levels and how to cope may be helpful to avoid potential burnout (Gottlieb, 1988).

The fact that existing network members have a rich history with the person needing support also needs to be addressed. In some cases, the history may be overwhelmingly positive and thus presents little problem in that person being a support provider. In other cases, network members may be a source of ambivalence and contain a mix of both positive and negative experiences and feelings. This is important because the provision of support resources such as emotional support may be viewed differently depending on the quality of the existing relationship. An emotionally supportive message such as "I'm sure you are strong enough to pull through this" may be viewed as a flippant remark if coming from a conflicted relationship.

In one study it was found that a sizable majority of older adults were able to recount particular acts of betrayal by members of their immediate family or support network (Hansson, Jones, and Fletcher, 1990). As noted by these researchers, many of these incidents occurred more than twenty to thirty years earlier but still maintained its significance in later life. Consistent with these findings, we have found across both young and older samples that network ties that are sources of ambivalence make up almost half of important network members (Uchino et al., 2001). The important implication here is under some circumstances, extended dyadic counseling may be needed to help individuals resolve the ambivalence in their relationships so the person can serve as a more effective support provider (Finch et al., 1989).

Another important consideration for such support interventions is whether to recruit broadly from the person's social network or focus on particular relationships (for example, family members). It has been found that the networks of older adults serve distinct functions (Rook and Shuster, 1996). Spouses and close family members are usually sources of emotional support, whereas other family members are more likely to be sources of personal care and tangible support. Friends, on the other hand, appear to be more a source of companionship and belonging support. If one was to rely on support norms as a guiding principle (Gottlieb, 2000), then depending on the issue facing older adults mobilizing support sources in their normative role might work best. Another possibility is to identify individuals in the network that are general sources of support, such as a confidant. The flexibility in these network members can be a real strength in the development of interventions. Of course, this would first necessitate a detailed analysis of each individual's social network.

Given the potential benefits of engagement in voluntary groups and social activities, it may also be possible for friends and family to gently encourage such practices. As argued by social control theorists, close network ties can play a role in helping individuals engage in behavioral change. Participation in such social activities can theoretically help affirm aspects of the self, provide increased life meaning, or provide access to other important sources of support (for example, organized support groups). However, as noted by such theorists, direct social control can be a source of stress, so more gentle strategies may be best (for example, simply making suggestions). This may be particularly important because recent perspectives in social identity suggest the benefits of social roles and ties that are voluntary (Berbrier and Schulte, 2000). Strong attempts at social control may undermine the support recipient's perception of how voluntary such participation is. Depending on the group or social activity, it may also be possible for support providers to mutually engage in such activities. This may be beneficial for support recipients who have less experience or feel less comfortable with strangers in social or group activities (Wing and Jeffery, 1999).

General Discussion of Support Intervention Approaches

In summary, the major approaches to support interventions include fostering professional, peer, and existing network sources of support

(Gottlieb, 1988; Hogan, Linden, and Najarian, 2002). The overall results of these interventions are promising in terms of altering behaviors, fostering adjustment, and sometime better survival (Hogan et
al.). However, these interventions are not without problems, and many
interesting questions are raised by this research. In this section I highlight the major issues that cut across these different types of interventions.

One of the most basic questions to ask before attempting a support intervention is related to its appropriateness to the situation and
population of interest. However, surprisingly few of these interventions appear to involve a thorough consideration of these basic issues
(Gottlieb, 2000). In my opinion, social support interventions can be
comprehensively described by a variant of the question historically
asked in the persuasion literature: "Who says what to whom with what
effect" (Smith, Lasswell, and Casey, 1946). In our case, the question becomes "Who *provides* what to whom with what effect." The "who" aspect of this statement describes the nature of the relationship between
the provider and recipient of support. It can range from relatively new
relationships such as between patients and practitioners to already established support members such as family and friends. The second aspect of this statement concerns "what" is being provided. It may be the
provision of emotional support or the acquisition of new social skills to
obtain needed support. The "whom" aspect refers to the target population of the intervention and can be healthy individuals or specific patient groups (for example, cancer or cardiovascular patients). Finally,
"with what effect" has to do with the pathways and outcomes that the
intervention is attempting to modify. The researcher will often need to
show an effect on some specified outcome (for example, smoking or
adherence) and that a person's social support was indeed altered by the
intervention.

This basic question of "Who provides what to whom with what
effect" makes salient the aspects that a well-designed intervention
should address. At the "who" stage it may be important to address issues of who is available in the person's network and what functions
they normally serve. If the person's network is impoverished due to
losses (for example, bereavement), or if they are socially isolated, support from a new relationship may be required (Gottlieb, 2000). In ad-

dition, "provides what to whom" will be highly contextual (for example, caregivers or cardiac patients), so these factors will need careful consideration in such intervention studies. One contextual consideration is the time frame for the interventions based on participant need. It may seem obvious, but longer-term interventions seem to be associated with better outcomes (Cutrona and Cole, 2000). However, in some cases long-term interventions may not be practical, and the use of "booster" sessions may be important. Booster sessions essentially bring participants back periodically to reinforce intervention skills and information.

Another important issue for these intervention studies revolves around the "with what effect" aspect of the question. Most intervention researchers have a set of defined outcomes they would like to impact, such as well-being, behavioral change, or mortality. However, there are two other aspects of this question that are worth repeating. First, it was surprising that many of these interventions failed to measure whether support levels were increased as a function of the intervention (Hogan, Linden, and Najarian, 2002). This can represent real problems in interpreting the results of an intervention. In some cases, however, it may be difficult to show changes in general perceptions of support availability because it tends to be quite stable and may have its origins in early childhood interactions. However, interventions can still address whether participants viewed that different support functions were exchanged, such as emotional support or informational support. This provides a support manipulation check that is firmly grounded in the intervention.

An emphasis on "with what effect" also makes salient the importance of examining the mechanisms by which the support intervention may be working. It is perfectly understandable why an intervention might be heavily focused on a primary outcome such as disease progression. However, intervention outcomes are a result of a process, and the need to understand this process is crucial to the reciprocal enterprise of theory building and practical application. The theoretical models covered in chapters 3 and 6 provide a starting point for examining relevant mechanisms. For instance, the stress-buffering model highlights the importance of self-esteem, feelings of control, and most of all appraisals of stress. These potential mechanisms need immediate attention in the social support research more generally, and experimental interventions may provide a sensitive test of these pathways.

One important question for support interventions is the cost-effectiveness of such an approach. In an ideal world social support interventions would be both helpful and cost-effective. Fortunately, several studies suggest that social support interventions are a cost-effective way to improve outcomes. In one study, researchers examined the effects of a one-year educational and support group intervention in patients with osteoarthritis. Combined across both types of interventions, the average cost savings during the subsequent two years was $1,279 per participant per year compared to a control condition. This difference was primarily due to a lower number of days spent in hospitalization for the intervention groups. In fact, it has been estimated that if support group participation was at the typical 3 percent among the 32 million arthritis sufferers, the four-year cost savings would be around $650 million (Davison, Pennebaker, and Dickerson, 2000). With increasing emphasis on medical cost containment, support interventions may be an increasingly viable option.

It is also important to note that much of the support interventions have focused on the individual or their family and friends. A relatively neglected area of inquiry is community-level interventions that increase social support (Gottlieb, 2000; Caplan, 1974). The importance of such community-level interventions is highlighted by research on social capital (Kawachi and Berkman, 2000). Such theorists suggest that community trust and collective action may be important pathways linking social relationships to health outcomes. Interventions that encourage group participation and facilitate greater community trust can serve as important pathways for increased social capital. Issues relating to the operationalization and definition of social capital, however, will need to be addressed in order to most effectively apply this research as an intervention strategy (Macinko and Starfield, 2001).

One excellent example of a community-level intervention is the North Karelia Project in Finland (Puska and Uutela, 1999). At the start of this project in the 1970s, residents had one of the highest rates of cardiovascular disease in the world. Drawing on various theories of health behavior change, the intervention targeted individuals with slightly elevated risk because these individuals represented a large segment of the population. The intervention gained the cooperation of the media (for example, television), community organizations, industry (for example, supermarkets), and worksites in a far-reaching attempt to change prevailing norms and behavior. Consistent with health behavior change models, this project also sought to increase social support for such behavioral change. Results of this impressive coordination revealed reductions in a variety of cardiovascular risk factors, including smoking, blood pressure, and cholesterol (Puska and Uutela). Importantly, reductions in cardiovascular mortality were obtained as well as a reduction of cancer rates. This project, although wide in scope, was successful and cost-effective. The promise of such community-level interventions is untapped in social support theory and research.

The North Karelia Project highlights a broader approach or class of interventions that do not simply include social support but a host of other psychosocial techniques that can help individuals live healthier lives. By and large these general psychosocial interventions appear quite effective in fostering adjustment in cardiac and cancer patients (Linden, Stossel, and Maurice, 1996; Rozanski, Blumenthal, and Kaplan, 1999). For example, one intervention by researchers evaluated the effects of a six-week structured group intervention that provided education, problem-solving skills, stress management, and social support to cancer patients (Fawzy et al., 1993). Importantly, a six-year follow-up revealed lower mortality rates in the structured group intervention compared to the no intervention condition.

One important question here relates to whether a specific social support or more broad psychosocial intervention approach is best. On the one hand, a broad approach maximizes potential benefits as participants are provided or taught a variety of skills and coping techniques. On the other hand, more specific approaches are better for theory testing but can undermine overall treatment because effects for any given psychosocial process may be smaller. The most controlled approach would obviously be to manipulate each aspect of such general interventions to determine its individual and combined effects. It may be that some of these components are not necessary, and this information can lead to fewer time-intensive and more cost-effective interventions. I will not endorse one approach over the other because each has its strengths and weaknesses. Both approaches are necessary, but a crucial

aspect of the more specific or general approach will be a good understanding and assessment of mechanisms. Thus, even for general interventions, researchers should try to get a good sense of the different
components that are influenced by the intervention via appropriate
measurement procedures.

Most of the social support interventions focus on individuals
who are most at risk or who already have psychological, behavioral, or
medical problems. An alternative way of thinking about support interventions is as a form of primary prevention that focuses on healthy individuals. Primary prevention refers to attempts to reduce the probability of a health problem developing (Kaplan, 2000). Good examples
include interventions to increase exercise or prevent smoking in
healthy individuals. In his compelling analysis, Robert Kaplan argued
for the promise of primary prevention efforts, especially in light of the
more limited public health benefits that seem to arise from secondary
prevention efforts that simply focus on the identification and treatment of disease.

Given that many chronic diseases have a long-term etiology and
develop over decades (for example, coronary artery disease), primary
prevention efforts in social support interventions may be particularly
important to consider. For instance, social support interventions may
be usefully applied early in children and adolescents to provide them
with general social support skills or encourage participation in a diversity of voluntary social groups or roles. According to existing social
support models covered in chapter 6, the cumulative effects of such an
intervention, if successful, should produce improvements in both life
quality and longevity over the lifespan.

A final general issue here is a comment echoed by many support
researchers: Do no harm (Cutrona and Cole, 2000; Gottlieb, 2000)!
Research reviewed in chapter 2 suggests that negative aspects of relationships are important predictors of decreased well-being. We need to
remember that although relationships have the tremendous potential
to heal, they can also be a significant source of interpersonal conflict,
which can add to a person's distress during a time of need. If we are not
careful, individuals in support interventions may get ineffective information, feel frustrated with their relationships, or feel let down by the
support provider. In addition, we need to be careful of the effects that

support interventions may have on a person's sense of control (Rowe and Kahn, 1987). Much of these issues can be addressed by carefully considering each aspect of the "who provides what to whom with what effect" question to the intervention. This question makes salient the importance of getting a comprehensive assessment of existing network functions, paying particular attention to the social skills and needs of the support seeker and provider, and being clear about the main pathways and outcomes of interest. Such research can play a crucial role in the testing and further refinement of theoretical models linking social support to health outcomes.

8

Future Directions
and Conclusions

The research reviewed in this book provides strong evidence that social support predicts lower mortality rates. In chapter 4, evidence was reviewed that structural aspects of relationships, such as participation in group activities, and functional aspects of relationships, such as the availability of emotional support, show reliable associations with lower mortality. An examination of specific diseases in chapter 5 suggested that social support is associated with lower mortality from cardiovascular disease, the major cause of death in the United States and most industrialized societies. Preliminary evidence was also found for a role of social support in other leading causes of death, including cancer and acquired immunodeficiency syndrome. In chapter 6, evidence for the pathways responsible for these effects was discussed. This resulted in "retuned" stress-related and direct effect models as well as a broader perspective on how social support may influence physical health. Finally, in chapter 7 the implications of these findings for social support interventions were discussed. Although evidence for the effectiveness of some types of interventions was evident, a consideration of the question "who provides what to whom with what effect" may be important in order to reconcile some findings and design more appropriate support interventions.

Given the myriad factors that ultimately influence mortality, the data linking social support to physical health are in many ways quite striking. These findings are consistent with a growing body of research on the importance of psychosocial factors such as personality, stress, and depression on morbidity and mortality (Linden, Stossel, and Maurice, 1996; Rozanski, Blumenthal, and Kaplan, 1999; Smith and Gallo, 2001). These associations are now generating greater attention in light of the zeitgeist for a more integrated approach to public health (Schneiderman et al., 1999). After all, the body does not exist in isolation. Disease processes unfold in environmental circumstances and interact in complex ways with a person's reactions to their sociocultural milieu. These observations make salient the crucial goal of more completely integrating biological and behavioral approaches to modern medicine.

In this concluding chapter, I would like to highlight what I perceive to be the main issues, questions, and directions for future inquiry into social support and physical health over the next fifteen to twenty years. These recommendations also have implications for the general goal of linking other psychosocial factors to physical health end points. They are not ordered in terms of priority. In general they represent what I view to be the critical directions or lapses in our knowledge of this important phenomenon.

The Need for Integrative Interdisciplinary Research

As highlighted throughout this book, social support is amazingly complex. It involves consideration of social structures, group or individual communication patterns, the perception of these processes, and personality and behavioral factors. Disease processes such as cardiovascular disorders and cancer are similarly complex at the biological level of analysis. As a result, interdisciplinary research teams, preferably with some degree of overlapping expertise, will be important to tackle future state-of-the-art questions concerning the links between social support and health.

I would like to highlight the potential importance of research teams with overlapping expertise. This would mean that social scientists would have some understanding and appreciation of the medical and biological perspective on disease and medical professionals would likewise understand and appreciate aspects of psychosocial risk factors. This facilitates a mutual understanding and respect for the complexity of the phenomena. It also provides the backbone for a sustained and generative program of research on these issues. Of course, this highlights gaps in our training programs that need to be systematically addressed for the next generation of researchers interested in making connections between psychosocial processes and health.

It may not be enough to promise a greater understanding of the phenomena that will emerge as a result of such interdisciplinary teams. Institutions and funding agencies will need to provide incentives for such approaches as well as foster dialogue on the structure and training to support such research teams. A good example here is the recent "mind-body" center grants funded by the National Institutes of Health to support integrative interdisciplinary teams with a programmatic focus. These issues regarding training programs and incentive structures are not easy to address but they may play a crucial role in future progress at the interface of social processes and health.

The Need to Understand More Fully What Is Social Support

At the beginning of chapter 2 we asked the question, What is social support? There is presently no universally agreed upon definition of support. In some cases it refers to aspects of the social network (groups, familial ties), at other times to specific behaviors (for example, emotional or informational support), and sometimes to our perceived availability of support resources that may be shaped via early childhood experiences. In fact, many attempts have been made to clarify these questions, knowing well that the lack of conceptual clarity may be one of the most serious roadblocks to progress in social support research (Vaux, 1988).

I have tried to take a more integrative approach and not rule out any potentially useful conceptualizations of support. As shown in this book, there is evidence for the utility of considering both structural and functional measures of support, and I have highlighted the links among these different assessments. For instance, structural measures of support provide the opportunity for supportive exchanges. These supportive exchanges may reinforce social support skills and lead to the development of a more diverse social network. Future research will be needed to test the plausibility of these bidirectional links, although existing research is consistent with the organizational framework presented in figure 2.1.

Research examining social support in the context of close relationships can contribute much to our understanding of what is social support (Badr et al., 2001; Gottlieb, 1985). Historically, the integration of social support and close relationships research has been complicated by their different areas of emphasis (Gottlieb). Close relationship researchers have often focused on social support as one of many important outcomes associated with our close ties. Social support researchers, on the other hand, have been more interested in the mental and physical health outcomes predicted by social ties. A simultaneous consideration of social support in the context of close relationships, however, can help us better understand the meaning of support by highlighting how and why support transactions unfold (or do not unfold) in a particular social context.

The issue of what is social support will also likely require complex analyses of childhood experiences and personality processes that influence how individuals negotiate their social world. Such an analysis of the antecedent processes influencing social support will be critical if we are to understand the development and maintenance of strong support networks that then facilitate a sense of identity and adjustment to life events.

It may not be the case that all aspects of social support will prove to be health relevant. However, in the absence of a clear understanding of how social support develops and is maintained, we will not know whether the aspects of support that predict health outcomes are simply more proximal factors in the chain of events. That is, other aspects of social support may be important, but at an earlier stage of the process (Cohen, Sherrod, and Clark, 1986). For instance, social support skills may influence one's ability to effectively mobilize one's network by influencing the choice of support providers and appropriate disclosure.

Ultimately, it may be the receipt of emotional support that proves health relevant, but the role of support skill should not be ignored in our thinking about social support processes or in developing interventions. Our ability to model these processes, however, will be dependent on our understanding of what is social support.

Greater Attention to Basic Measurement Issues

One basic but easy to overlook issue is the measurement of social support and its proposed mediating variables. Social support in some mortality studies was measured with single-item indicators that can limit their measurement reliability and validity. Such measurement issues significantly hinder our ability to detect and understand associations between social support and health outcomes. There are a number of structural and functional social support scales with well-documented measurement properties that could be used more systematically in future studies (see chapter 2). Many large epidemiological studies, however, require brief measurement devices because social support may be one of many different risk factor assessments. The development and validation of short forms of these social support scales would be useful for future use in such studies. More generally, the use of scales with multiple indicators is highly recommended, and future studies should also document the measurement properties of their assessment, especially for less utilized or validated scales of social support.

A similar problem appears to exist in the measurement of potential mediators in social support and mortality studies. In some of the studies reviewed in this book, both social support and the potential mediators (that is, health behaviors) were measured with single-item indices that are of suspect reliability and validity. In other cases, social support was measured using validated measures, but the "control variables" were measured much less carefully. It is important to emphasize that testing these mechanisms in future research means that they are given the same attention as social support. That is, these mediators need to be measured with good measurement reliability and validity. The testing of mechanisms will require more complex models that demand better measurement reliability and validity. Such studies will be more time intensive but well worth the potential statistical and conceptual gains of evaluating associations and mediating mechanisms.

The Need to Test Theoretical Models Evaluating Mechanisms at Different Levels of Analysis

The need to test the proposed theoretical mechanisms is one of the most pressing issues in this literature. The research reviewed in this book spans some twenty-two years but represents only the first wave of research examining links between social support and health outcomes. The next generation of studies will need to test the process models and mechanisms by which social support has its effects on morbidity and mortality. The research reviewed in this book highlights the importance of esteem, control, stress appraisals, loneliness, and health behaviors as a few mediators of these effects. The elucidation of mechanisms will be important in helping us build accurate theories and in the design of effective interventions.

In testing these theoretical models, there are statistical and conceptual issues that need strong consideration. As discussed above, one issue is the valid and reliable measurement of social support and the proposed pathways. Another issue, however, is that of the studies that test theoretical mediators in social support research, many attempt to analyze single mediators. This practice assumes that there is a single dominant pathway at work, but research reviewed in this book suggests that there are multiple mediating processes that may or may not be overlapping. For instance, the psychological and behavioral pathways in the direct effect models are not necessarily competing perspectives, and each may highlight important processes ultimately linking social support to effects on health.

One question to consider is how to best test these more complex theoretical models. Most of the literature on social support and physical health utilized correlational designs that related naturalistic social support to health outcomes over time. However, experimental laboratory and intervention studies that are able to examine health-related processes in a more controlled manner provide a complementary approach to address mechanistic questions. For instance, a number of experimental studies have shown that social support reduces cardiovascular reactivity during stress (Lepore, 1998). Future studies that model the processes responsible for these effects can provide important data on the conceptual perspectives highlighted in this book.

For testing these models in future correlational studies, one straightforward and widely available approach is covariance structural modeling (Bollen, 1989). This technique allows for the specification of complex models and can test specific pathways but also provides indices of overall model fit. It also encourages a strong consideration of measurement issues as multiple indicators of a construct aid in the power of such tests. There are other more complex approaches to modeling pathways that should receive more attention in future studies. These include multilevel models and latent growth curve modeling that can nicely incorporate change over time (Cheong, MacKinnon, and Khoo, 2003; Singer, 1998).

One difficulty in examining the theoretical models is that a strong design of the primary end points of interest (morbidity and mortality) necessarily entails a long-term study. I would thus like to highlight the theoretical and practical importance of also examining more "intermediate" processes associated with support effects. Social support ultimately influences physical health via biological processes. Measures such as resting blood pressure, ambulatory blood pressure, coronary artery scans, and functional immune assays have been linked to a variety of health outcomes. Studies linking social support to these more intermediate outcomes would allow us to make links to the more distal health outcomes of interest (for example, cardiovascular disease or infectious diseases) as well as provide information on mediating biological mechanisms. However, we will ultimately need to test the full model that includes social support, physiological processes, and actual health outcomes.

In our evaluation of theoretical pathways it will be crucial for us to take an integrative perspective and consider the question of mechanisms at multiple levels of analyses (see figures 6.3 and 6.4). The links between social support and the disease processes covered in this book may continue to defy explanation in the absence of such a perspective that acknowledges the complexity of this phenomenon at different levels of analysis (for example, cultural influences on social support). These levels of analysis range from the sociocultural to the biological as these appear most relevant to explaining the links between social support and health outcomes. Future research with such a perspective can serve to clarify the levels of analysis that are most important and inform and refine our understanding of the conditions under which social support is health promoting.

The Need to Develop and Evaluate Comprehensive Theory-Based Interventions

Chapter 7 highlights some important studies and approaches to performing social support interventions. However, it was surprising that many of these studies did not obtain checks to see whether support was modified as a result of the intervention (Hogan, Linden, and Najarian, 2002). In addition, few studies seem to have carefully considered the complex issues involved in determining the suitability of the intervention to the situation and population of interest (Gottlieb, 2000).

Future interventions that address the question "who provides what to whom with what effect" will need to be carefully considered in light of the existing theoretical models linking social support to health. These interventions will also need to include more intermediate outcomes and have more of a focus on the process by which the intervention may work. In general, these support interventions provide an excellent means to test the theoretical models outlined earlier. These theoretical models also highlight the possible effectiveness of social support interventions that focus on primary prevention efforts. Such interventions that focus on healthy individuals are in need of greater dialogue and consideration (Kaplan, 2000).

We also need to be more creative in designing conceptually appropriate support intervention. Most interventions are focused at the individual level of analysis. However, community-based social support interventions may be worthwhile to influence norms and feelings of integration that can have widespread influences on health (Kawachi and Berkman, 2000; Gottlieb, 1988). We also need to be open to different modes of influencing social support. For instance, the Internet is quickly changing the way people communicate, and it may be possible to utilize this medium to perform different types of support interventions. Finally, we need to examine the cost-effectiveness of social support interventions. Most psychosocial interventions appear cost-effective in the long term, but we will be increasingly asked to provide such information in consideration of its more widespread implementation.

Incorporation of a Successful Aging or Lifespan Approach

The biological aging process has been of considerable interest to medical researchers because of its links to disease susceptibility. One striking aspect of health and disease is the individual variability in the aging process. Some individuals just seem to age more successfully than others by maintaining satisfying relationships, their sense of well-being, and physical health. In fact, there is increasing appreciation for the role of psychosocial and behavioral factors in the aging process (Rowe and Kahn, 1998). These observations have led to the concept of successful aging that acknowledges the factors that help individuals maintain functionality throughout the years (Rowe and Kahn, 1987).

The potential role of social support in successful aging was acknowledged more than fifteen years ago in the seminal review by Rowe and Kahn (1987), which was based on some of the early social support and mortality studies covered in this book. Given more recent research linking social support with lower mortality, the successful aging perspective has much to contribute to social support research and vice versa. The mending of these concepts highlights the importance of linking social support to aging throughout the lifespan. These links are highlighted by evidence suggesting that perceptions of support availability may be established early in life and serve as the basis for "working models" of the trustworthiness of others over time.

These perceptions of support may cast long shadows on the person's development. As a simple example, consider the lives of two young individuals, one who has access to support (individual A) or another who has limited access to support (individual B). Taking a lifespan approach to the models covered in chapter 6 highlights the amazing potential differences in life trajectories of these individuals. Individual A is expected to be exposed to less life stress, have better self-esteem, and have a greater sense of meaning or control in life. Extend

this process over some forty or fifty years and one can start to appreciate the cumulative wear and tear on individual B compared to individual A. Although this overly simplistic example ignores other potentially important factors (for example, genetics, socioeconomic status),
this snapshot gives you an idea of the kind of difference that may
emerge over time for these two individuals who initially differ only in
their level of social support.

Of course, this does not mean that individuals who have poor social support are doomed to life problems. The study of resilience makes
clear the enormous potential of individuals to rise above their circumstances (Jessor, 1993). In addition, the interventions covered earlier
suggest the possibility of successful support changes. One implication
of the successful aging perspective, however, is the benefit of primary
prevention efforts that establish these positive profiles early in life instead of the more costly and painful way of intervention once individuals already have developed established behavioral patterns.

The successful aging approach also makes salient the importance
of considering the stage of disease that may be influenced by social support. Little direct research exists demonstrating the exact stage(s) of
disease that may be influenced by social support (see chapter 5). For instance, although social support is clearly linked to cardiovascular mortality, its role in the development of cardiovascular disease is less clear.
Of course, these issues need to be incorporated into any comprehensive model of social support and health and in the design of appropriate interventions.

The Need to Consider Both Positive and
Negative Aspects of Relationships

Research on social support is rather unique in the context of main-
stream psychology. Psychology as a field has often been criticized for
emphasizing the negative aspects of the human condition (for example, biases or clinical pathology). This criticism in part has led to the recent emphasis on "positive psychology" that highlights the processes
that promote positive behavioral, psychological, and social outcomes
(Sheldon and King, 2001). Social support, on the other hand, has historically focused on the positive role of relationships on health and

well-being and been criticized for ignoring the negative aspects or "costs" associated with relationships (Rook and Pietromonaco, 1987).

Repeatedly throughout this book I have cautioned about the negative aspects of relationships and the need to consider them in the context of social support processes (Coyne and DeLongis, 1986). As covered in chapter 2, they can complicate the interpretation of both structural and functional measures of support. The simple existence of social ties and links to various groups and organizations does not guarantee that they are health promoting. It is clear that social ties may also serve as significant sources of stress or become models for deviant or unhealthy behaviors (Burg and Seeman, 1994).

Although functional aspects of support would seem less prone to this problem, research indicates that many network ties are characterized by co-occurring positive and negative feelings regarding their supportiveness (Barrera, 1980; Uchino et al., 2001). These network ties that an individual feels "ambivalent" about may serve as additional sources of stress and interfere with the seeking or efficacy of any received support. For instance, communications of emotional support appear more effective in the context of a positive rather than more mixed relationship (Major et al., 1997). We will need to be keenly aware of this co-occurring negativity in relationships because it may weaken associations between social support and health outcomes. In fact, it is my view that some of the inconsistencies in the effects of relationships on health may be attributable to this practice of ignoring the co-occurring negative feelings that exist in many of our relationships. Taking into account this complexity in our relationships can serve to inform and refine existing theoretical models of social support.

The Need to Integrate Social Support with Other Psychosocial Risk Factor Models

In the examination of psychosocial factors and disease, it is common to focus on one or two processes given the complexity of these links. In this book I have focused on the link between social support and physical health outcomes. At various points, however, I have also referred to other psychosocial risk factors such as socioeconomic status, hostility, depression, and stress. In some studies these psychosocial risk factors are treated as competing hypotheses. For instance, researchers may look at the link between social support and health while treating depression as a control variable.

Researchers are gaining a greater appreciation for the interactions and common pathways by which psychosocial processes may contribute to physical health outcomes. One obvious example here is the stress-buffering model of support that suggests the combination of low support and high life stress may be particularly unhealthy. I also reviewed a few studies that looked at the combination of having low social support and certain personality profiles such as Type A (Orth-Gomér and Undén, 1990). These studies suggest that such individuals are at more of an increased risk than they are when considering any one of these factors alone. These examples make the point that social support is part of a more complex system of associations. Better predictive utility may be gained by examining the interaction between social support and other conceptually relevant factors.

More recently, Timothy Smith and colleagues argued that a more comprehensive system of examining risk factors may be obtained via the interpersonal circumplex (Smith and Ruiz, 2002). The interpersonal circumplex can locate traits and behaviors along two dimensions: friendliness-hostility and dominance-submission (Kiesler, 1991). According to this approach, social support and hostility may anchor the ends of the friendliness dimension, with varying degrees of dominance. This perspective makes the important point that there may be more comprehensive ways to organize risk factors than has been appreciated in past research. In fact, these risk factors may have common developmental antecedents that then influence the expression of these processes in later life (Gallo and Smith, 1999). Promoting a more integrated approach to these questions will be important so that we can start to build more comprehensive risk factor models.

Conclusions

At the beginning of this book I started with the Gilbert O'Sullivan song "Alone Again (Naturally)." Readers can now appreciate with greater faith my early statement on the tragedy of the circumstances outlined in his song. Being habitually alone fosters a sense of isolation and despair that is only deepened when faced with life's challenges. In contrast, the strength of social bonds manifests in the joy, sense of acceptance, and resources we experience as part of our relationships. This not only promotes positive mental health, but can also influence how long one lives. Evidence in this book suggests the role of social support in predicting lower all-cause as well as disease specific mortality. This conclusion is based on more than twenty years of research conducted in Asia, Europe, and North America with tens of thousands of research participants.

There is still much more work that needs to be done to understand scientifically how social support ultimately influences health outcomes. The models developed in this book are based on prior frameworks and the extant literature on social support and physical health outcomes. It is meant to guide the next generation of studies that seeks to test more specific mechanisms and develop conceptually driven intervention strategies. I look forward to the next twenty years of research that will bring us closer to the ultimate goal of understanding and harnessing the incredible potential of our relationships to help us live happier, healthier, and longer lives.

References

References marked with an asterisk indicate studies included in the social support and mortality review.

Abbas, A. K., Lichtman, A. H., and Pober, J. S. (1997). *Cellular and molecular immunology* (3rd ed.). Philadelphia: Harcourt Brace.

Acitelli, L. K. and Young, A. M. (1996). Gender and thought in relationships. In G. J. O. Fletcher and J. Fitness (Eds.), *Knowledge structures in close relationships: A social psychological approach* (pp. 147–168). Mahwah, NJ: Erlbaum.

Ader, R., Felton, D. L., and Cohen, N. (2001). *Psychoneuroimmunology* (3rd ed.). New York: Academic Press.

Adler, N. E., Boyce, T., Chesney, M. A., Cohen, S., Folkman, S., Kahn, R. L., and Syme, S. L. (1994). Socioeconomic status and health: The challenge of the gradient. *American Psychologist, 49,* 15–24.

Ainsworth, M. D. S., Blehar, M. C., Waters, E., and Wall, S. (1978). *Patterns of attachment: A psychological study of the strange situation.* Hillsdale, NJ: Erlbaum.

Alferi, S. M., Carver, C. S., Antoni, M. H., Weiss, S., and Duran, R. E. (2001). An exploratory study of social support, distress, and life disruption among low-income Hispanic women under treatment for early stage breast cancer. *Health Psychology, 20,* 41–46.

Altman, I., and Taylor, D. A. (1973). *Social penetration: The development of interpersonal relationships.* New York: Holt, Rinehart and Winston.

American Cancer Society. (2001). *Cancer facts and figures 2001.* Atlanta: American Cancer Society.

American Heart Association. (2001). *2001 Heart and stroke statistical update.* Dallas: American Heart Association.

Anders, S. L., and Tucker, J. S. (2000). Adult attachment style, interpersonal communication competence, and social support. *Personal Relationships, 7,* 379–389.

Andersson, L. (1985). Intervention against loneliness in a group of elderly women: An impact evaluation. *Social Science and Medicine, 20,* 355–364.

Angerer, P., Siebert, U., Kothny, W., Muhlbauer, D., Mudra, H., and von Schacky, C. (2000). Impact of social support, cynical hostility and anger expression on progression of coronary atherosclerosis. *Journal of the American College of Cardiology, 36,* 1781–1788.

Antonucci, T. C., and Israel, B. A. (1986). Veridicality of social support: A comparison of principal and network members' responses. *Journal of Consulting and Clinical Psychology, 54*, 432–437.

Aspinwall, L. G., and Taylor, S. E. (1997). A stitch in time: Self-regulation and proactive coping. *Psychological Bulletin, 121*, 417–436.

Atienza, A. A., Collins, R., and King, A. C. (2001). The mediating effects of situational control on social support and mood following a stressor: A prospective study of dementia caregivers in their natural environment. *Journal of Gerontology: Social Sciences, 56B*, S129-S139.

*Avlund, K., Damsgaard, M. T., and Holstein, B. E. (1998). Social relations and mortality: An eleven year follow-up study of 70-year-old men and women in Denmark. *Social Science and Medicine, 47*, 635–643.

Badr, H., Acitelli, L., Duck, S., and Carl, W. J. (2001). Weaving social support and relationships together. In B. Sarason and S. Duck (Eds.), *Personal relationships: Implications for clinical and community psychology* (pp. 1–14). West Sussex, England: Wiley.

Barbee, A. P., Gulley, M. R., and Cunningham, M. R. (1990). Support seeking in personal relationships. *Journal of Social and Personal Relationships, 7*, 531–540.

Baron, R. M., and Kenny, D. A. (1986). The moderator-mediator distinction in social psychological research: Conceptual, strategic, and statistical considerations. *Journal of Personality and Social Psychology, 51*, 1173–1182.

Baron, R. S., Cutrona, C. E., Hicklin, D., Russell, D. W., and Lubaroff, D. M. (1990). Social support and immune function among spouses of cancer patients. *Journal of Personality and Social Psychology, 59*, 344–352.

Barrera, M. (1980). A method for the assessment of social support networks in community survey research. *Connections, 3*, 8–13.

Barrera, M. (1986). Distinctions between social support concepts, measures, and models. *American Journal of Community Psychology, 14*, 413–445.

Barrera, M. (1988). Models of social support and life stress: Beyond the buffering hypothesis. In L. Cohen (Ed.), *Life events and psychological functioning: Theoretical and methodological issues* (pp. 211–236). London: Sage.

Barrera, M. (2000). Social support research in community psychology. In J. Rappaport and E. Seidman (Eds.), *Handbook of community psychology* (pp. 215–245). New York: Kluwer Academic/Plenum.

Barrera, M., Sandler, I. N., and Ramsey, T. B. (1981). Preliminary development of a scale of social support: Studies on college students. *American Journal of Community Psychology, 9*, 435–447.

Bartholomew, K. (1990). Avoidance of intimacy: An attachment perspective. *Journal of Social and Personal Relationships, 7*, 147–178.

Benjamin, L. S. (1996). *Interpersonal diagnosis and treatment of personality disorders*. New York: Guilford.

Berbrier, M., and Schulte, A. (2000). Binding and nonbinding integration: The relational costs and rewards of social ties on mental health. *Research in Community and Mental Health, 11,* 3–27.

Berkman, L. F. (1986). Social networks, supports, and health: Taking the next step forward. *American Journal of Epidemiology, 123,* 559–562.

Berkman, L. F. (1995). The role of social relations in health promotion. *Psychosomatic Medicine, 57,* 245–254.

Berkman, L. F., and Glass, T. (2000). Social integration, social networks, social support, and health. In L. Berkman and I. Kawachi (Eds.), *Social epidemiology* (pp. 137–173). New York: Oxford.

Berkman, L. F., Glass, T., Brissette, I., and Seeman, T. E. (2000). From social integration to health: Durkheim in the new millennium. *Social Science and Medicine, 51,* 843–857.

*Berkman, L. F., Leo-Summers, L., and Horwitz, R. I. (1992). Emotional support and survival after myocardial infarction: A prospective, population-based study of the elderly. *Annals of Internal Medicine, 117,* 1003–1009.

*Berkman, L. F., and Syme, S. L. (1979). Social networks, host resistance, and mortality: A nine-year follow-up study of Alameda county residents. *American Journal of Epidemiology, 109,* 186–204.

Berscheid, E. (1985). Interpersonal attraction. In G. Lindzey and E. Aronson. (Eds.). *Handbook of social psychology* (3rd ed.). San Francisco: Freeman.

Berscheid, E., and Reis, H. T. (1998). Attraction and close relationships. In D. T. Gilbert, S. T. Fiske, and G. Lindzey (Eds.), *The Handbook of Social Psychology* (Volume 2, pp. 193–281). New York: Oxford University Press.

*Blazer, D. G. (1982). Social support and mortality in an elderly community population. *American Journal of Epidemiology, 115,* 684–694.

Blomkvist, V., Theorell, T., Jonsson, H., Schulman, S., Berntorp, E., and Stigendal, L. (1994). Psychosocial self-prognosis in relation to mortality and morbidity in hemophiliacs with HIV infection. *Psychotherapy and Psychosomatics, 62,* 185–192.

Bloom, J. R., Stewart, S. L., Johnston, M., Banks, P., and Fobair, P. (2001). Sources of support and the physical and mental well-being of young women with breast cancer. *Social Science and Medicine, 53,* 1513–1524.

Bolger, N., Foster, M., Vinokur, A. D., and Ng, R. (1996). Close relationships and adjustment to a life crisis: The case of breast cancer. *Journal of Personality and Social Psychology, 70,* 283–294.

Bolger, N., Zuckerman, A., and Kessler, R. C. (2000). Invisible support and adjustment to stress. *Journal of Personality and Social Psychology, 79,* 953–961.

Bollen, K. A. (1989). *Structural equations with latent variables.* New York: Wiley.

Bourgeois, M. S., Schulz, R., and Burgio, L. (1996). Interventions for caregivers of patients with Alzheimer's disease: A review and analysis of content, process, and outcomes. *International Journal of Aging and Human Development, 43,* 35–92.

Bowlby, J. (1982). *Attachment and loss: Attachment* (2nd ed.). New York: Basic Books.

*Bowling, A. (1988–1989). Who dies after widow(er) hood? A discriminant analysis. *Omega, 19,* 135–153.

Brissette, I., Cohen, S., and Seeman, T. E. (2000). Measuring social integration and social networks. In S. Cohen, L. G. Underwood, and B. H. Gottlieb (Eds.), *Social support measurement and intervention: A guide for health and social scientists* (pp. 53–85). New York: Oxford University Press.

Broadhead, W. E., Kaplan, B. H., James, S. A., Wagner, E. H., Schoenbach, V. J., Grimson, R., Heyden, S., Tibblin, G., and Gehlbach, S. H. (1983). The epidemiological evidence for a relationship between social support and health. *American Journal of Epidemiology, 117,* 521–537.

Brown, G. W. and Harris, T. (1978). *Social origins of depression: A study of psychiatric disorder in women.* New York: Free Press.

*Brummett, B. H., Barefoot, J. C., Siegler, I. C., Clapp-Channing, N. E., Lytle, B. L., Bosworth, H. B., Williams, R. B., Jr., and Mark, D. B. (2001). Characteristics of socially isolated patients with coronary artery disease who are at elevated risk for mortality. *Psychosomatic Medicine, 63,* 267–272.

*Bryant, S., and Rakowski, W. (1992). Predictors of mortality among elderly African-Americans. *Research on Aging, 14,* 50–67.

Burg, M. M., and Seeman, T. E. (1994). Families and health: The negative side of social ties. *Annals of Behavioral Medicine, 16,* 109–115.

Burleson, B. R., and Goldsmith, D. J. (1998). How the comforting process works: Alleviating emotional distress through conversationally induced reappraisals. In P. A. Andersen and L. K. Guerrero (Eds.), *Handbook of communication and emotion: Research, theory, applications, and contexts* (pp. 245–280). San Diego: Academic Press.

Burroughs, T. E., Harris, M. A., Pontius, S. L., and Santiago, J. V. (1997). Research on social support in adolescents with IDDM: A critical review. *The Diabetes Educator, 23,* 438–448.

Cacioppo, J. T., and Berntson, G. G. (1992). Social psychological contributions to the decade of the brain: Doctrine of multilevel analysis. *American Psychologist, 47,* 1019–1028.

Cacioppo, J. T., and Berntson, G. G. (in press). Balancing demands of the internal and external milieu. In H. Friedman and S. Cohen (Eds.), *Oxford handbook of health psychology.* New York: Oxford.

Cacioppo, J. T., Hawkley, L. C., Berntson, G. G., Ernst, J. M., Gibbs, A. C., Stickgold, R., and Hobson, J. A. (in press). Do lonely days invade the night?: Potential social modulation of sleep efficiency. *Psychological Science.*

Cacioppo, J. T., Hawkley, L. C., Crawford, L. E., Ernst, J. M., Burleson, M. H., Kowalewski, R. B., Malarkey, W. B., Van Cauter, E., and Berntson, G. G.

(2002). Loneliness and health: Potential mechanisms. *Psychosomatic Medicine, 64,* 407–417.

Caplan, G. (1974). *Support systems and community mental health: Lectures on concept development.* New York: Behavioral Publications.

*Case, R. B., Moss, A. J., Case, N., McDermott, M., and Eberly, S. (1992). Living alone after myocardial infarction: Impact on prognosis. *Journal of the American Medical Association, 267,* 515–519.

Cassell, J. (1976). The contribution of the social environment to host resistance. *American Journal of Epidemiology, 104,* 107–123.

Cassidy, J., and Shaver, P. R. (1999). *Handbook of attachment: Theory, research, and clinical applications.* New York: Guilford.

*Cassileth, B. R., Lusk, E. J., Miller, D. S., Brown, L. L., and Miller, C. (1985). Psychosocial correlates of survival in advanced malignant disease? *New England Journal of Medicine, 312,* 1551–1555.

*Cassileth, B. R., Walsh, W. P., and Lusk, E. J. (1988). Psychosocial correlates of cancer survival: A subsequent report 3 to 8 years after cancer diagnosis. *Journal of Clinical Oncology, 6,* 1753–1759.

Catz, S. L., Kelly, J. A., Bogart, L. M., Benotsch, E. G., and McAuliffe, T. L. (2000). Patterns, correlates, and barriers to medication adherence among persons prescribed new treatments for HIV disease. *Health Psychology, 19,* 124–133.

*Cerhan, J. R., and Wallace, R. B. (1997). Change in social ties and subsequent mortality in rural elders. *Epidemiology, 8,* 475–481.

*Ceria, C. D., Masaki, K. H., Rodriguez, B. L., Chen, R., Yano, K., and Curb, J. D. (2001). The relationship of psychosocial factors to total mortality among older Japanese-American men: The Honolulu heart program. *Journal of the American Geriatric Society, 49,* 725–731.

*Chacko, R. C., Harper, R. G., Gotto, J., and Young, J. (1996). Psychiatric interview and psychometric predictors of cardiac transplant survival. *American Journal of Psychiatry, 153,* 1607–1612.

Cheong, J., MacKinnon, D. P., and Khoo, S. T. (2003). An investigation of mediational processes using latent growth curve modeling. *Structural Equation Modeling, 10,* 238–262.

Christenfeld, N., Gerin, W., Linden, W., Sanders, M., Mathur, J., Deich, J. D., and Pickering, T. G. (1997). Social support effects on cardiovascular reactivity: Is a stranger as effective as a friend? *Psychosomatic Medicine, 59,* 388–398.

*Christensen, A. J., Dornink, R., Ehlers, S. L., and Schultz, S. K. (1999). Social environment and longevity in schizophrenia. *Psychosomatic Medicine, 61,* 141–145.

Christensen, A. J., and Smith, T. W. (1993). Cynical hostility and cardiovascular reactivity during self-disclosure. *Psychosomatic Medicine, 55,* 193–202.

*Christensen, A. J., Wiebe, J. S., Smith, T. W., and Turner, C. W. (1994). Predictors of survival among hemodialysis patients: Effect of perceived family support. *Health Psychology, 13,* 521–525.

Chrousos, G. P., and Gold, P. W. (1992). The concepts of stress and stress system disorders: Overview of physical and behavioral homeostasis. *Journal of the American Medical Association, 267,* 1244–1252.

Clark, M. S., and Mills, J. (1993). The difference between communal and exchange relationships: What it is and is not. *Personality and Social Psychology Bulletin, 19,* 684–691.

Cobb, S. (1976). Social support as a moderator of life stress. *Psychosomatic Medicine, 38,* 300–314.

*Cohen, C. I., Teresi, J., and Holmes, D. (1986–1987). Social networks and mortality in an inner-city elderly population. *International Journal of Aging and Human Development, 24,* 257–269.

Cohen, S. (1988). Psychosocial models of the role of social support in the etiology of physical disease. *Health Psychology, 7,* 269–297.

Cohen, S., Doyle, W. J., Skoner, D. P., Rabin, B. S., and Gwaltney, J. M. (1997). Social ties and susceptibility to the common cold. *Journal of the American Medical Association, 277,* 1940–1944.

Cohen, S., Frank, E., Doyle, W. J., Skoner, D. P., Rabin, B. S., and Gwaltney, J. M., Jr. (1998). Types of stressors that increase susceptibility to the common cold in healthy adults. *Health Psychology, 17,* 214–223.

Cohen, S., and Herbert, T. B. (1996). Health psychology: Psychological factors and physical disease from the perspective of human psychoneuroimmunology. *Annual Review of Psychology, 47,* 113–142.

Cohen, S., Kaplan, G. A., and Salonen, J. T. (1999). The role of psychological characteristics in the relation between socioeconomic status and perceived health. *Journal of Applied Social Psychology, 29,* 445–468.

Cohen, S., Kessler, R. C., and Gordon, L. U. (1995). *Measuring stress: A guide for health and social scientists.* New York: Oxford University Press.

Cohen, S., and McKay, G. (1984). Social support, stress and the buffering hypothesis: A theoretical analysis. In A. Baum, S. E. Taylor, and J. E. Singer (Eds.), *Handbook of psychology and health* (pp. 253–267). Hillsdale, NJ: Erlbaum.

Cohen, S., Mermelstein, R. J., Kamarck, T., and Hoberman, H. M. (1985). Measuring the functional components of social support. In I. G. Sarason and B. Sarason (Eds.), *Social support: Theory, research and applications* (pp. 73–94). The Hague, Holland: Martines Niijhoff.

Cohen, S., Sherrod, D. R., and Clark, M. S. (1986). Social skills and the stress-protective role of social support. *Journal of Personality and Social Psychology, 50,* 963–973.

Cohen, S., Underwood, L. G., and Gottlieb, B. H. (2000). *Social support measurement and intervention.* New York: Oxford.

Cohen, S., and Wills, T. A. (1985). Stress, social support, and the buffering hypothesis. *Psychological Bulletin, 98,* 310–357.

Collins, N. L., and Feeney, B. C. (2000). A safe haven: An attachment theory perspective on support seeking and caregiving in intimate relationships. *Journal of Personality and Social Psychology, 78,* 1053–1073.

*Cornell, L. L. (1992). Intergenerational relationships, social support, and mortality. *Social Forces, 71,* 53–62.

Coyne, J. C. (1976). Depression and the response of others. *Journal of Abnormal Psychology, 85,* 186–193.

Coyne, J. C., and Anderson, K. K. (1999). Marital status, marital satisfaction, and support processes among women at high risk for breast cancer. *Journal of Family Psychology, 13*(4), 629–641.

Coyne, J. C., and DeLongis, A. (1986). Going beyond social support: The role of social relationships in adaptation. *Journal of Consulting and Clinical Psychology, 54,* 454–460.

*Coyne, J. C., Rohrbaugh, M. J., Shoham, V., Sonnega, J. S., Nicklas, J. M., and Cranford, J. A. (2001). Prognostic importance of marital quality for survival of congestive heart failure. *American Journal of Cardiology, 88,* 526–529.

Coyne, J. C., Wortman, C. B., and Lehman, D. R. (1988). The other side of support: Emotional overinvolvement and miscarried help. In B. H. Gottlieb (Ed.), *Marshalling Social Support* (pp. 305–330). London: Sage.

Croyle, R. T., and Hunt, J. R. (1991). Coping with health threat: Social influence processes in reactions to medical test results. *Journal of Personality and Social Psychology, 60,* 382–389.

Cutrona, C. E. (1986). Behavioral manifestations of social support: A microanalytic investigation. *Journal of Personality and Social Psychology, 51,* 201–208.

Cutrona, C. E., and Cole, V. (2000). Optimizing support in the natural network. In S. Cohen, L. G. Underwood, and B. H. Gottlieb (Eds.), *Social support measurement and intervention: A guide for health and social scientists* (pp. 278–308). New York: Oxford University Press.

Cutrona, C. E., and Russell, D. (1987). The provisions of social relationships and adaptation to stress. In W. Jones and D. Perloff (Eds.), *Advances in personal relationships* (pp. 37–67). Greenwich, CT: JAI Press.

Cutrona, C. E., and Russell, D. W. (1990). Type of social support and specific stress: Towards a theory of optimal matching. In B. R. Sarason, I. G. Sarason, and G. R. Pierce (Eds.), *Social support: An interactional view* (pp. 319–366). New York: Wiley.

Dakof, G. A., and Taylor, S. E. (1990). Victims' perceptions of social support: What is helpful from whom. *Journal of Personality and Social Psychology, 58,* 80–89.

*Dalgard, O. S., and Haheim, L. L. (1998). Psychosocial risk factors and mortality: A prospective study with special focus on social support, social participation, and locus of control in Norway. *Journal of Epidemiology Community Health, 52,* 476–481.

Davis, M. H., Morris, M. M., and Kraus, L. A. (1998). Relationship-specific and global perceptions of social support: Associations with well-being and attachment. *Journal of Personality and Social Psychology, 74,* 468–481.

Davison, K. P., Pennebaker, J. W., and Dickerson, S. S. (2000). Who talks? The social psychology of illness support groups. *American Psychologist, 55,* 205–217.

*Denollet, J., Sys, S. U., and Brutsaert, D. L. (1995). Personality and mortality after myocardial infarction. *Psychsomatic Medicine, 57,* 582–591.

*Devins, G. M., Mann, J., Mandin, H., Paul, L. C., Hons, R. B., Burgess, E. D., Taub, K., Schorr, S., Letourneau, P. K., and Buckle, S. (1990). Psychosocial predictors of survival in end-stage renal disease. *Journal of Nervous and Mental Disease, 178,* 127–133.

Diamond, L. A. (2001). Contributions of psychophysiology to research on adult attachment: Review and recommendations. *Personality and Social Psychology Review, 5,* 276–295.

Dilworth-Anderson, P., and Marshall, S. (1996). Social support in its cultural context. In G. R. Pierce, B. R. Sarason, and I. G. Sarason (Eds.), *Handbook of Social Support and the Family* (pp. 67–79). New York: Plenum Press.

Dressler, W. W. (1991). Social support, lifestyle incongruity, and arterial blood pressure in a southern Black community. *Psychosomatic Medicine, 53,* 608–620.

Dressler, W. W. (1994). Cross-cultural differences and social influences in social support and cardiovascular disease. In S. A. Shumaker and S. M. Czajkowski (Eds.), *Social Support and Cardiovascular Disease* (pp. 167–192). New York: Plenum Press.

Dressler, W. W. (1995). *Culture, social support, and health status in Brazil.* Paper presented at the 94th Annual Meeting of the American Anthropological Association, Washington, DC.

Dressler, W. W., Balieiro, M. C., and Dos Santos, J. E. (1997). The cultural construction of social support in Brazil: Associations with health outcomes. *Culture, Medicine and Psychiatry, 21,* 303–335.

Dressler, W. W., and Bindon, J. R. (2000). The health consequences of cultural consonance: Cultural dimensions of lifestyle, social support, and arterial blood pressure in an African American community. *American Anthropologist, 102,* 244–260.

Dressler, W. W., Dos Santos, J. E., and Viteri, F. E. (1986). Blood pressure, ethnicity, and psychosocial resources. *Psychosomatic Medicine, 48,* 509–519.

Dressler, W. W., Mata, A., Chavez, A., Viteri, F. E., and Gallagher, P. (1986). Social support and arterial blood pressure in a central Mexican community. *Psychosomatic Medicine, 48,* 338–350.

Dunkel-Schetter, C., and Bennett, T. L. (1990). Differentiating the cognitive and behavioral aspects of social support. In B. R. Sarason, I. G. Sarason, and G. R. Pierce (Eds.), *Social support: An interactional view* (pp. 267–296). New York: Wiley.

Dunkel-Schetter, C., Folkman, S., and Lazarus, R. S. (1987). Correlates of social support receipt. *Journal of Personality and Social Psychology, 53,* 71–80.

Durkheim, E. (1951). *Suicide: A study in sociology.* London: Free Press.

*Eaker, E. D., Pinsky, J., and Castelli, W. P. (1992). Myocardial infarction and coronary death among women: Psychosocial predictors from a 20-year follow-up of women in the Framingham study. *American Journal of Epidemiology, 135,* 854–864.

Effros, R. B., and Walford, R. L. (1987). Infection and immunity in relation to aging. In E. A. Goidl (Ed.), *Aging and the immune response* (pp. 45–65). New York: Marcel Dekker.

Eggert, L. L., Thompson, E. A., Herting, J. R., Nicholas, L. J., and Dicker, B. G. (1994). Preventing adolescent drug abuse and high school dropout through an intensive school-based social network development program. *American Journal of Health Promotion, 8,* 202–215.

Eizenman, D. R., Nesselroade, J. R., Featherman, D. L., and Rowe, J. W. (1997). Intraindividual variability in perceived control in an older sample: The MacArthur successful aging studies. *Psychology and Aging, 12,* 489–502.

Ell, K. (1996). Social networks, social support and coping with serious illness: The family connection. *Social Science and Medicine, 42,* 173–183.

*Ell, K., Nishimoto, R., Medianski, L., Mantell, J., and Hamovitch, M. (1992). Social relations, social support and survival among patients with cancer. *Journal of Psychosomatic Research, 36,* 531–541.

*Engedal, K. (1996). Mortality in the elderly: A 3-year follow-up of an elderly community sample. *International Journal of Geriatric Psychiatry, 11,* 467–471.

Engel, G. L. (1977). The need for a new medical model: A challenge for biomedicine. *Science, 196,* 129–136.

*Falk, A., Hanson, B. S., Isacsson, S.-O., and Östergren, P.-O. (1992). Job strain and mortality in elderly men: Social network, support, and influence as buffers. *American Journal of Public Health, 82,* 1136–1139.

*Farmer, I. P., Meyer, P. S., Ramsey, D. J., Goff, D. C., Wear, M. L., Labarthe, D. R., and Nichaman, M. Z. (1996). Higher levels of social support predict greater survival following acute myocardial infarction: The Corpus Christi Heart project. *Behavioral Medicine, 22,* 59–66.

Fawzy, F. I., Fawzy, N. W., Hyun, C. S., Gutherie, D., Fahey, J. L., and Morton, D. (1993). Malignant melanoma: Effects of an early structured psychiatric intervention, coping, and affective state on recurrence and survival six years later. *Archives of General Psychiatry, 50,* 681–689.

Feldman, P. J., Dunkel-Schetter, C., Sandman, C. A., and Wadhwa, P. D. (2000). Maternal social support predicts birth weight and fetal growth in human pregnancy. *Psychosomatic Medicine, 62,* 715–725.

Fijneman, Y.-A., Willemsen, M.-E., and Poortinga, Y.-H. (1996). Individualism-collectivism: An empirical study of a conceptual issue. *Journal of Cross Cultural Psychology, 27,* 381–402.

Finch, J. F., Barrera, M., Okun, M. A., Bryant, W. H. M., Pool, G. J., and Snow-Turek, A. (1997). The factor structure of received social support: Dimensionality and the prediction of depression and life satisfaction. *Journal of Social and Clinical Psychology, 16,* 323–342.

Finch, J. F., Okun, M. A., Barrera, M., Zautra, A. J., and Reich, J. W. (1989). Positive and negative social ties among older adults: Measurement models and the prediction of psychological distress and well-being. *American Journal of Community Psychology, 17,* 585–605.

Fincham, F. D., and Linfield, K. J. (1997). A new look at marital quality: Can spouses feel positive and negative about their marriages? *Journal of Family Psychology, 11,* 489–502.

Flaherty, J. A., and Richman, J. A. (1986). Effects of childhood relationships on the adult's capacity to form social supports. *American Journal of Psychiatry, 143,* 851–855.

Flaherty, J., and Richman, J. (1989). Gender differences in the perception and utilization of social support: Theoretical perspectives and an empirical test. *Social Science and Medicine, 28,* 1221–1228.

Fleming, R., Baum, A., Gisriel, M. M., and Gatchel, R. J. (1982). Mediating influences of social support on stress at Three Mile Island. *Journal of Human Stress, 8,* 14–22.

Folkman, S., and Lazarus, R. S. (1985). If it changes it must be a process: Study of emotion and coping during three stages of a college examination. *Journal of Personality and Social Psychology, 48,* 150–170.

*Forster, L. E., and Stoller, E. P. (1992). The impact of social support on mortality: A seven-year follow-up of older men and women. *Journal of Applied Gerontology, 11,* 173–186.

*Frasure-Smith, N., Lesperance, F., Gravel, G., Masson, A., Juneau, M., Talajic, M., and Bourassa, M. G. (2000). Social support, depression, and mortality during the first year after myocardial infarction. *Circulation,* 1919–1924.

Frasure-Smith, N., Lesperance, F., Prince, R., Verrier, P., Garber, R. A., Juneau, M., Wolfson, C., and Bourassa, M. G. (1997). Randomised trial of home-based psychosocial nursing intervention for patients recovering from myocardial infarction. *Lancet, 350,* 473–479.

Frasure-Smith, N., and Prince, R. (1985). The ischemic heart disease life stress monitoring program: Impact on mortality. *Psychosomatic Medicine, 47,* 431–445.

*Fried, T. R., Pollack, D. M., and Tinetti, M. E. (1998). Factors associated with six-month mortality in recipients of community-based long-term care. *Journal of the American Geriatric Society, 46,* 193–197.

Gallo, L. C., and Matthews, K. A. (1999). Do negative emotions mediate the association between socioeconomic status and health? *Annals of the New York Academy of Sciences, 896,* 226–245.

Gallo, L. C., and Smith, T. W. (1999). Patterns of hostility and social support: Conceptualizing psychosocial risk factors as characteristics of the person *and* the environment. *Journal of Research in Personality, 33,* 281–310.

Gallup Organization, The. (2000, October 13). *Gallup poll analyses: Americans are overwhelmingly happy and optimistic about the future of the United States.* Retrieved from http://www.gallup.com/poll/releases/pr001013.asp

*Ganzini, L., Smith, D. M., Fenn, D. S., and Lee, M. A. (1997). Depression and mortality in medically ill older adults. *Journal of the American Geriatrics Society, 45,* 307–312.

Gerin, W., Pieper, C., Levy, R., and Pickering, T. G. (1992). Social support in social interaction: A moderator of cardiovascular reactivity. *Psychosomatic Medicine, 54,* 324–336.

Glaser, R., Kiecolt-Glaser, J. K., Bonneau, R., Malarkey, W., Hughes, J. (1992). Stress-induced modulation of the immune response to recombinant hepatitis B vaccine. *Psychosomatic Medicine, 54,* 22–29.

Glass, T. A., Mendes De Leon, C. F., Seeman, T. E., and Berkman, L. F. (1997). Beyond single indicators of social networks: A LISREL analysis of social ties among the elderly. *Social Science and Medicine, 44,* 1503–1517.

Goodkin, K., Blaney, N. T., Feaster, D., Fletcher, M. A., Baum, M. K., Mantero-Atienza, E., Klimas, N. G., Millon, C., Szapocznik, J., and Eisdorfer, C. (1992). Active coping style is associated with natural killer cell cytotoxicity in asymptomatic HIV-1 seropositive homosexual men. *Journal of Psychosomatic Research, 36,* 635–650.

Goodwin, P. J., Leszca, M., Ennis, M., Koopmans, J., Vincent, L., Guther, H., Drysdale, E., Hundleby, M., Chochinov, H. M., Navarro, M., Speca, M., and Hunter, J. (2001). The effect of group psychosocial support on survival in metastatic breast cancer. *New England Journal of Medicine, 345,* 1719–1726.

Gore, S. (1981). Stress-buffering functions of social supports: An appraisal and clarification of research models. In B. Dohrenwend and B. Dohrenwend (Eds.), *Stressful life events and their context* (pp. 202–222). New York: Prodist.

Gottlieb, B. (1985). Social support and the study of personal relationships. *Journal of Social and Personal Relationships, 2,* 351–375.

Gottlieb, B. (1988). Support interventions: A typology and agenda for research.

In S. W. Duck (Ed.), *Handbook of Personal Relationships* (pp. 519–541). New York: Wiley.

Gottlieb, B. H. (2000). Selecting and planning support interventions. In S. Cohen, L. G. Underwood and B. H. Gottlieb (Eds.), *Social support measurement and intervention: A guide for health and social scientists* (pp. 195–220). New York: Oxford University Press.

*Grand, A., Grosclaude, P., Bocquet, H., Pous, J., and Albarede, J. L. (1990). Disability, psychosocial factors and mortality among the elderly in a rural French population. *Journal of Clinical Epidemiology, 43,* 773–782.

Granovetter, M. S. (1973). The strength of weak ties. *American Journal of Sociology, 78,* 1360–1380.

Graves, P. L., Want, N.-Y., Mead, L. A., Johnson, J. V., and Klag, M. J. (1998). Youthful precursors of midlife social support. *Journal of Personality and Social Psychology, 74,* 1329–1336.

Green, B. B., McAfee, T., Hindmarsh, M., Madsen, L., Caplow, M., and Buist, D. (2002). Effectiveness of telephone support in increasing physical activity levels in primary care patients. *American Journal of Preventive Medicine, 22,* 177–183.

Green, L. R., Richardson, D. S., Lago, T., and Schatten-Jones, E. (2001). Network correlates of social and emotional loneliness in young and older adults. *Personality and Social Psychology Bulletin, 27,* 281–288.

Greenspan, F. S., and Baxter, J. D. (1994). *Basic and clinical endocrinology.* Norwalk, CT: Appleton and Lange.

Grunberg, N. E., and Baum, A. (1985). Biological commonalities of stress and substance abuse. In S. Shiffman and T. A. Wills (Eds.), *Coping and substance abuse* (pp. 25–62). Orlando, FL: Academic Press.

Gump, B. B., Polk, D. E., Kamarck, T. W., and Shiffman, S. M. (2001). Partner interactions are associated with reduced blood pressure in the natural environment: Ambulatory monitoring evidence from a healthy, multiethnic adult sample. *Psychosomatic Medicine, 63,* 423–433.

*Hanson, B. S., Isacsson, S.-O., Janzon, L., and Lindell, S.-E. (1989). Social network and social support influence mortality in elderly men: The prospective population study of "men born in 1914," Malmo, Sweden. *American Journal of Epidemiology, 130,* 100–111.

Hansson, R. O., Jones, W. H., and Fletcher, W. L. (1990). Troubled relationships in later life: Implications for support. *Journal of Social and Personal Relationships, 7,* 451–463.

Harris, T., Brown, G. W., and Robinson, R. (1999). Befriending as an intervention for chronic depression among women in an inner city. I: Randomised controlled trial. *British Journal of Psychiatry, 174,* 219–224.

*Haug, M. R., Breslau, N., and Folmar, S. J. (1989). Coping resources and selective survival in mental health of the elderly. *Research on Aging, 11,* 468–491.

Hawkley, L. C., Burleson, M. H., Berntson, G. G., and Cacioppo, J. T. (2003). Loneliness in everyday life: Cardiovascular activity, psychosocial context, and health behaviors. *Journal of Personality and Social Psychology*, 85, 105–120.

*Haynes, S. G., and Feinleib, M. (1980). Women, work and coronary heart disease: Prospective findings from the Framingham heart study. *American Journal of Public Health*, 70, 133–141.

Hazan, C., and Shaver, P. (1987). Romantic love conceptualized as an attachment process. *Journal of Personality and Social Psychology*, 52, 511–524.

Helgeson, V. S. (1993). Two important distinctions in social support: Kind of support and perceived versus received. *Journal of Applied Social Psychology*, 10, 825–845.

Helgeson, V. S., and Cohen, S. (1996). Social support and adjustment to cancer: Reconciling descriptive, correlational, and intervention research. *Health Psychology*, 15, 135–148.

Helgeson, V. S., Cohen, S., Schulz, R., and Yasko, J. (2000). Group support interventions for women with breast cancer: Who benefits from what? *Health Psychology*, 19, 107–114.

Heller, K., Thompson, M. G., Trueba, P. E., Hogg, J. R., and Vlachos-Weber, I. (1991). Peer support telephone dyads for elderly women: Was this the wrong intervention? *American Journal of Community Psychology*, 19, 53–74.

Henderson, L., and Zimbardo, P. G. (2001). Shyness as a clinical condition: The Stanford model. In W. Crozier and L. Alden (Eds.), *International handbook of social anxiety: Concepts, research and interventions relating to the self and shyness* (pp. 431–447). New York: Wiley.

*Hibbard, J. H., and Pope, C. R. (1992). Women's employment, social support, and mortality. *Women and Health*, 18, 119–133.

*Hibbard, J. H., and Pope, C. R. (1993). The quality of social roles as predictors of morbidity and mortality. *Social Science and Medicine*, 36, 217–225.

*Ho, S. C. (1991). Health and social predictors of mortality in an elderly Chinese cohort. *American Journal of Epidemiology*, 133, 907–921.

Hobfoll, S. E. (1989). Conservation of resources: A new attempt at conceptualizing stress. *American Psychologist*, 44, 513–524.

Hobfoll, S. E., Jackson, A. P., Lavin, J., Britton, P. J., and Shepherd, J. B. (1994). Reducing inner-city women's AIDS risk activities: A study of single, pregnant women. *Health Psychology*, 13, 397–403.

Hogan, B. E., Linden, W., and Najarian, B. (2002). Social support interventions: Do they work? *Clinical Psychology Review*, 22, 381–440.

Holahan, C. J., and Moos, R. H. (1990). Life stressors, resistance factors, and improved psychological functioning: An extension of the stress resistance paradigm. *Journal of Personality and Social Psychology*, 58, 909–917.

Horsten, M., Mittleman, M. A., Wamala, S. P., Schenck-Gustafsson, K., and Orth-Gomér, K. (1999). Social relations and the metabolic syndrome in middle-aged Swedish women. *Journal of Cardiovascular Risk*, 6, 391–397.

House, J. S. (2001). Social isolation kills, but how and why? *Psychosomatic Medicine, 63,* 273–274.

House, J. S., Landis, K. R., and Umberson, D. (1988). Social relationships and health. *Science, 241,* 540–545.

*House, J. S., Robbins, C., and Metzner, H. L. (1982). The association of social relationships and activities with mortality: Prospective evidence from the Tecumseh Community Health Study. *American Journal of Epidemiology, 116,* 123–140.

Hughes, M., and Gove, W. R. (1981). Living alone, social integration, and mental health. *American Journal of Sociology, 87,* 48–74.

Humphreys, K., Mankowski, E. S., Moos, R. H., and Finney, J. W. (1999). Do enhanced friendship networks and active coping mediate the effect of self-help groups on substance abuse? *Annuals of Behavioral Medicine, 21,* 54–60.

Humphreys, K., and Noke, J. M. (1997). The influence of posttreatment mutual help group participation on the friendship networks of substance abuse patients. *American Journal of Community Psychology, 25,* 1–17.

*Irvine, J., Basinski, A., Baker, B., Jandciu, S., Paquette, M., Cairns, J., Connolly, S., Roberts, R., Gent, M., and Dorian, P. (1999). Depression and risk of sudden cardiac death after acute myocardial infarction: Testing for the confounding effects of fatigue. *Psychosomatic Medicine, 61,* 729–737.

Janes, C. R., and Pawson, I. G. (1986). Migration and biocultural adaptation: Samoans in California. *Social Science and Medicine, 22,* 821–834.

Jessor, R. (1993). Successful adolescent development among youth in high-risk settings. *American Psychologist, 48,* 117–126.

Johnson, C. L., and Johnson, F. A. (1975). Interaction rules and ethnicity: The Japanese and Caucasians in Honolulu. *Social Forces, 54,* 452–466.

*Johnson, J. V., Hall, E. M., and Theorell, T. (1989). Combined effects of job strain and social isolation on cardiovascular disease morbidity and mortality in a random sample of the Swedish male working population. *Scandinavian Journal of Work Environmental Health, 15,* 271–279.

*Johnson, J. V., Stewart, W., Hall, E. M., Fredlund, P., and Theorell, T. (1996). Long-term psychosocial work environment and cardiovascular mortality among Swedish men. *American Journal of Public Health, 86,* 324–331.

*Jorm, A. F., Henderson, A. S., Kay, D. W. K., and Jacomb, P. A. (1991). Mortality in relation to dementia, depression and social integration in an elderly community sample. *International Journal of Geriatric Psychiatry, 6,* 5–11.

*Jylhä, M., and Aro, S. (1989). Social ties and survival among the elderly in Tampere, Finland. *International Journal of Epidemiology, 18,* 158–164.

Kamarck, T., Everson, S., Kaplan, G., Manuck, S., Jennings, R., Salonen, R., Salonen, J. (1997). Exaggerated blood pressure responses during mental stress are associated with enhanced carotid atherosclerosis in middle-aged Finnish men. *Circulation, 96,* 3842–3848.

Kamarck, T. W., Manuck, S. B., and Jennings, J. R. (1990). Social support reduces cardiovascular reactivity to psychological challenge: A laboratory model. *Psychosomatic Medicine, 52,* 42–58.

*Kaplan, G. A., Salonen, J. T., Cohen, R. D., Brand, R. J., Syme, S. L., and Puska, P. (1988). Social connections and mortality from all causes and from cardiovascular disease: Prospective evidence from Eastern Finland. *American Journal of Epidemiology, 128,* 370–380.

*Kaplan, G. A., Wilson, T. W., Cohen, R. D., Kauhanen, J., Wu, M., and Salonen, J. T. (1994). Social functioning and overall mortality: Prospective evidence from the Kuopio ischemic heart disease risk factor study. *Epidemiology, 5,* 495–500.

Kaplan, N. M. (1989). The deadly quartet: Upper body adiposity, glucose intolerance, hypertriglyceridaemia and hypertension. *Archives of Internal Medicine, 148,* 1514–1520.

Kaplan, R. M. (2000). Two pathways to prevention. *American Psychologist, 55,* 382–396.

Kawachi, I., and Berkman, L. (2000). Social cohesion, social capital, and health. In L. F. Berkman and I. Kawachi (Eds.), *Social Epidemiology* (pp. 174–190). New York: Oxford University Press.

*Kawachi, I., Colditz, G. A., Ascherio, A., Rimm, E. B., Giovannucci, E., Stampfer, M. J., and Willett, W. C. (1996). A prospective study of social networks in relation to total mortality and cardiovascular disease in men in the USA. *Journal of Epidemiology and Community Health, 50,* 245–251.

*Kawachi, I., Kennedy, B. P., Lochner, K., and Prothrow-Stith, D. (1997). Social capital, income inequality, and mortality. *American Journal of Public Health, 87,* 1491–1498.

Kelly, J. A., Murphy, D. A., Sikkema, K. J., and Kalichman, S. C. (1993). Psychological interventions to prevent HIV infection are urgently needed: New priorities for behavioral research in the second decade of AIDS. *American Psychologist, 10,* 1023–1034.

Kelly, J. A., Otto-Salaj, L. L., Sikkema, K. J., Pinkerton, S. D., and Bloom, F. R. (1998). Implications of HIV treatment advances for behavioral research on AIDS: Protease inhibitors and new challenges in HIV secondary prevention. *Health Psychology, 17,* 310–319.

*Kennedy, B. P., Kawachi, I., and Brainerd, E. (1998). The role of social capital in the Russian mortality crisis. *World Development, 26,* 2029–2043.

Kennell, J., Klaus, M., McGrath, S., Robertson, S., and Hinkley, C. (1991). Continuous emotional support during labor in a US hospital. *Journal of the American Medical Association, 265,* 2197–2201.

Kernis, M. H., Paradise, A. W., Whitaker, D. J., Wheatman, S. R., and Goldman, B. N. (2000). Master of one's psychological domain: Not likely if one's self-esteem is unstable. *Personality and Social Psychology Bulletin, 26,* 1297–1305.

Kessler, R. C., Mickelson, K. D., and Zhao, S. (1997). Patterns and correlates of self-help group membership in the United States. *Social Policy, 27,* 27–46.

Kiecolt-Glaser, J. K., Dura, J. R., Speicher, C. E., Trask, O. J., and Glaser, R. G. (1991). Spousal caregivers of dementia victims: Longitudinal changes in immunity and health. *Psychosomatic Medicine, 53,* 345–362.

Kiecolt-Glaser, J. K., and Glaser, R. (1995). Psychoneuroimmunology and health consequences: Data and shared mechanisms. *Psychosomatic Medicine, 57,* 269–274.

Kiecolt-Glaser, J. K., and Newton, T. L. (2001). Marriage and health: His and hers. *Psychological Bulletin, 127,* 472–503.

Kiecolt-Glaser, J. K., Newton, T., Cacioppo, J. T., MacCallum, R. C., Glaser, R., and Malarkey, W.B. (1996). Marital conflict and endocrine function: Are men really more physiologically affected than women? *Journal of Consulting and Clinical Psychology, 64,* 324–332.

*Kiely, D. K., Simon, S. E., Jones, R. N., and Morris, J. N. (2000). The protective effect of social engagement on mortality in long-term care. *Journal of the American Geriatric Society, 48,* 1367–1372.

Kiesler, D. J. (1991). Interpersonal methods of assessment and diagnosis. In C. R. Snyder and D. R. Forsyth (Eds.), *Handbook of social and clinical psychology: The health perspective.* Elmsford, New York: Pergamon Press.

Knox, S. S., Adelman, A., Ellison, C. R., Arnett, D. K., Siegmund, K. D., Weidner, G., and Province, M. A. (2000). Hostility, social support, and carotid artery atherosclerosis in the National Heart, Lung, and Blood Institute Family Heart Study. *American Journal of Cardiology, 86,* 1086–1089.

Knox, S. S., Siegmund, K. D., Weidner, G., Ellison, C. R., Adelman, A., and Paton, C. (1998). Hostility, social support, and coronary heart disease in the National Heart, Lung, and Blood Institute Family Heart Study. *American Journal of Cardiology, 82,* 1192–1196.

Knox, S. S., and Uvnas-Moberg, K. (1998). Social isolation and cardiovascular disease: An atherosclerotic pathway? *Psychoneuroendocrinology, 23,* 877–890.

Kobak, R. R., and Sceery, A. (1988). Attachment in late adolescence: Working models, affect regulation, and representations of self and others. *Child Development, 59,* 135–146.

*Korten, A. E., Jorm, A. F., Jiao, Z., Letenneur, L., Jacomb, P. A., Henderson, A. S., Christensen, H., and Rodgers, B. (1999). Health, cognitive, and psychosocial factors as predictors of mortality in an elderly community sample. *Journal of Epidemiology and Community Health, 53,* 83–88.

Krantz, D. S., Helmers, K. F., Bairey, N., Nebel, L. E., Hedges, S. M., and Rozanski, A. (1991). Cardiovascular reactivity and mental stress-induced myocardial ischemia in patients with coronary artery disease. *Psychosomatic Medicine, 53,* 1–12.

Krause, N. (1987a). Chronic financial strain, social support, and depressive symptoms among older adults. *Psychology and Aging, 2,* 185–192.

Krause, N. (1987b). Life stress, social support, and self-esteem in an elderly population. *Psychology and Aging, 2,* 349–356.

*Krause, N. (1997). Received support, anticipated support, social class, and mortality. *Research on Aging, 19,* 387–422.

Krause, N. (2001). Social support. In R. H. Binstock and L. K. George (Eds.)., *Handbook of Aging and the Social Sciences* (5th ed.) (pp. 272–294). New York: Academic Press.

Krause, N., and Borawski-Clark, E. (1995). Social class differences in social support among older adults. *Gerontologist, 35,* 498–508.

Krause, N., Liang, J., and Keith, V. (1990). Personality, social support, and psychological distress in later life. *Psychology and Aging, 5,* 315–326.

Krause, N., and Shaw, B. A. (2000). Role-specific feelings of control and mortality. *Psychology and Aging, 15,* 617–626.

Kulik, J. A., Mahler, H. I. M., and Moore, P. J. (1996). Social comparison and affiliation under threat: Effects on recovery from major surgery. *Journal of Personality and Social Psychology, 71,* 967–979.

Lakey, B., and Cohen, S. (2000). Social support theory and measurement. In S. Cohen, L. G. Underwood, and B. H. Gottlieb (Eds.), *Social support measurement and intervention: A guide for health and social scientists* (pp. 29–52). Oxford: Oxford University Press.

Lando, H. A., Pirie, P. L., Roski, J., McGovern, P. G., and Schmid, L. A. (1996). Promoting abstinence among relapsed chronic smokers: The effect of telephone support. *American Journal of Public Health, 86,* 1786–1790.

Lang, F. R., Featherman, D. L., and Nesselroade, J. R. (1997). Social self-efficacy and short-term variability in social relationships: The MacArthur successful aging studies. *Psychology and Aging, 12,* 657–666.

LaRocco, J. M., House, J. S., and French, J. R. P. (1980). Social support, occupational stress, and health. *Journal of Health and Social Behavior, 21,* 202–218.

Larose, S., and Bernier, A. (2001). Social support processes: Mediators of attachment state of mind and adjustment in late adolescence. *Attachment and Human Development, 3,* 96–120.

*LaVeist, T. A., Sellers, R. M., Brown, K. A. E., and Nickerson, K. J. (1997). Extreme social isolation, use of community-based senior support services, and mortality among African American elderly women. *American Journal of Community Psychology, 25,* 721–732.

Lazarus, R. S., and Folkman, S. (1984). *Stress, appraisal, and coping.* New York: Springer-Verlag.

*Lee, M., and Rotheram-Borus, M. J. (2001). Challenges associated with increased survival among parents living with HIV. *American Journal of Public Health, 91,* 1303–1309.

Lehman, D. R., Ellard, J. H., and Wortman, C. B. (1986). Social support for the bereaved: Recipients' and providers' perspectives on what is helpful. *Journal of Consulting and Clinical Psychology, 54,* 438–446.

Lepore, S. J. (1995). Cynicism, social support, and cardiovascular reactivity. *Health Psychology, 14,* 210–216.

Lepore, S. J. (1998). Problems and prospects for the social support-reactivity hypothesis. *Annuals of Behavioral Medicine, 20,* 257–269.

Lepore, S. J., Allen, K. A., and Evan, G. W. (1993). Social support lowers cardiovascular reactivity to an acute stressor. *Psychosomatic Medicine, 55,* 518–524.

Leppin, A., and Schwarzer, R. (1990). Social support and physical health: An updated meta-analysis. In L. R. Schmidt, P. Schwenkmezger, J. Weinman, and S. Maes (Eds.), *Theoretical and applied aspects of health psychology* (pp. 185–202). Amsterdam, Netherlands: Harwood Academic Publishers.

Levenson, D. (Ed.). (1994). *Mind, body, and medicine: A history of the American Psychosomatic Society.* McLean, VA: Williams and Wilkins.

Levine, D. M., Green, L. W., Deeds, S. G., Chwalow, J., Russell, R. P., Finlay, J. (1979). Health education for hypertensive patients. *Journal of the American Medical Association, 241,* 1700–1703.

Levy, S. M., Herberman, R. B., Whiteside, T., Sanzo, K., Lee, J., and Kirkwood, J. (1990). Perceived social support and tumor estrogen/progesterone receptor status as predictors of natural killer cell activity in breast cancer patients. *Psychosomatic Medicine, 52,* 73–85.

Lewin, K. (1951). *Field theory in social science.* New York: Harper and Brothers Publishers.

Lewis, M. A., and Rook, K. S. (1999). Social control in personal relationships: Impact on health behaviors and psychological distress. *Health Psychology, 18,* 63–71.

Ley, P. (1977). Psychological studies of doctor-patient communication. In S. Richman (Ed.), *Contributions to Medical Psychology* (Vol. 1). Oxford: Pergamon.

Libby, P., Ridker, P. M., and Maseri, A. (2002). Inflammation and atherosclerosis. *Circulation, 105,* 1135–1143.

Light, K. C., Dolan, C. A., Davis, M. R., and Sherwood, A. (1992). Cardiovascular responses to an active coping challenge as predictors of blood pressure patterns 10 to 15 years later. *Psychosomatic Medicine, 54,* 217–230.

Lin, N. (1982). Social resources and instrumental action. In P. Marsden and N. Lin (Eds.), *Social structure and network analysis* (pp. 131–145). Beverly Hills, CA: Sage.

Lin, N. (1986). Modeling the effects of social support. In N. Lin, A. Dean, and

W. Ensel (Eds.), *Social support, life events, and depression* (pp. 173–209). Orlando, FL: Academic Press.

Linden, W., Chambers, L., Maurice, J., and Lenz, J. W. (1993). Sex differences in social support, self-deception, hostility, and ambulatory cardiovascular activity. *Health Psychology, 12,* 376–380.

Linden, W., Stossel, C., and Maurice, J. (1996). Psychosocial interventions for patients with coronary artery disease. *Archives of Internal Medicine, 156,* 745–752.

Liu, W. T., and Duff, R. W. (1972). The strength in weak ties. *Public Opinion Quarterly, 36,* 361–366.

*Liu, X., Hermalin, A. I., and Chuang, Y. -L. (1998). The effect of education on mortality among older Taiwanese and its pathways. *Journal of Gerontology: Social Sciences, 2,* S71-S82.

Lloyd-Jones, D. M., Evans, J. C., Larson, M. G., O'Donnell, C. J., and Levy, D. (1999). Differential impact of systolic and diastolic blood pressure level on JNC-VI staging. Joint national committee on the prevention, detection, evaluation, and treatment of high blood pressure. *Hypertension, 34,* 381–385.

*Lund, R., Modvig, J., Due, P., and Holstein, B. E. (2001). Stability and change in structural social relations as predictor of mortality among elderly women and men. *European Journal of Epidemiology, 16,* 1087–1097.

Lynch, J. J. (1977). *The broken heart: The medical consequences of loneliness.* New York: Basic Books.

Macinko, J., and Starfield, B. (2001). The utility of social capital in research on health determinants. *Milbank Quarterly, 79,* 387–427.

MacKinnon, D. P., Goldberg, L., Clarke, G. N., Elliot, D. L., Cheong, J., Lapin, A., Moe, E. L., and Krull, J. L. (2001). Mediating mechanisms in a program to reduce intentions to use anabolic steroids and improve exercise self-efficacy and dietary behavior. *Prevention Science, 2,* 15–28.

MacMahon, S., Peto, R., Cutler, J., Collins, R., Sorlie, P., Neaton, J., Abbott, R., Godwin, J., Dyer, A., and Stamler, J. (1990). Blood pressure, stroke, and coronary heart disease. Part 1, prolonged differences in blood pressure: Prospective observational studies corrected for the regression dilution bias. *Lancet, 335,* 765–774.

Major, B., Zubek, J. M., Cooper, M. L., and Richards, C. (1997). Mixed messages: Implications of social conflict and social support within close relationships for adjustment to a stressful life event. *Journal of Personality and Social Psychology, 72,* 1349–1363.

Manne, S., and Glassman, M. (2000). Perceived control, coping efficacy, and avoidance coping as mediators between spouses' unsupportive behaviors and cancer patients' psychological distress. *Health Psychology, 19,* 155–164.

Manne, S. L., Pape, S. J., Taylor, K. L., and Dougherty, J. (1999). Spouse support, coping, and mood among individuals with cancer. *Annuals of Behavioral Medicine, 21,* 111–121.

Manuck, S. B. (1994). Cardiovascular reactivity in cardiovascular disease: "Once more unto the breach." *International Journal of Behavioral Medicine, 1,* 4–31.

Markus, H. R., and Kitiyama, S. (1991). Culture and the self: Implications for cognition, emotion, and motivation. *Psychological Review, 98,* 224, 253.

*Marottoli, R. A., Berkman, L. F., Leo-Summers, L., and Cooney, L. M. (1994). Predictors of mortality and institutionalization after hip fracture: The New Haven EPESE cohort. *American Journal of Public Health, 84,* 1807–1812.

Mead, G. H. (1934). *Mind, self, and society.* Chicago: University of Chicago Press.

Menaghan, E. C. (1989). Role changes and psychological well-being: Variations in effects by gender and role repertoire. *Social Forces, 67,* 693–714.

*Merlo, J., Ostergren, P. O., Mansson, N. O., Hanson, B. S., Ranstam, J., Blennow, G., Isacsson, S. O., and Melander, A. (2000). Mortality in elderly men with low psychosocial coping resources using anxiolytic-hypnotic drugs. *Scandinavian Journal of Public Health, 28,* 294–297.

*Mertens, J. R., Moos, R. H., and Brennan, P. L. (1996). Alcohol consumption, life context, and coping predict mortality among late-middle-aged drinkers and former drinkers. *Alcoholism: Clinical and Experimental Research, 20,* 313–319.

Miller, G. E., and Cole, S. W. (1998). Social relationships and the progression of human immunodeficiency virus infection: A review of evidence and possible underlying mechanisms. *Annuals of Behavioral Medicine, 20,* 181–189.

Miller, T. Q., Smith, T. W., Turner, C. W., Guijarro, M. L., and Hallett, A. J. (1996). A meta-analytic review of research on hostility and physical health. *Psychological Bulletin, 119,* 322–348.

Morisky, D. E., DeMuth, N. M., Field-Fass, M., Green, L. W., and Levine, D. M. (1985). Evaluation of family health education to build social support for long-term control of high blood pressure. *Health Education Quarterly, 12,* 35–50.

Morisky, D. E., Levine, D. M., Green, L. W., Shapiro, S., Russell, P., and Smith, C. R. (1983). Five-year blood pressure control and mortality following health education for hypertensive patients. *American Journal of Public Health, 73,* 153–162.

*Murberg, T. A., and Bru, E. (2001). Social relationships and mortality in patients with congestive heart failure. *Journal of Psychosomatic Research, 51,* 521–527.

Nadler, A., and Fisher, J. D. (1986). The role of threat to self-esteem and perceived control in recipient reaction to help: Theory development and empirical validation. In L. Berkowitz (Ed.), *Advances in Experimental Social Psychology* (pp. 81–122). New York: Academic Press.

Noller, P. (1980). Misunderstandings in marital communication: A study of couples' nonverbal communication. *Journal of Personality and Social Psychology, 39*(6), 1135–1148.

Norbeck, J. S., Dejoseph, J. F., and Smith, R. T. (1996). A randomized trial of an empirically-derived social support intervention to prevent low birthweight among African American women. *Social Science and Medicine, 43,* 947–954.

Norris, F. H., and Kaniasty, K. (1996). Received and perceived social support in times of stress: A test of the social support deterioration deterrence model. *Journal of Personality and Social Psychology, 71,* 498–511.

Nuckolls, K. B., Cassel, J., and Kaplan, B. H. (1972). Psychosocial assets, life crisis, and the prognosis of pregnancy. *American Journal of Epidemiology, 95,* 431–441.

O'Brien, M. K., Petrie, K., and Raeburn, J. (1992). Adherence to medical regimens: Updating a complex medical issue. *Medical Care Review, 49,* 435–454.

Ognibene, T. C., and Collins, N. L. (1998). Adult attachment styles, perceived social support and coping strategies. *Journal of Social and Personal Relationships, 15,* 323–345.

Olds, D. L., and Kitzman, H. (1993). Review of research on home visiting for pregnant women and parents of young children. *Future of Children, 3,* 53–92.

*Olsen, R. B., Olsen, J., Gunner-Sevensson, F., and Waldstrom, B. (1991). Social networks and longevity. A 14 year follow-up study among elderly in Denmark. *Social Science and Medicine, 33,* 1189–1195.

O'Reilly, P., and Thomas, H. E. (1989). Role of support networks in maintenance of improved cardiovascular health status. *Social Science and Medicine, 28,* 249–260.

*Orth-Gomér, K., and Johnson, J. V. (1987). Social network interaction and mortality: A six year follow-up study of a random sample of the Swedish population. *Journal of Chronic Diseases, 40,* 949–957.

*Orth-Gomér, K., Rosengren, A., and Wilhelmsen, L. (1993). Lack of social support and incidence of coronary heart disease in middle-aged Swedish men. *Psychosomatic Medicine, 55,* 37–43.

*Orth-Gomér, K., and Undén, A.-L. (1990). Type A behavior, social support, and coronary risk: Interaction and significance for mortality in cardiac patients. *Psychosomatic Medicine, 52,* 59–72.

O'Sullivan, G. (1972). *Alone again (naturally).* Jersey, England: Grand Upright Music.

*Oxman, T. E., Freeman, D. H., and Manheimer, E. D. (1995). Lack of social participation or religious strength and comfort as risk factors for death after cardiac surgery in the elderly. *Psychosomatic Medicine, 57,* 5–15.

Patterson, T. L., Shaw, W. S., Semple, S. J., Cherner, M., McCutchan, J. A., Atkinson, J. H., Grant, I., and Nannis, E. (1996). Relationship of psychosocial factors to HIV progression. *Annals of Behavioral Medicine, 18,* 30–39.

Peirce, R. S., Frone, M. R., Russell, M., and Cooper, M. L. (1996). Financial stress, social support, and alcohol involvement: A longitudinal test of the buffering hypothesis in a general population survey. *Health Psychology, 15,* 38–47.

Penninx, B. W. J. H., van Tilburg, T., Boeke, A. J. P., Deeg, D. J. H., Kriegsman, D. M. W., and van Eijk, J. T. M. (1998). Effects of social support and personal coping resources on depressive symptoms: Different for various chronic diseases? *Health Psychology, 17,* 551–558.

*Penninx, B. W. J. H., van Tilburg, T., Kriegsman, D. M. W., Deeg, D. J. H., Boeke, A. J. P., and van Eijk, J. T. M. (1997). Effects of social support and personal control resources on mortality in older age: The longitudinal aging study Amsterdam. *American Journal of Epidemiology, 146,* 510–519.

Perloff, D., Sokolow, M., and Cowan, R. (1983). The prognostic value of ambulatory blood pressure. *Journal of the American Medical Association, 249,* 2793–2798.

Perry, S., Fishman, B., Jacobsberg, L., and Frances, A. (1992). Relationships over 1 year between lymphocyte subsets and psychosocial variables among adults with infection by human immunodeficiency virus. *Archives of General Psychiatry, 49,* 396–401.

Persson, L., Gullberg, B., Hanson, B. S., Moestrup, T., and Ostergren, P. O. (1994). HIV infection: Social network, social support, and CD4 lymphocyte values in infected homosexual men in Malmo, Sweden. *Journal of Epidemiology and Community Health, 48,* 580–585.

Pierce, G. R., Lakey, B., Sarason, I. G., Sarason, B. R., and Joseph, H. J. (1997). Personality and social support processes: A conceptual overiew. In G. R. Pierce, B. Lakey, I. G. Sarason, and B. R. Sarason (Eds.), *Sourcebook of Social Support and Personality* (pp. 3–18). New York: Plenum Press.

Pierce, G. R., Lakey, B., Sarason, I. G., and Sarason, B. R. (1997). *Sourcebook of Social Support and Personality.* New York: Plenum Press.

Pierce, G. R., Sarason, I. G., and Sarason, B. R. (1991). General and relationship-based perceptions of social support: Are two constructs better than one? *Journal of Personality and Social Psychology, 61,* 1028–1039.

Pinquart, M., and Sorensen, S. (2001). Influences on loneliness in older adults: A meta-analysis. *Basic and Applied Social Psychology, 23,* 245–266.

Prisant, L. M., Carr, A. A., Wilson, B., and Converse, S. (1990). Ambulatory blood pressure monitoring and echocardiographic left ventricular wall thickness and mass. *American Journal of Hypertension, 3,* 81–89.

Puska, P., and Uutela, A. (1999). Community intervention in cardiovascular health promotion: North Karelia, 1972–1999. In N. Schneiderman,

M. Speers, J. Silva, H. Tomes, and J. Gentry (Eds.), *Integrating behavioral and social sciences with public health* (pp. 73–96). Washington, DC: American Psychological Association.

Putnam, R. D. (1995). Bowling alone: America's declining social capital. *Journal of Democracy, 6,* 65–78.

Raikkonen, K., Matthews, K. A., and Kuller, L. H. (2001). Trajectory of psychological risk and incident hypertension in middle-aged women. *Hypertension, 38,* 798–802.

*Reed, D., McGee, D., Yano, K., and Feinleib, M. (1983). Social networks and coronary heart disease among Japanese men in Hawaii. *American Journal of Epidemiology, 117,* 384–396.

*Rehm, J., Fichter, M. M., and Elton, M. (1993). Effects on mortality of alcohol consumption, smoking, physical activity, and close personal relationships. *Addiction, 33,* 101–112.

Rejeski, W. J., Thompson, A., Brubaker, P. H., and Miller, H. S. (1992). Acute exercise: Buffering psychosocial stress responses in women. *Health Psychology, 11,* 355–362.

*Reynolds, P., and Kaplan, G. A. (1990). Social connections and risk for cancer: Prospective evidence from the Alameda County study. *Behavioral Medicine, 16,* 101–110.

Rico, A., Fraile, M., and Gonzalez, P. (1999). Regional decentralization of health policy in Spain: Social capital does not tell the whole story. *Western European Politics, 21,* 180–199.

Rodin, J. (1986). Aging and health: Effects of the sense of control. *Science, 233,* 1271–1276.

Rook, K. S. (1998). Investigating the positive and negative sides of personal relationships: Through a lens darkly? In B. H. Spitzberg and W. R. Cupach (Eds.), *The dark side of close relationships* (pp. 369–393). Mahwah, NJ: Erlbaum.

Rook, K. S., and Pietromonaco, P. (1987). Close relationships: Ties that heal or ties that bind. *Advances in Personal Relationships, 1,* 1–35.

Rook, K. S., and Shuster, T. L. (1996). Compensatory processes in the social networks of older adults. In G. Pierce, B. Sarason, and I. Sarason (Eds.), *The handbook of social support and the family* (pp. 219–248). New York: Plenum.

*Rosengren, A., Orth-Gomér, K., Wedel, H., and Wilhelmsen, L. (1993). Stressful life events, social support, and mortality in men born in 1933. *British Medical Journal, 307,* 1102–1105.

Rosenman, R. H., Brand, R. J., Jenkins, C. D., Friedman, M., Straus, R., and Wurm, M. (1975). Coronary heart disease in the Western Collaborative Group Study: Final follow-up experience of 8 1/2 years. *Journal of the American Medical Association, 233,* 872–877.

Ross, R. (1999). Mechanisms of disease: Atherosclerosis—An inflammatory disease. *New England Journal of Medicine, 340,* 115–126.

Ross, R., and Glomset, J. A. (1976). The pathogenesis of atherosclerosis (Part 1). *New England Journal of Medicine, 295,* 369–377.

Rowe, J. W., and Kahn, R. L. (1987). Human aging: Usual and successful. *Science, 237,* 143–149.

Rowe, J. W., and Kahn, R. L. (1998). *Successful aging: The MacArthur Foundation study.* New York: Pantheon Books.

*Roy, A. W., FitzGibbon, P. A., and Haug, M. M. (1996). Social support, household composition, and health behaviors as risk factors for four-year mortality in an urban elderly cohort. *Journal of Applied Gerontology, 15,* 73–86.

Rozanski, A., Bairey, N., Krantz, D. S., Friedman, J., Resser, K. J., Morell, M., Hilton-Chalfen, S., Herstrin, L., Bietendorf, J., and Berman, D. S. (1988). Mental stress and the induction of silent myocardial ischemia in patients with coronary artery disease. *New England Journal of Medicine, 318,* 1005–1012.

Rozanksi, A., Blumenthal, J. A., and Kaplan, J. (1999). Impact of psychological factors on the pathogenesis of cardiovascular disease and implications for therapy. *Circulation, 99,* 2192–2217.

*Ruberman, W., Weinblatt, E., Goldberg, J. D., and Chaudhary, B. S. (1984). Psychosocial influences on mortality after myocardial infarction. *New England Journal of Medicine, 311,* 552–559.

Rumberger, J. A., Brundage, B. H., Rader, D. J., and Kondos, G. (1999). Electron beam computed tomographic coronary calcium scanning: A review and guidelines for use in asymptomatic persons. *Mayo Clinic Proceedings, 74,* 243–252.

Russell, D. W., and Cutrona, C. E. (1991). Social support, stress, and depressive symptoms among the elderly: Test of a process model. *Psychology and Aging, 6,* 190–201.

Russell, D., Peplau, L., and Cutrona, C. (1980). The revised UCLA loneliness scale: Concurrent and discriminant validity evidence. *Journal of Personality and Social Psychology, 39,* 472–480.

*Sabin, E. P. (1993). Social relationships and mortality among the elderly. *Journal of Applied Gerontology, 12,* 44–60.

Sandler, I. N., and Barrera, M. (1984). Toward a multimethod approach to assessing the effects of social support. *American Journal of Community Psychology, 12,* 37–52.

Sapolsky, R. M., Krey, L. C., and McEwen, B. S. (1986). The neuroendocrinology of stress and aging: The glucocorticoid cascade hypothesis. *Endocrine Reviews, 7,* 284–301.

Sarason, B. R., Sarason, I. G., and Gurung, R. A. R. (2001). Close personal relationships and health outcomes: A key to the role of social support. In B. Sarason and S. Duck (Eds.), *Personal relationships: Implications for clinical and community psychology* (pp. 15–41). West Sussex, England: Wiley.

Sarason, B. R., Sarason, I. G., Hacker, A., and Basham, R. B. (1985). Concomitants of social support: Social skills, physical attractiveness, and gender. *Journal of Personality and Social Psychology, 49*(2), 469–480.

Sarason, B. R., Sarason, I. G., and Pierce, G. R. (1990). *Social support: An interactional view.* New York: Wiley.

Sarason, I. G., Levine, H. M., Basham, R. B., and Sarason, B. R. (1983). Assessing social support: The social support questionnaire. *Journal of Personality and Social Psychology, 44,* 127–139.

Sarason, I. G., and Sarason, B. R. (1986). Experimentally provided social support. *Journal of Personality and Social Psychology, 50,* 1222–1225.

Sarason, I. G., Sarason, B. R., and Shearin, E. N. (1986). Social support as an individual difference variable: Its stability, origins, and relational aspects. *Journal of Personality and Social Psychology, 50,* 845–855.

Schneiderman, N., Speers, M. A., Silva, J. M., Tomes, H., and Gentry, J. H. (1999). *Integrating behavioral and social sciences with public health.* Washington, DC: American Psychological Association.

*Schoenbach, V. J., Kaplan, B. H., Fredman, L., and Kleinbaum, D. G. (1986). Social ties and mortality in Evans County, Georgia. *American Journal of Epidemiology, 123,* 577–591.

Schulz, R., and Beach, S. R. (1999). Caregiving as a risk factor for mortality: The caregiver health effects study. *Journal of the American Medical Association, 282,* 2215–2219.

Scott, J. (Ed.). (2000). *Social network analysis: A handbook* (2nd ed.). Thousand Oaks, CA: Sage.

Seeman, T. E. (1996). Social ties and health: The benefits of social integration. *Annals of Epidemiology, 6,* 442–451.

Seeman, T. E., Berkman, L. F., Blazer, D., and Rowe, J. W. (1994). Social ties and support and neuroendocrine function: The MacArthur studies of successful aging. *Annals of Behavioral Medicine, 16,* 95–106.

Seeman, T. E., Berkman, L. F., Kohout, F., LaCroix, A., Glynn, R., and Blazer, D. (1993). Intercommunity variations in the association between social ties and mortality in the elderly: A comparative analysis of three communities. *Annals of Epidemiology, 3,* 325–335.

*Seeman, T. E., Kaplan, G. A., Knudsen, L., Cohen, R., and Guralnik, J. (1987). Social network ties and mortality among the elderly in the Alameda County Study. *American Journal of Epidemiology, 126,* 714–723.

Seeman, T. E., and Robbins, R. J. (1994). Aging and the hypothalamic-pituitary-adrenal response to challenge in humans. *Endocrine Reviews, 15,* 233–260.

Seeman, T. E., and Syme, L. (1987). Social networks and coronary artery disease: A comparison of the structure and function of social relations as predictors of disease. *Psychosomatic Medicine, 49,* 341–354.

Sheldon, K. M., and King, L. (2001). Why positive psychology is necessary. *American Psychologist, 56,* 216–217.

Sheps, D. S., McMahon, R. P., Becker, L.,Carney, R. M., Freedland, K. E., Cohen, J. D., Sheffield, D., Goldberg, D. A., Ketterer, M. W., Pepire, C. J., Raczynski, J. M., Light, K., Krantz, D. S., Stone, P. H., Knatterud, G. L., and Kaufman, P. G. (2002). Mental stress-induced ischemia and all-cause mortality in patients with coronary artery disease. *Circulation, 105,* 1780–1784.

Sherbourne, C. D., Hays, R. D., Ordway, L., DiMatteo, M. R., and Kravitz, R. L. (1992). Antecedents of adherence to medical recommendations: Results from the medical outcomes study. *Journal of Behavioral Medicine, 15,* 447–468.

Shrock, D., Palmer, R. F., and Taylor, B. (1999). Effects of a psychosocial intervention on survival among patients with stage I breast and prostate cancer: A matched case-control study. *Alternative Therapies in Health and Medicine, 5,* 49–55.

Shumaker, S. A., and Hill, D. R. (1991). Gender differences in social support and health. *Health Psychology, 10,* 102–111.

*Shye, D., Mullooly, J. P., Freeborn, D. K., and Pope, C. R. (1995). Gender differences in the relationship between social network support and mortality: A longitudinal study of an elderly cohort. *Social Science and Medicine, 41,* 935–947.

Simpson, J. A., Rholes, W. S., and Nelligan, J. S. (1992). Support seeking and support giving within couples in an anxiety-provoking situation: The role of attachment styles. *Journal of Personality and Social Psychology, 62,* 434–446.

Singer, J. D. (1998). Using SAS PROC MIXED to fit multilevel models, hierarchical models, and individual growth models. *Journal of Educational and Behavioral Statistics, 23,* 323–355.

Smith, B. L., Lasswell, H. D., and Casey, R. D. (1946). *Propaganda, communication, and public opinion.* Princeton, NJ: Princeton University Press.

Smith, T. W. (1992). Hostility and health: Current status of a psychosomatic hypothesis. *Health Psychology, 11,* 139–150.

Smith, T. W., and Gallo, L. C. (2001). Personality traits as risk factors for physical illness. In A. Baum, T. Revenson, and J. Singer (Eds.), *Handbook of health psychology* (pp. 139–172). Hillsdale, NJ: Erlbaum.

Smith, T. W., and Ruiz, J. M. (1999). Methodological issues in adult health psychology. In P. C. Kendall, J. N. Butcher, and G. N. Holmbeck (Eds.), *Handbook of research methods in clinical psychology* (pp. 499–536). New York: Wiley.

Smith, T. W., and Ruiz, J. M. (2002). Psychosocial influences on the development and course of coronary heart disease: Current status and implications for research and practice. *Journal of Consulting and Clinical Psychology, 70,* 548–568.

*Sorlie, P. D., Backlund, E., and Keller, J. B. (1995). US mortality by economic, demographic, and social characteristics: The national longitudinal mortality study. *American Journal of Public Health, 85,* 949–956.

*Spector, W. D., and Takada, H. A. (1991). Characteristics of nursing homes that affect resident outcomes. *Journal of Aging and Health, 3,* 427–454.

Spiegel, D. (2001). Mind matters—group therapy and survival in breast cancer. *New England Journal of Medicine, 345,* 1767–1768.

Spiegel, D., Bloom, J. R., Kraemer, H. C., and Gottheil, E. (1989). Effect of psychosocial treatment on survival of patients with metastatic breast cancer. *Lancet, 2,* 888–891.

Spitzberg, B. H., and Cupach, W. R. (1998). *The dark side of close relationships.* London: Erlbaum.

Spitzer, S. B., Llabre, M. M., Ironson, G. H., Gellman, M. D., and Schneiderman, N. (1992). The influence of social situations on ambulatory blood pressure. *Psychosomatic Medicine, 54,* 79–86

*Steinbach, U. (1992). Social networks, institutionalization, and mortality among elderly people in the United States. *Journal of Gerontology: Social Sciences, 47,* S183-S190.

Steptoe, A., Lundwall, K., and Cropley, M. (2000). Gender, family structure and cardiovascular activity during the working day and evening. *Social Science and Medicine, 50,* 531–539.

Stone, A. A., Mezzacappa, E. S., Donatone, B. A., and Gonder, M. (1999). Psychosocial stress and social support are associated with prostate-specific antigen levels in men: Results from a community screening program. *Health Psychology, 18,* 482–486.

Stroebe, W., and Stroebe, M. (1996). The social psychology of social support. In E. T. Higgins and A. W. Kruglanski (Eds.), *Social psychology: Handbook of basic principles* (pp. 597–621). New York: Guilford Press.

Stroebe, W., Stroebe, M., Abakoumkin, G., and Schut, H. (1996). The role of loneliness and social support in adjustment to loss: A test of attachment versus stress theory. *Journal of Personality and Social Psychology, 70,* 1241–1249.

Stryker, S., and Burke, P. J. (2000). The past, present, and future of an identity theory. *Social Psychology Quarterly, 63,* 284–297.

*Sugisawa, H., Liang, J., and Liu, X. (1994). Social networks, social support, and mortality among older people in Japan. *Journal of Gerontology: Social Sciences, 49,* S3-S13.

Suh, T., Mandell, W., Latkin, C., and Kim, J. (1997). Social network characteristics and injecting HIV-risk behaviors among street injection drug users. *Drug and Alcohol Dependence, 47,* 137–143.

Suitor, J. J., Pillemer, K., and Keeton, S. (1995). When experience counts: The effects of experiential and structural similarity on patterns of support and interpersonal stress. *Social Forces, 73,* 1573–1588.

Tamparo, C. D., and Lewis, M. A. (1995). *Diseases of the human body.* Philadelphia: F. A. Davis.

Taylor, S. E., Klein, L. C., Lewis, B. P., Gruenewald, T. L., Gurung, R. A. R., and Updegraff, J. A. (2000). Biobehavioral responses to stress in females: Tend-and-befriend, not fight-or-flight. *Psychological Review, 107*, 411–429.

Taylor, S. E., and Seeman, T. E. (1999). Psychosocial resources and the SES-health relationship. *Annals of the New York Academy of Sciences, 896*, 210–225.

Teichman, B. J., Burker, E. J., Weiner, M., and Egan, T. M. (2000). Factors associated with adherence to treatment regimens after lung transplantation. *Progress in Transplantation, 10*, 113–121.

Theorell, T., Blomkvist, V., Jonsson, H., Schulman, S., Berntorp, E., and Stigendal, L. (1995). Social support and the development of immune function in human immunodeficiency virus infection. *Psychosomatic Medicine, 57*, 32–36.

Thoits, P. A. (1983). Multiple identities and psychological well-being: A reformulation and test of the social isolation hypothesis. *American Sociological Review, 48*, 174–187.

Thoits, P. A. (1986). Social support as coping assistance. *Journal of Consulting and Clinical Psychology, 54*, 416–423.

Thoits, P. A. (1992). Identity structures and psychological well-being: Gender and marital status comparisons. *Social Psychology Quarterly, 55*, 236–256.

Thoits, P. A. (1995a). Identity-relevant events and psychological symptoms: A cautionary tale. *Journal of Health and Social Behavior, 36*, 72–82.

Thoits, P. A. (1995b). Stress, coping, and social support processes: Where are we? What next? *Journal of Health and Social Behavior* [extra issue], 53–79.

Thoits, P. A. (2001, April). *Personal agency in the accumulation of multiple role-identities.* Paper presented at the Mini-Conference on Identity Theory and Research, Bloomington, IN.

Thoits, P. A., Hohmann, A. A., Harvey, M. R., and Fletcher, B. (2000). Similar-other support for men undergoing coronary artery bypass surgery. *Health Psychology, 19*, 264–273.

Toobert, D. J., Glasgow, R. E., Nettekoven, L. A., and Brown, J. E. (1998). Behavioral and psychosocial effects of intensive lifestyle management for women with coronary heart disease. *Patient Education and Counseling, 35*, 177–188.

Trobst, K. K. (2000). An interpersonal conceptualization and quantification of social support transactions. *Personality and Social Psychology Bulletin, 26*, 971–986.

Turner-Cobb, J. M., Sephton, S. E., Koopman, C., Blake-Mortimer, J., and Spiegel, D. (2000). Social support and salivary cortisol in women with metastatic breast cancer. *Psychosomatic Medicine, 62*, 337–345.

Uchino, B. N., Cacioppo, J. T., and Kiecolt-Glaser, J. K. (1996). The relationship between social support and physiological processes: A review with emphasis on underlying mechanisms and implications for health. *Psychological Bulletin, 119,* 488–531.

Uchino, B. N., Cacioppo, J. T., Malarkey, W., Glaser, R., and Kiecolt-Glaser, J. K. (1995). Appraisal support predicts age-related differences in cardiovascular function in women. *Health Psychology, 14,* 556–562.

Uchino, B. N., and Garvey, T. G. (1997). The availability of social support reduces cardiovascular reactivity to acute psychological stress. *Journal of Behavioral Medicine, 20,* 15–27.

Uchino, B. N., Holt-Lunstad, J., Uno, D., and Betancourt, R. (1999). Social support and age-related differences in cardiovascular function: An examination of potential mediators. *Annals of Behavioral Medicine, 21,* 135–142.

Uchino, B. N., Holt-Lunstad, J., Uno, D., and Flinders, J. B. (2001). Heterogeneity in the social networks of young and older adults: Prediction of mental health and cardiovascular reactivity during acute stress. *Journal of Behavioral Medicine, 24,* 361–382.

Uchino, B. N., Kiecolt-Glaser, J. K., and Glaser, R. (2000). Psychological modulation of cellular immunity. In J. T. Cacioppo, L. G. Tassinary, and G. G. Berntson (Eds.), *Handbook of Psychophysiology* (pp. 397–424). New York: Cambridge University Press.

Uchino, B. N., Uno, D., and Holt-Lunstad, J. (1999). Social support, physiological processes, and health. *Current Directions in Psychological Science, 8,* 218–221.

Umberson, D. (1987). Family status and health behaviors: Social control as a dimension of social integration. *Journal of Health and Social Behavior, 28,* 306–319.

UNAIDS/WHO (2001, December). *AIDS epidemic update.* Geneva, Switzerland. Retrieved from www.unaids.org/epidemic_update/report_deco1/index.html

U.S. Department of Health and Human Services (1996). *Physical Activity and Health: A report of the surgeon general.* Atlanta, GA: U.S. Department of Health and Human Services, Centers for Disease Control and Prevention, National Center for Chronic Disease Prevention and Health Promotion.

Uno, D., Uchino, B. N., and Smith, T. W. (2002). Relationship quality moderates the effect of social support given by close friends on cardiovascular reactivity in women. *International Journal of Behavioural Medicine, 9*(3), 243–262.

Uvnas-Moberg, K. (1998). Oxytocin may mediate the benefits of positive social interaction and emotions. *Psychoneuroendocrinology, 23,* 819–835.

Vasan, R. S., Larson, M. G., Leip, E. P., Evans, J. C., O'Donnell, C. J., Kannel, W. B., and Levy, D. (2001). Impact of high-normal blood pressure on the risk of cardiovascular disease. *New England Journal of Medicine, 345,* 1291–1297.

Vaux, A. (1988). *Social support: Theory, research, and intervention.* New York: Praeger.

Villar, J., Farnot, U., Barros, F., Victoria, C., Langer, A., and Belizan, J. M. (1992). A randomized trial of psychosocial support during high-risk pregnancies. The Latin American network for perinatal and reproductive research. *New England Journal of Medicine, 327,* 1266–1271.

Vitaliano, P. P., Scanlan, J. M., Zhang, J., Savage, M. V., Brummett, B., Barefoot, J., and Siegler, I. C. (2001). Are the salutogenic effects of social supports modified by income? A test of an "added value hypothesis." *Health Psychology, 20,* 155–165.

*Vogt, T. M., Mullooly, J. P., Ernst, D., Pope, C. R., and Hollis, J. F. (1992). Social networks as predictors of ischemic heart disease, cancer, stroke, and hypertension: Incidence, survival, and mortality. *Journal of Clinical Epidemiology, 45,* 659–666.

Walker, M. E., Wasserman, S., and Wellman, B. (1994). Statistical models for social support networks. In S. Wasserman and J. Galaskiewicz (Eds.), *Advances in social network analysis: Research in the social and behavioral sciences* (pp. 53–78). Thousand Oaks, CA: Sage.

Wasserman, S., and Galaskiewicz, J. (Eds.), (1994). *Advances in social network analysis: Research in the social and behavioral sciences.* Thousand Oaks, CA: Sage.

Watson, D. L., and Tharp, R. G. (1997). *Self-directed behavior: Self modification for personal adjustment.* Pacific Grove, CA: Brooks/Cole.

Weiss, R. (1973). *Loneliness: The experience of emotional and social isolation.* Cambridge: MIT Press.

*Welin, C., Lappas, G., and Wilhelmsen, L. (2000). Independent importance of psychosocial factors for prognosis after myocardial infarction. *Journal of Internal Medicine, 247,* 629–639.

*Welin, L., Larsson, B., Svärdsudd, K., Tibblin, B., and Tibblin, G. (1992). Social network and activities in relation to mortality from cardiovascular diseases, cancer and other causes: A 12 year follow up of the study of men born in 1913 and 1923. *Journal of Epidemiology and Community Health, 46,* 127–132.

*Welin, L., Tibblin, G., Svärdsudd, K., Tibblin, B., Ander-Peciva, S., Larsson, B., and Wilhelmsen, L. (1985, April 20). Prospective study of social influences on mortality: The study of men born in 1913 and 1923. *Lancet,* 915–918.

Wellman, B., and Wortley, S. (1990). Different strokes from different folks: Community ties and social support. *American Journal of Sociology, 96,* 558–588.

Wethington, E., and Kessler, R. C. (1986). Perceived support, received support, and adjustment to stressful life events. *Journal of Health and Social Behavior, 27,* 78–89.

Whitehead, M. (2001). Social capital and health: tip-toeing through the mine-field of evidence. *Lancet, 358,* 165.

Whiteside, T. L., and Herberman, R. B. (1994). Role of human natural killer cells in health and disease. *Clinical and Diagnostic Laboratory Immunology, 1,* 125–133.

*Williams, R. B., Barefoot, J. C., Califf, R. M., Haney, T. L., Saunders, W. B., Pryor, D. B., Hlatky, M. A., Siegler, I. C., and Mark, D. B. (1992). Prognostic importance of social and economic resources among medically treated patients with angiographically documented coronary artery disease. *Journal of the American Medical Association, 267,* 520–524.

Wills, T. A. (1985). Supportive functions of interpersonal relationships. In S. Cohen and S. L. Syme (Eds.), *Social support and health* (pp. 61–82). San Diego, CA: Academic Press.

Wills, T. A., Gibbons, F. X., Gerrard, M., and Brody, G. H. (2000). Protection and vulnerability processes relevant for early onset of substance use: A test among African American children. *Health Psychology, 19,* 253–263.

Wing, R. R., and Jeffery, R. W. (1999). Benefits of recruiting participants with friends and increasing social support for weight loss and maintenance. *Journal of Consulting and Clinical Psychology, 67,* 132–138.

Wood, J. V. (1989). Theory and research concerning social comparisons of personal attributes. *Psychological Bulletin, 106,* 231–248.

Writing Group for the Activity Counseling Trial Research Group. (2001). Effects of physical activity counseling in primary care: The activity counseling trial: A randomized controlled trial. *Journal of the American Medical Association, 286,* 677–687.

*Yasuda, N., Zimmerman, S. I., Hawkes, W., Fredman, L., Hebel, J. R., and Magaziner, J. (1997). Relation of social network characteristics to 5-year mortality among young-old versus old-old white women in an urban community. *American Journal of Epidemiology, 145,* 516–523.

*Zuckerman, D. M., Kasl, S. V., and Ostfeld, A. M. (1984). Psychosocial predictors of mortality among the elderly poor: The role of religion, well-being, and social contacts. *American Journal of Epidemiology, 119,* 410–423.

Index

Page numbers followed by "t" indicate tables